"Steve Pope is a marvelous Teacher, Scholar and Mystic. This book provides a modern way of approaching ancient Biblical texts and a practical roadmap to spiritual awakening. Through clear and penetrating insights, Steve helps the reader discover the deeper meaning hidden in the western mystical teachings."
Rev. Dr. Megan Wagner, PhD, Author of *The Sapphire Staff*, Provost and Director of Spiritual Psychology at The Chaplaincy Institute in California, USA.

"*Patterns of Creation* brings the reader into the creative power of the present. Written with great clarity and considerable scholarship, this book achieves its aim, that of awakening the reader to a greater awareness of the spiritual consciousness that exists in each of us, enfolding us within the greater circle of life of which so many people are largely unaware.
Natasha Hoffman, Author, with Hamilton Hill, of *Let the Standing Stones Speak* (O-Books), and with Carolyn North, of *Voices Out of Stone* (Findhorn Press).

As a longtime student of the Hebrew Kabbalah, or *receiving*, Steve Pope writes with authority about the symbolism of the Gospel of John, which conceals spiritual messages derived from its Hellenistic origins. He deals at length with the key word *Logos*, the Word of God, the divine essence of Life, and explains how important it is to be conscious of the life force within us that animates body and mind through the Soul. This exegesis is well illustrated with geometric diagrams, which will interest many people, who will gain much from the numerous meditations and breathing exercises which illuminate the text, all aimed at release from the dominance of the ego. This is recommended reading that many will find useful and rewarding.

Hamilton Hill M.A. (Oxon), Author with Natasha Hofffman of *Let the standing Stones Speak* (O-Books).

The author's overarching perspective and focus is the ceaseless unfolding of being into becoming, through the Logos itself; and that the "perennial wisdom" must be constantly experienced and enacted if it is to bear fruit. His words have real substance, and a clarity and simplicity that enhances the content of the book and makes it readily accessible to a wide audience. I believe this is a much-needed book with a much-needed message that will not disappoint, and I recommend it wholeheartedly.

Ingrid Walton MA Lit. Hum. (Oxon.); Dip. Information Science (City) Translator of Classical Greek and Latin texts.

Patterns of Creation

Logos and the Tree of Life
in the Gospel of John

Patterns of Creation

Logos and the Tree of Life
in the Gospel of John

Stephen Pope BD. MA

AXIS MUNDI
BOOKS

Winchester, UK
Washington, USA

First published by Axis Mundi Books, 2012
Axis Mundi Books is an imprint of John Hunt Publishing Ltd., Laurel House, Station Approach,
Alresford, Hants, SO24 9JH, UK
office1@jhpbooks.net
www.johnhuntpublishing.com
www.axismundi-books.com

For distributor details and how to order please visit the 'Ordering' section on our website.

ISBN: 978 1 78099 117 7

A CIP catalogue record for this book is available from the British Library.

Design: Stuart Davies

Printed and bound by CPI Group (UK) Ltd, Croydon, CR0 4YY

We operate a distinctive and ethical publishing philosophy in all
areas of our business, from our global network of authors to
production and worldwide distribution.

CONTENTS

Acknowledgments

Nobody ever writes a book alone and this is the work of many people, too many to mention by name. I would like to thank all those who worked with the meditations and ideas presented in the book over the years at workshops and seminars. I am grateful to Andrea Mestanek, Gwen Cuthbert, Megan Wagner and Jim Larkin, Marie-Elsa Bragg, Dion McDonald and Joanne and Kurt Browne with whom I shared so much in conversation and meditation. I would particularly like to give thanks to Eleanor O'Hanlon for reading and editing the manuscript, and for all your love and support in helping it come to print. To Joyce Foxcroft for her hard work on early versions of the manuscript and to Ingrid Walton for her meticulous checking of the Greek translations and suggestions for the book. To Jeremy Linden and Martin Wilson for their work on the diagrams and support for the book. And to all my teachers who have helped me awaken and deepen my understanding of the Unity of life.

Introduction

In the beginning was the Logos: the essence and unity of Life. I have written this book because these opening words to the Gospel of John have always spoken to me of the deep connection of all life, the patterns of creation. They always seemed to point to something beyond me, to a greater sense of life and the unity of all things. Only as that sense of *something* and *me* began to diminish did I begin to feel the reality of greater awareness that continually flows into all things, where there is no fear, need, or separation. This book, like the Gospel itself, is about that revelation, which is bound to occur within every awakening human being, because spiritual consciousness is the essence of who we really are.

Although this book presents a new look at the mystical teachings found in the Gospel of John, it is not a commentary; its primary purpose is the same as that of the Gospel itself: to help you awaken to the greater consciousness that exists as the core of your *being,* and to begin to live from your spiritual heart or center, which connects you with the entire circle of life. This realization requires that we strip away centuries of dogmas and doctrines, and all the mind made images of God that obscure the essence of its teachings.

There are many names and words used to describe the unseen unity of life we call God. This is beyond anything that your mind can conceive of as anything, yet exists as your essence deep within you. This is what the concept of Logos reveals to us, the simple and intimate essence of life. It is the mind with all its distractions that brings the illusion that your spiritual Being, your connection with God, is far from you, hidden in some deep mystery that can only be realized in some future time.

The secret of the Gospel is that everything it describes exists within you *now.* And it is you and no one else who will bring it to life. Everything in life, everything you see and touch, and everyone you meet, reflects that inner reality. It is your perception of that reflection of life that changes as you awaken spiritually. This is equally true of reading spiritual writing such as John's Gospel.

One of our problems in the modern world is that we have become conditioned by the Western concept of thinking, intellect and mind, which influences our understanding of words, reading and writing. This makes it difficult for us to experience the reading of sacred texts as meditation or contemplation, in which the observing consciousness meets with the reality behind the symbols contained in the writings. Instead, these symbols have been turned into mental concepts, which means that we no longer allow them to open out, so that what they represent can be felt as living reality within.

Before reading any sacred text, it is important to begin by being as present as you can; to still and silence the mind, since the text can only mirror back your own level of awareness.

For this reason, Chapters Two to Thirteen of this book contain exercises to help you raise awareness before you begin to meditate on the symbolism in the text. The book also contains visual meditations or inner journeys that can be used to help you deepen your awareness of the teachings in the Gospel of John. It is only as we learn to suspend, and go beyond, the thinking mind that our awareness deepens, and the reality of the teachings begins to take effect in us.

The teachings of the Gospel are not something to be believed or disbelieved — they can only be *known*. To begin to understand this, first learn *To Be*, and so allow all things, all creatures, and all people, *To Be*. To be present as fully as possible wherever, and in whatever situation you may find yourself is the essence and simplicity of the mystical teachings found in John's Gospel.

Chapter One

In the Beginning

The opening lines of the Gospel of John are one of the world's great spiritual poems. These few short lines weave together the most profound teachings on the relationship between God, existence, creation and humanity. The words, like those of all true sacred writing, are uttered on the edge of silence: they are the last words that can be spoken before language itself is no longer of use. The opening words "In the beginning" refer us back to the opening line of the creation story contained in the Book of Genesis. But for the Jewish mystics the creation — *Bereshith (In Hebrew)* — was not a story to be read and believed in, or a series of events that had taken place in the remote past. Creation is the continual outpouring of life *in the ever present now,* understood through direct experience as continually unfolding out of this eternal present moment, within all forms of life.

This knowledge and understanding came through the practice of Merkabah, a word that means "Chariot" and its practitioners were referred to as the "Riders in the Chariot." The chariot is a symbol for the Soul, the vehicle in which we journey through life, and which takes us in what the chariot riders called the mystical ascent or descent: the inner journey of awakening consciousness from the depths of physical matter, through the lower halls of psychological form, to the upper halls of creative pattern, into union with our Divine source: I Am — *Being.* In the language of John's Gospel, this is to experience Logos, the Greek concept normally translated as Word, which in fact is untranslatable. We will explore the deeper meanings of Logos throughout this book.

By the first century of the Common Era, Jewish mystical

3

teachers had begun to refer to the passing of this knowledge from one generation to the next by the Hebrew word Kabbal, which means, "to receive." It is from this Hebrew word that the term Kabbalah has come. In order to receive we have to create an inner space of silence and stillness; go beyond the constraints of the thinking, analytical, time bound mind, and leave behind the distractions that block our connection with our true self and the abundance of life we call God. Learning to find our still center and inner silence is the primary purpose of Kabbalah, and all mystical teachings.

The Tree of Life: Symbol of Living Torah

The word Torah is normally associated with the first five books of the Old Testament. However, Torah means *teachings on the laws of life* and these cannot be contained by the written word. Every living creature, every human being, is a manifestation of the laws of life. They are in our breath and blood, in the great web of life from the smallest subatomic particles to the great galaxies of the Cosmos. We ourselves become *the teaching* when we realize our spiritual center, our own *Being*; when we hear, see, and feel its creative patterns come alive in ourselves, and in all our fellow creatures in the world around us. This is depicted in the symbol of the great Tree of Life: the single source of created existence, from which consciousness expresses and realizes itself through bearing the fruit of all life forms, holding them in their interconnected patterns. For this reason, it was said by the Jewish mystics that the Torah given to Moses on the mythical Mount Sinai was, and remains oral. It was to be written down only in order that it might not be forgotten. It is the oral tradition, consciously carried on the breath that connects, that brings any teaching and the seeds it contains to life, because it is the living creative source of life that the written Torah can only point to.

The teachings in the Gospel of John that we have inherited today are part of this living tradition. First taught by word of mouth, some of its teachings were eventually written down a century or more later. What is essential is to realize *now* that the Gospel story is speaking of your own individual relationship to life and God — whatever that means to you. The teachings and your own unique understanding of them come to life as you awaken spiritually to the great circle of life.

Throughout the book, you will find geometric diagrams that are synonymous with Kabbalah. The ratio and patterns in these mandalas are contained within the teaching stories of the Gospel. You can use them as the basis for your own meditation and contemplation, and they will help to clarify the different levels of conscious awareness that are woven into the text of the Gospel. The individuals that we meet in this story, the landscape through which they move and the way in which they meet, converse, and relate to one another personify the archetypal Divine, spiritual, and psycho-somatic patterns that exist within you, and which are depicted on the Tree of Life diagram you see overleaf.

experience - personal understanding & connection

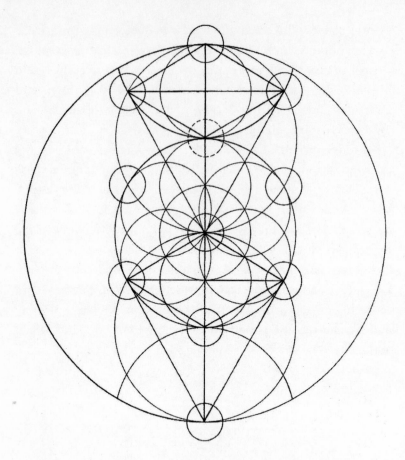

Everything presented in the Gospel stories points to your inner awakening: realizing your own consciousness. This awakening is represented here in the geometric form of the Tree of Life.

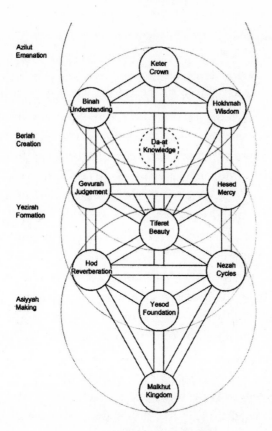

Sefirotic Tree of Life

The classical depiction of the Kabbalistic Tree of Life with English translations of the four worlds, ten Sephirot and 22 interconnecting paths. The names of the four worlds and the Sephirot come from Old Testament texts, and the 22 paths represent the letters of the Hebrew alphabet.

John 21 chptrs
Nof 22 ?

The Gospel story maps out your inner spiritual journey and each of the characters you meet represent your own inner levels of awareness: states of unconsciousness and consciousness that you must first recognize, then integrate and transform on your journey through life. This is not portrayed as a purely transcendent journey: it shows that you also need to have your feet firmly planted in the Earth, and live consciously in your physical body.

In the Gospel, the figure of Jesus becomes the personification of the Logos, the good shepherd, and the redeeming Sun God. The symbolism is not concerned with the historical Jesus but with the perennial archetypes that the symbolic name Joshua–Jesus and Christos–Messiah represent. In the translation of the Gospel I have prepared for this book, Jesus tells his disciples "walk with me, step by step." This is because *Logos* is your eternal *Being* on your journey through life. It is not separate from who you really are, and when you consciously realize *Being*, you become at-one with the whole of life.

The Gospels use the ancient symbol of a point within a circle to represent unity and wholeness, the One, *Being*, source of all life. This circle is subdivided into four, and then twelve equal divisions, to symbolize the multiplicity and diversity of life, which come from the One source. In the Old Testament first Moses, then the Anointed Joshua son of Nun take up the central point around which the twelve tribes of Israel revolve. Exactly the same motif is used in the New Testament. The term Anointed means the Messiah, and the Anointed — or Christ Jesus in Greek — stands at the center, with the twelve disciples revolving around this central stillness. As in the Old Testament, these twelve divisions — also known through the Zodiac — represent twelve aspects of Cosmic life through which humanity passes: all humanity, both male and female, and all the races and creeds we might identify with, reflecting the One Divine source at the center of all life. This center exists within you, here and now, and only the illusions that exist within the mind keep you separate from it.

Because male names are attributed to all of these aspects, and to the figure at the central core, this spiritual motif, taken literally, has given the false impression that the whole scheme of spiritual enlightenment is exclusively masculine, and that the Gospel teachings were spread, without exception, by men. So many of us

8

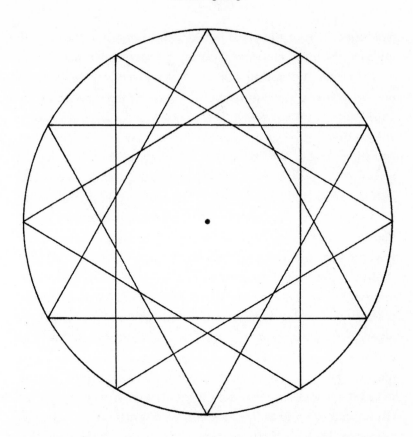

assume this to be true when reading Bible stories, because it has been deeply woven into the fabric of our religious and social culture for thousands of years.

Reawakening to the Feminine

The marginalization of Women and the Divine Feminine in religion and society is part of our increasingly destructive behavior towards the natural world and each other. The figure of Mary, one of the few feminine figures to make it into the Gospel stories, has been so reduced that she is only a shadow of the great Triple Goddess, the feminine face of the One, Isis-Sophia, which she truly represents. In the New Testament, she plays minor supporting roles to the central male figure — the masculine face of the One. But this has done nothing to stop millions of women and men from being drawn to her sacred sites, caves, wells, and springs, or consciously connecting with the beauty of the natural world and the fellow creatures we share life with. This natural upwelling of the energy of the Divine feminine still pours through us because it courses through the life we see and experience within and about us, and it naturally increases as we awaken spiritually. Without it, we remain fragmented and divided — devoid of our potential to realize Logos, and reflect the circle of life. This suppression and disempowerment of the feminine needs to be urgently, and consciously redressed, if we are to truly realize our place within the circle of life, and end our destructive behavior towards it.

Spiritual awakening involves realizing equal balance between the feminine and masculine within the circle of life. The names given to the authors of the four Gospels, Matthew, Mark, Luke and John, depict the four types of humanity, both women and men: in the classical world, that of action, thinking, feeling and intuition. Many other Gospels were also written, one was the Gospel according to Mary (Magdalene), fragments of which were found in the Nag Hammadi manuscripts and also some later texts, circa fifth century, belonging to the Coptic Church. Her teachings focus on the dissolution of thought forms in which we are entrapped, the end of the illusions of separation from the One and the Good. The Magdalene is key to the deeper understanding of the Gospel teachings on re-unification; we look at her role in greater depth in Chapter Twelve and explore the figure of Mary as Great Mother in Chapter Ten on the marriage at Cana. (The symbolism of the Divine Feminine can be understood more fully by reading Chapter Fourteen on the history of symbols and ideas.)

Text and Translation
This book concentrates on the ideas and symbols at the beginning

and end of the Gospel. I look in depth at the first two chapters and at the symbolism of the crucifixion, death and resurrection at the end. Beginning and end act as a framework that take you into the deeper layers contained within the Gospel and within your Self. This helps to give a deeper understanding of the parables and teaching stories, which are framed by beginning and end.

It is important to note that there is no single original copy of the Gospel, and that there are many minor variations in the surviving texts. The stories in the Gospel were first transmitted by word of mouth in the language of Aramaic. This was a form of Hebrew, which was the spoken language of the Middle Eastern world in which the drama is set, and was the primary medium of the teachings. There are Aramaic manuscripts of the Gospel, which I have cross-referenced whilst preparing the translation. Arguments as to whether the original text of the Gospel was in Greek or Aramaic do not concern the teachings presented in this book, as there are no great differences in the Aramaic and Greek versions of the text covered in the book.

The mystical teachers of ancient Palestine were steeped in the esoteric and philosophical concepts of what was to become the Hebrew Bible, whilst those of the Jewish Diaspora were deeply rooted in the Hellenistic cultures and were instrumental in bringing the two traditions together. Biblical Greek and Hebrew words are containers for spiritual ideas — the texts lose much of their depth when translated, particularly when they are translated without awareness of the different levels of consciousness they represent. Many of the Greek and Hebrew words can be compared to icons: they contain images that, in meditation and contemplation, open out like the corolla of a flower to reveal an inner world, the core of which lies within each of us.

In addition, the Old Testament quotations in the text of the Gospel are cross-referenced with their Hebrew sources. Some simple explanations of the Jewish and Semitic language roots relevant to the Gospel are also given in the book. Indeed, since the Greek text is the work of a Jewish mystical school, it cannot be properly understood without the Jewish mystical framework in which it is set.

It is not necessary to have any knowledge of Kabbalah to read this book. However, if you are unfamiliar with its teachings and terminology, and would like to explore them further, you will find a section that will help orientate you in its symbolic language in Chapter Fifteen.

For those of you who would like to explore the historical development of the ideas and images discussed here, in more detail, you can turn to the separate history section, which you will find in Chapter Fourteen.

Chapter Two

The Relationship of God to Existence

The Gospel of John opens with a metaphysical poem, which has been divided into eighteen verses by later scribes. They are described as the testimony of John, (the meaning of the name will be explained later, where it appears in the text.) The first five verses set the scene for what follows. As with any poetry, it is essential to allow space for contemplation and meditation rather than reading it as an intellectual exercise. It is also important to understand that however resonant the English translation of these opening verses may be, it cannot reveal the extraordinary depth that is contained and expressed in the biblical Greek.

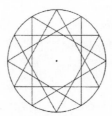

1:1 In the beginning the Logos was, and the Logos was next to God, and the Logos was Divine.

These opening words "In the beginning" immediately recall the first words of the creation story of the *Book of Genesis*. To understand the first line of the poem, we have to know that the author wants us to stand at the still point in existence, out of which creation continually emerges. The opening line of the Genesis narrative itself is concerned with the unfolding of creation — not of the physical universe, but of *the spiritual universe of metaphysical ideas*. The author assumes that their students already know this, for without this knowledge the rest of the poem loses its transformative power.

In Hebrew the creation is called Bereshith — "beginnings" or "beginnings of principles of power" — and the created universe is called Beriah, which comes from the Hebrew root Bara, "to create." Neither concept denotes the physical universe, nor is the creation a past event: it is a continual outpouring from the eternal Now. To stand here we need to still and silence the mind and breathe from a point of stillness deep within.

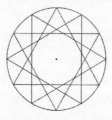

Take a conscious breath: breathe with awareness. Through the breath, be aware of your Solar Plexus as a radiant point, beneath and behind the heart and lungs. Be aware of your spinal column from the coccyx at the base of the spine to the first of the seven cervical vertebrae at the top. As you breathe from the solar plexus, feel the spine supporting you, allowing your life force to expand with each breath, releasing any tensions you are holding in your body. Become aware of the central stillness out of which each breath emerges, and into which it returns. If you can be aware that all movement is supported by stillness, then you are beginning to experience something of the meaning of Logos.

The verse says that the Logos *was* in the beginning. The Greek word translated as "was" literally means "to be" and indicates the eternally present "Now." It appears in the Greek text in the past tense to show that the Logos already exists at the point when creation — the first movement out of Unity — begins. That is to say, the Logos is experienced, from within the time and space of creation, as the pre-existent and un-created Divine universe of *Being*, containing all that is, was, and shall be in the eternal Now.

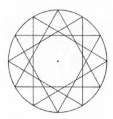

Stillness, before and behind any movement; the pause between the in-breath and the out-breath. Continue to breathe consciously from your center at the Solar Plexus, drawing the breath up from the base of the spine to deepen your awareness.

"*In the beginning the Logos was*" tells us that something completely different is occurring: if there is a beginning then there must also be an end. Movement, time unfolding in space, marks a point of departure from unity, the unity of the eternal Divine world of *Being* — the Logos — which is all time, held in a single, eternal, moment. As you stand at your still center, you are given the overview of the difference between created existence — experienced as movement — and the pre-existent Divine universe: stillness. *The breath moves; consciousness is still. That which "is" witnesses every movement. This is Logos.*

In the second part of the verse, we are told that, "*the Logos was next to God, and the Logos was Divine.*" The Greek word *pros* translated as "next to" also means "near" "by the side of" and "with." In Hebrew, the word used for the Divine universe is *Atzilut,* and one of its meanings is "to stand next to." So what does it mean that Logos is "next to" God and the Logos is Divine?

In these mystical teachings, God is Absolute, limitless, and the limitless cannot be confined to, or contained by, existence. God does not exist in any of the terms that we understand by existence. God is no-thing that we can say is anything. If we say that God *is* anything then we limit God to our own mental concepts or images as someone or something. The Logos — *Divine Being* — *exists*: total consciousness; total presence. Brought forth out of the No-thing of the Absolute, it is the contained potentiality — the essence — of all that will unfold as the created universe. However there is no beginning, no movement: it is eternal, *Being*, the perfect reflection of the Absolute.

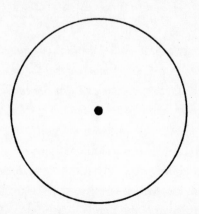

Logos and its relationship to God can be understood through the symbol of the point within the circle. The circle represents the Logos; timeless eternal presence, the perfect reflection of God the Absolute, which cannot be contained within the circle of existence, and does not exist in the terms that the mind understands as existence. The center of the circle exists within every living thing, beyond form, the unifying principle of all life; the unique seed of the Absolute unknowable God.

so is not God?

reflection of God, what is a reflection?

Logos: Timeless Eternal presence yet the impression is still that it came after God/Absolute

Does to exist need/imply a pre-requisite of time?

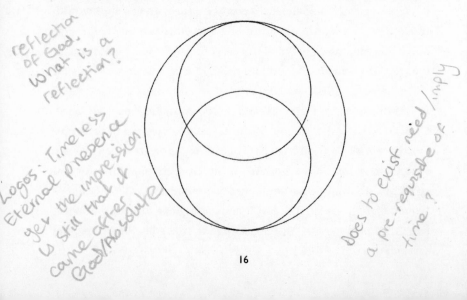

made by? How? [handwritten]

The beginning signifies the first movement out of the unity of Being. This is symbolized by two interlacing circles. The upper circle and the outer circle represent Unity, Stillness, the timeless eternal One. The lower circle represents the spiritual universe of metaphysical ideas — time unfolding in space.

— or movement #15 [handwritten]

This first verse states: In the beginning [of created existence — the primary movement out of unity] the Logos was, [pre-existed] and the Logos was next to The Absolute [a full and perfect reflection], and the Logos was Divine [Being — eternal presence]. Almost but not exactly [handwritten]

This is why the end of the verse, which is usually translated *left right — Yin Yang ?* [handwritten] as, *and the Word was God,* should read, *and the Logos was Divine.* The Greek text makes a distinction between God as Absolute, and *god* as Divine being. The word for God in Greek is *Theos.* When it is referred to in the absolute sense, it is prefixed by the definite article, in English "the." It therefore means "The Absolute — God," but when it is left without the definite article it means "a God," which is Divinity or Logos. This interpretation of the text is the same in the Aramaic text, which also makes a distinction between God as Absolute and *the Miltha* — an ‡ 20 [handwritten] Aramaic term which means the manifestation of God in the sense of pattern, and equates with the Greek term Logos. *The word: Logos: Creation: The first sign of God.* [handwritten]

Yin or Yang ? [handwritten] The Logos, which is the Absolute's immanence in existence, continually gives birth to the unfolding of creative pattern. The Logos is the eternal timeless presence of existence — and it is through the Divine universe that the Absolute wills the process of creative unfolding, time in space. *Logos Yang or Yin ?* [handwritten]

Most translations give Logos as *"the Word."* Although poetic, this is misleading and inaccurate. Logos is a concept that cannot be properly translated, and "Word" barely hints at its depths. At a superficial level, Logos was used to denote speech, literally "to speak, a discourse or account." Other meanings assigned to it are "to lay out" or "arrange in sequence." It is not words or speech, but the creative potential of sequential movement that opens its depth of meaning.

Logos is an ancient Pagan, Greek concept. Its first use as a description of Divinity is attributed to the philosopher-mystic Heraclitus in around 600 BCE. (See Chapter Fourteen). For Heraclitus and other Greek philosopher mystics, Logos represented the Divine essence that underlies the whole of existence and directs the unfolding of creation: the stillness behind every movement, the silence behind every sound. It expressed the very core and source of life that indwells every human being and everything that exists.

As the very essence of Life and Humanity, the concept of Logos is neither male nor female, but contains the potential expression of both. In this way, Logos was understood as *"the cause of causes,"* the instrument through which the unknowable Absolute-God acts within existence, and the expression of God's will for existence. Logos also denotes the principles of creation: mediation, balance, and harmony between extremes; order or pattern, ratio or proportion and the power of reason. Logos can only be understood and experienced when you awaken to the beauty and harmony of pattern and ratio that support the diversity of life within the Cosmos, our solar system, the natural world, and within you. These same patterns that express themselves in the beauty of form and matter are what connect you to the stars, and beyond to the formless universe of creation; and the stillness of Being, out of which creation continually emerges.

By using Logos in this context, the author of the poem is consciously binding together ideas on Divinity and creation drawn from both the Jewish and Greek traditions into a whole. Because Logos describes the essence of life out of which creation is born, it was therefore used to denote *the Torah*, which is primarily oral, and means *"teaching,"* the transmission of mystical knowledge by word of mouth from generation to generation, a living tradition given to those who are consciously

[handwritten margin note at top: # I keep thinking of the 'stillness behind" as the ... Absolute, not Logos — then having to take a step back — If Logos is stillness what is the Absolute?]

receptive to life.

Torah is not merely the writings of the five books of Moses, and cannot be contained in the written word. Torah is often translated as Law, but as Law, it is mistranslated to mean legalism. If we refer to Torah as Law, it means the universal codes, which govern the web of life and its unfolding patterns. Logos — Torah is the essence of life, the codes of life, which become Ideas, and then take on diverse forms that manifest as the physical universe — the Cosmos.

[handwritten margin note: The Laws]

Everything that exists, from the cells in your body, to the stars in the Cosmos, are governed by the same principals of ratio, harmony, balance, and beauty, expressed by Logos. These patterns allow life to unfold out of Unity, and express themselves in the complexity of diverse forms we experience in nature through the symmetry of a flower, the passage of the planets in the solar system, and turning of the myriad formations of the stars of our galaxy observed in a clear night sky.

[handwritten margin notes: Change stillness; Chaos Calm; opposites; Reaching]

This brings us to the next verse, which is a confirmation of the unity of existence.

[handwritten margin note: outward & inward erm.]

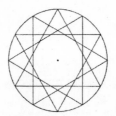

1:2 This One had its Being in the beginning next to God.
Verse two, is usually translated as, "He was in the beginning with God." The Greek word translated into English as "He" is *houtos*, which simply means "This One," and again the Aramaic equivalent is identical in meaning. "This One" refers to the Logos. It is a careful reiteration that existence and all of creation originates from a single source: Logos — *Divine Being of the*

[handwritten margin note: [reflection]?]

Absolute — God or Logos ?

Absolute.

Both the Jewish and Greek mystical and philosophical traditions understood God to be nothing that we can say is anything. God cannot be said to exist by the terms that we understand as existence, and God is therefore a term for the unknowable One Source of *Being*. In these traditions, there is one source of all life, which the author of the poem calls Logos. *Being — the Divine attribute or name of the Absolute.*

God or Logos #17 Absolute

In these mystical teachings, we hold no forms of God, we make no graven images. There are over ten Divine attributes of God used in the Old Testament, but these names — such as *Jahveh* and *Elohim* — are not God, but *names of God*. That is, they are combinations of Hebrew letters that are ways of expressing — *Being, Presence, the essence of all life, and creative power.* Here in the Gospel poem Logos is the collective name of all these Divine attributes.

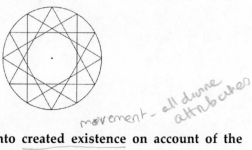

movement — all divine attributes

1:3 All things came into created existence on account of the Logos, and without the Logos not even one created thing came into created existence.

Everything in created existence comes from one source: Logos. First, I need to repeat an essential point, which must be clarified before we go any further into the text. The author of the Gospel poem assumes that the reader or hearer already has the mystical understanding of the creation story in Genesis. The opening verses of the Genesis creation story speak of the origins of life at a spiritual or metaphysical level without form or physical substance. This is not a series of physical acts, nor is it subject to

20

(Azilut)
Beriah
Yetzirah
Asiyyah

our ideas of physical or psychological time. The verses in Genesis describe the unfolding of life at the level of abstract Idea *Beriah* in power or principle, and this is true of all that is depicted in the first chapter. The second chapter describes the emergence of *Yetzirah* forms out of Idea, and the third chapter physical substance *Asiyyah* emerging out of form. The Hebrew text makes this very clear by using three different concepts for the different universes of existence: Bara, to create, Yatzar to form, and Asah to make.

In the English translation of the Gospel poem, verse three reads, "All things were made through him, and without him was not anything made that was made." There are a number of problems with this translation. Firstly, the Greek word *autos*, which is translated as "him" refers directly to the Logos, which in Greek grammar takes the masculine form. The word *autos* which is translated as "he" in English is *not* exclusively masculine: it can be interpreted as "Self" in the sense of possessing both masculine and feminine in balance. This is why, in the translation, I have continued to use the noun Logos, rather than its connecter, the pronoun *autos*.

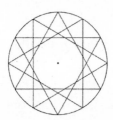

Logos contains within itself the essence of male and female. We attribute Gender to Divinity, for our own reasons, and as a result of our own experiences. But God and Goddess are only descriptive references for active and passive creative dynamics. These creative dynamics are held in union, as potencies, within the Divine universe.

Secondly, the Greek word *egeneto*, translated into English as "made," more accurately means, "to come into existence by an act of creation." The term "created existence" refers again to chapter one of Genesis, the spiritual universe of Beriah, containing all life as seed or Idea, without form or material substance. In Greek, the word *Cosmos*, which appears later in the Gospel, is used specifically for the physical universe and the universe of psychological forms.

The text states that created existence — the universe of spiritual ideas — is brought into existence by the Logos. All life has one source or origin; all life is connected. To emphasize this unity it says, *"without the Logos not even one created thing came into created existence."* All that exists does, so on account of Logos: the creative potential, or seed, of every living thing, human, animal, vegetable or mineral, archangelic ideas, and angelic forms — everything we know to exist is sustained by and originates from Logos.

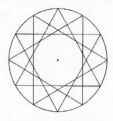

1:4 In the Logos life had Being, and the life was the radiance of Humanity.

In the RSV (The Revised Standard Version of the English Bible) this verse reads, "In him was life and life was the light of men." Again it is the Logos that is being referred to, and the verse states unequivocally that all of humanity — the Greek Anthropos which is used in the verse above, means humanity and not male gender — has Divine origins. The verse could also be translated: *In Logos the vitality of life had Being, and the abundant flow of life was the radiance of Universal Humanity.*

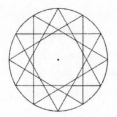

To realize the vitality of abundant life is to know that you are deeply connected to every living thing. Logos is the essence of all life, every created thing, and all of humanity. *"And the life was the radiance of Universal Humanity."* When, through spiritual consciousness, you realize Logos as the essence of life, you become a human — *Being.*

According to Genesis, The Elohim creates a spiritual universe in which it is eternally present. During the sixth cycle of creation, *The Elohim (Divine Being) creates Adam (universal humanity).* Elohim is your eternal source, Being, that exists within you now. The created Human Spirit is androgynous, containing both masculine and feminine in union, which is why the Gospel poem uses the Greek Anthropos to speak of universal humanity. Your Spiritual Body is a garment of creative patterns, a vessel for Being to move within the unfolding expressions of the universe of creation. It is only at the level of form that male and female appear as objective to each other, and as we enter the physical realm, we inhabit separate bodies as men and women.

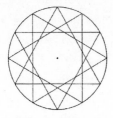

1:5 And the light was made visible in the spiritual darkness, and the spiritual darkness could not take possession of it.
The light is the emanation of Logos; Being — the abundance of

23

Skotia   Darkness / Sin / Polarity

life, all that *is*, held in the eternal present as it pours into created existence. The Greek word *skotia* means darkness, not simply the darkness of night, but spiritual darkness, that is, blindness, ignorance, wickedness and its resultant misery. This is a condition unique to humanity. Spiritual darkness is the unconscious, lower, human mind. We might say that part of us that generates evil.

Evil is a much-misused word, especially by those who seek to hold religious or political authority. The only source of evil is the unconscious human mind. Cut off from Being, and spiritual awareness — and spiritual awareness simply means conscious awareness — the individual and collective unconscious mind believes itself to be separate from the Unity of life, and seeks to be powerful, to possess and control life. It seeks power through the accumulation of wealth for its own sake. This has nothing to do with building a house or business, buying a car, piece of artwork, or beautiful clothes. It is a malady that makes us feel important and special, and we amass possessions, power and wealth to reinforce this belief.

Cut off from knowledge of abundant life, the unconscious egocentric mind becomes increasingly parasitical, as it can only take life from those around it. With sufficient skill and awareness to manipulate the psychological world, it makes others weak and vulnerable in order to exploit them. This further increases the desire for the life force of others through their enslavement. Moreover, everything in the natural world becomes a commodity to exploit; as this insanity becomes manifest as external pollution, it brings about the willful destruction of the web of life on Earth, decimating and destroying whole species, whole regions and ecosystems.

All that is darkness in humanity, must itself become the light: This is understood in some of the meanings attributed to Logos: equilibrium, harmony, ratio, and beauty. In the Gospel poem, darkness symbolizes more than the unconscious mind, or our

24

concepts of evil. With created existence and the beginning of
movement (time) in space, comes the first separation from the
Unity of Being. In the biblical language of Genesis chapter 2:9,
this spiritual universe is referred to as *"The Tree of Knowledge of
good and evil."*

The following translation of Genesis 2:9 brings out the deeper
meaning of the Hebrew text that the Gospel is referring to. *And
JHVH-Elohim (the intense power of Absolute life) caused to spring
forth from the seedbed of life, every Tree (self fructifying creative
patterns — worlds within worlds). And they were desirable to the inner
vision (experience) and good to sustain the growth of life (as form).
And in the midst of the garden (abundant fertile life) was the Tree of
Life (Being) and from it the Tree of Knowledge of Good and Evil (the
up-building and down-breaking cycles of life.) (My translation.)*

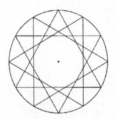

*The Tree of Life is the timeless center of existence; the Tree of
Knowledge the creative tension of polarity that gives space to life; the
Garden of Eden the beauty of divergent forms, that continually bloom
and die, and re-emerge as new forms of life: intense dynamic pressure,
continual flow, movement and change.*

We have to take care to understand the original Hebrew of
this translation. The Hebrew word Etz, can be translated as tree,
but it also means the spinal cord, and building blocks — the
structures that shape life. Tov is translated as good and also
means the beautiful and pleasant — the will to build up and
expand. Ratz, translated as evil, also means to break down,
shatter, and crush — the will to contract and dissolve.
Everything that is built up in creation meets resistance; is broken

down again — nothing in created existence, or the Cosmos is permanent or static. This is the intensity of creative power into which humanity must evolve, and which constitutes the essential nature of who we are.

These forces — *Tov and Ratz* — are polarized opposites, symbolized by light and darkness. Thus, consciousness is held in a dynamic setting where life unfolds through movement in space. The statement that the spiritual darkness was not able to overcome the light illustrates the balance of the tension of opposites that allows the creative process to take place, and encourages all life to grow through evolutionary pressure. The function of the force of resistance within creation is to test, or to temper, the expansive force of life. The dynamic opposites of *Tov and Ratz* should be understood as the polar tension of opposites allowing life to develop, diversify and evolve in equilibrium.

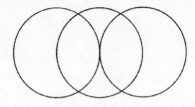

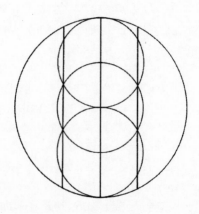

The three interlacing circles at the top represent equilibrium (center) active (right) and passive (left) dynamics. If they are turned vertically, they can be seen to represent Creation, formation and manifestation held within the One, represented by the outer circle. The principles of active and passive polarities, and equilibrium, are shown via the three vertical lines as present within the whole of existence.

It is this creative polarity, emerging out of stillness that enables the dynamic movement of ideas to manifest as the form and matter of the Cosmos. The physical universe, the Earth and the body come from the Logos, and are inherently good and sacred. Evil, in the common understanding of the word, is something different, being limited to, and only operating within, the unconscious human mind. Humans can consciously choose to evolve, and to affect the general evolutionary progress of creation. This light of the Logos is made visible to us by choosing to join with the rest of life in the creative process. With this choice comes the ability to illuminate the ideas that already reside in this world. The spiritual darkness of the unconscious human mind is limited by its own destructive force and will consume itself. As the poem puts it, it is incapable of taking possession of the creative light of the Logos, because it cannot comprehend the Logos.

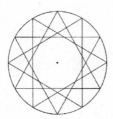

Human evolution is synonymous with spiritual awakening — to become conscious of being conscious. When the mind is still, and silenced, greater awareness emerges. To breathe consciously aids you to become present, here and now.

Meditation

To comprehend the teachings in the first five verses of the poem more fully, to have something approaching an inner experience of what is being expressed in the text, I suggest that you try the following exercise. This is the first of a series of meditations to help bring living experience to the teachings.

Before starting any meditation, you need to create a sacred space. You may start by lighting a candle, and choosing an invocation or prayer that has special significance for you. The most important part of creating a sacred space is to be alert, and to breathe consciously. You do this in order to prepare yourself to enter a higher state of consciousness, set apart from your mind made distractions, and the concerns and problems of the outside world.

Sit in a comfortable position, and relax your body through a deep breathing rhythm, in which the in breath matches the out breath in a balanced harmony. The spine should be straight but relaxed, with dropped shoulders, allowing the head to be carried and supported. Spend a few moments relaxing your muscles and frame, using the breath to release any blocks or tensions that you become aware of. As you breathe, do not force the breath, aim for a steady, easy flow like the tide of a tranquil sea. To breathe consciously from your center, which can be felt behind the Heart and the Solar Plexus, helps you to realize inner balance and peace.

Now be aware of the spinal cord. The first vertebra at the top of the spine is called the atlas, because it bears the direct weight of the skull. Through the breath, we allow the spine to support the skull without tension in the jaw and neck. The atlas vertebra rests upon the axis vertebra, which is the second of the seven cervical vertebrae, and allows rotational movement of the skull. As you breathe, you are allowing space and finding freedom of movement; nothing is forced, or subjected to the fears and anxieties or frustrations of the mind. Watch the mind, become the observing consciousness, and whenever you notice any thoughts appearing, use the conscious breath to bring you back to the present, and be still.

Below the seven cervical vertebrae are the thoracic vertebrae, the middle twelve in the vertebral column. From here, you can expand your awareness from your center to connect with the great circle of life. As you expand your peripheral vision you are realizing space in which creative life unfolds. Again, you are breathing life into the spine, freeing up space within you, allowing all tensions held in the body to release on the out-breath, allowing the spine to lengthen. And as you breathe in, become aware of the energy in your body, sustaining your body.

Below them are the five lumbar vertebrae, which are above the fused vertebrae of the sacrum. Breathing into this space draws you into your connection with the diversity and abundance of life, the continual flow of life into and out of form and matter.

At the base of the spine is the coccyx or "tailbone" which gives you your foundation in the Cosmos and places your feet firmly upon the Earth. As you continue to breathe consciously, be aware of the soles of your feet, visualize and feel that the breath is being drawn up from a point inside the body around the coccyx at the base of the spine. Be aware of the toes and heels connecting you with the Earth, and allowing you to grow up into the heavens above the crown of your head.

Now focus all of your attention on the ever-present stillness beneath and behind each movement of the breath, the supporting space that allows all movement to unfold. From deep within yourself, you bring forth on each breath, "In the beginning." This, the first act of creation, is happening now, movement continually unfolding in space, out of the eternal present moment. Without your inner *Being* having to move, you observe the unfolding out of the stillness, which holds the cycles of life, the cycles of the breath. Feel the stillness of your center with all your attention, the space between the in-drawing and outpouring of the breath. Remember that whenever you breathe consciously you connect with your life source, which is the eternal presence out of which all movement continually emerges.

After a few minutes, bring your attention to your feet on the floor, the air in your lungs, and the beating of your heart. Open your eyes, be fully aware of your surroundings, and feel your connection with the Earth as fully as possible through your feet. Close the meditation consciously, using an invocation or prayer if that helps you. As you go back to your everyday life, remember to take conscious breaths and to be aware your inner core or center. Be aware of the beauty and harmony of the patterns of unfolding life in the world about you, and your inner connection with all that you observe.

This analogy — and it is only an analogy — conveys something of the relationship of *Being* to the unfolding of creative pattern. Existence has *Being* through the will of the Absolute. There is no duality, only a polarity, in the sense of night and day, and active and passive dynamic, which begins with the first movement out of unity in the beginning of creation.

Continue to practice the breathing exercise and posture as you go through this book. *More important is to remember to breathe consciously in your daily life, to still the mind and create the conditions in which you begin to experience a sense of inner peace.*

Chapter Three

Awakening the Soul

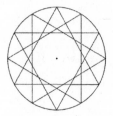

1:6 A human being named John came into created existence as an envoy of the Logos.

The sixth verse introduces John with the Greek word *Anthropos*. In the poem, *Anthropos* is used to describe the inner, spiritual nature of an individual, and of collective humanity: consciousness, lucid awareness, spiritual presence, in both women and men. John is also called an envoy. The Greek *Apostolos* (Apostle in English) means the bearer of a message as an envoy or agent rather than someone who simply passes on a message. To be an envoy means that we are aware of the contents and meaning of the message and speak it in our own words. Spiritually, it means we engage with the deeper awareness through which we can initiate change in ourselves. Each of us has the capacity to act as initiator for greater consciousness, which has nothing to do with changing others. It is the inner awakening that brings realization of our own spiritual consciousness, our *Being*. Without this realization, we fall victim to illusions: seeing ourselves as God's messenger, representative, or chosen, needing to guide, convince, and convert others to what we imagine to be "the truth."

It is imperative to understand that these mystical teachings are concerned with the present, *here, now*, not a mind made past or future. The poem speaks to us directly out of the present, calling us to be consciously present in all that we do, and awaken to the unity of life.

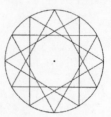

As in the first verse of the poem, we are asked to become conscious: still and centered, aware of what John is within us. Begin by breathing consciously; feel the air drawing into your body, feel the energy field of the body beneath the skin, from the top of your head right down to the soles of your feet. And when you breathe out, be aware of your posture, and your connection with your surroundings.

The name John, in Hebrew, can be translated as "whom Jahveh gave," or "Jah is gracious." The Hebrew letters JHVH (Jahveh) mean "To Be Being," and JH (Jah) "Being." This grace and giving is the "abundant life" that continually emerges out of Being. The grace is not concerned with a historical figure, but with becoming conscious of the life force within that gives life to mind and body through the Soul. There are two Hebrew words used to describe the Soul and both are concerned with the breath: *Neshamah* — to breathe, and *Nephesh* — breath.

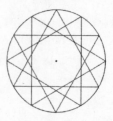

Breathing consciously and fully, you awaken higher awareness, and connect with your vital body, which connects you with the whole of life.

conscious awareness
+ the physical/psychological

Be conscious of the breath even as you read these words; there is no effort: the bodies' vital energy is breathing through you; as you awaken to it, you increase your presence.

In many Orthodox Church icons, John is depicted with long unkempt hair and beard, wearing animal skins and living off the things of the wilderness. This is not merely the image of an ascetic who has rejected the world. Human consciousness at the natural — or psycho-somatic — level contains within it the animal, vegetable and mineral consciousness that we see manifest in many forms in the world around us, from the rock formations of the Earth's crust, to the diverse flora and fauna; from the most basic to the most highly-evolved. John personifies our psychosomatic bodies, the vital energies, which can be felt within the mind and physical form, encompassing all our drives and desires. John is concerned with refining and focusing these psychological and physical energies under the will of higher consciousness; in Hebrew, this is called *Tipheret*.

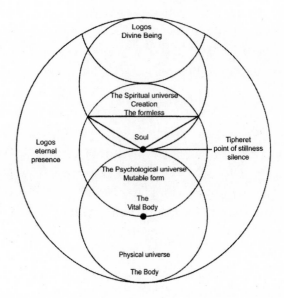

The Divine universe of eternal presence is represented through the outer circle, and the half circle at the top of the diagram. The spiritual

universe of creation is represented by the top circle, the universe of Soul and form by the central circle, and the outer manifestation of physical appearances by the bottom circle. This is better understood as moving from the still center of unity of life, into its expression in formless creative idea, and on to diversity in form and its multiple expression in the world of outer appearances.

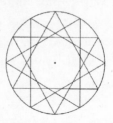

תפארת Tipheret the Center of all Things

Often translated as beauty, goodness or truth, *Tipheret* means: *absolute life held in balance; consciously held space, simultaneously containing and releasing creative pattern — never ceasing to be, never holding onto forms.* When you awaken to this creative space within you, and learn to live and move from it, you become aware that all your actions originate out of stillness, a lucidity, which brings the whole circle of life into conscious awareness. As your awareness deepens, you connect with the spirits of the natural world, and simultaneously observe and deepen your own inner life, detached from the thoughts, feelings, and deeper emotions that cling to your ego and obscure the light of consciousness.

Just as the Sun contains the solar system within its aura, and gives light to all life on Earth, so too Tipheret illuminates — gives life — to our natural humanity, the vital forces that make and sustain the physical body, and the psychological body of the ordinary, everyday mind of the ego and psyche. The part of us that thinks, feels, dreams, desires, and lives and breathes through the passions and drives of the mind and body. Through our natural humanity, we live and move within the universes of form and matter and use this life force to build a home, earn a living, raise a family, and master our chosen profession.

The Lower Human Nature

Wherever we live, whatever the nature of our work, the danger is to fall into a psychological sleep where we identify solely with the ego, and become hostage to our unconscious thought patterns and emotions. We then become susceptible to the collective unconscious thought patterns and desires of the society we live in and become overwhelmed, cut off from true creativity and higher faculties of awareness, through enslavement to the individual and collective unconscious — the lower human nature.

The natural world and all its creatures are always present, continually creating life in the now. To be disconnected from this rich and diverse web of life means we are not present, and do not live in a balanced way. With no roots in *Being*, we enter a living death, neither conscious of Soul and Spirit, nor consciously inhabiting our physical body. Suspended in an ego driven, virtual reality where we feel free to exploit and destroy the physical environment, we become unable or unwilling to realize that these unconscious patterns are unraveling the life force within and around us.

It is important to be clear that the lower human nature is not caused by the drives of the physical body. Rather, the unconscious thought patterns of the ego driven mind, which are detached from both spiritual awareness and the vital energy of the body, take us over and construct an illusory reality. Without the conscious presence of the Soul, we give our life energy away to the ego driven mind, which seeks the feelings of power that accompanies illusions of being separate and special. If, on the other hand, we believe ourselves to be small and insignificant, we may associate with other egos in groups to gain a sense of greater power; in this way, we become susceptible to giving our energy away to those who seek to manipulate and control others.

The world of politics and finance and religion easily give rise to institutions that serve only the lower human nature. These institutions seek to defend themselves against a supposedly hostile world, attacking perceived enemies, whose existence is in fact necessary to preserve their special status.

As the ego is never satisfied, it continually seeks to accumulate further power through control and fear. This turns into greed, a deliberately destructive entity that seeks to consume everything around it. It is through total identification with the ego that we come to believe ourselves to be separate entities within the circle of life.

All ego entities are maintained through illusions and lies that cannot survive in higher consciousness. The truth is that we are one with life in all its forms, even when submerged in the civilized life that has become a reflection of our unconscious and fragmented state. When we awaken higher consciousness of *Neshamah*, *Nephesh* through Tipheret, we do everything necessary to sustain ourselves, our families and communities, but we do it in awareness of Soul, which sustains our life in the natural world, and integrates us with it. Through the creativity of inner space, we allow ourselves to be, and from there allow all life forms to be.

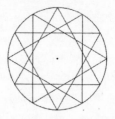

John is your awakened Soul; at its center is Tipheret; the awakened Soul is the vessel that contains within it all that we perceive as external life. To live from our center brings us into union with the great circle of life, inner and outer known as One. This is Peace.

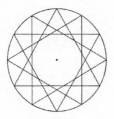

1:7 This John came as a witness, in order that there might be a witness about the light, so that all might believe through that light.
1:8 This John is not the light, but is a testimony concerning the light.

The Greek *martys*, translated in this verse as "witness," is where the term martyr comes from. Martyrdom is a term much abused by religious fanatics to indicate their pain and suffering, and to inflict this inner disquiet upon others. To use a teaching from the Bible, *God does not require blood sacrifices.* The root *martys* literally means to testify, to be steadfast and honest, and to view life with impartiality and honesty. It describes the observer or witness, who is able to obtain an objective overview of life or a particular situation, through creating space in which the mind and emotions are stilled. This implies something quite different to what is usually understood by the term martyrdom. A martyr is someone who is being called to maintain an honest position, not to lay down their life in selfless sacrifice for a cause. The sacrifice we make through *martys* is psychological: the pain of losing a cherished image of ourselves, giving up an important position, or fantasies of being special, are more difficult for the egocentric mind than the thought of physical death.

The second half of verse seven says that there has to be "a witness about the Divine light so that all might believe through this light." John, the awakened natural human, is the inner witness — lucid awareness. The Greek root translated here as "believe" also means, "to be convinced of something." To be convinced, in this case, does not refer to a mental position, but to the internal awakening in which we experience the light of consciousness directly, and see, hear and touch the beauty that is abundant life.

To experience higher consciousness, however briefly, brings increased awareness and changes our life forever. It gives the possibility of making a truly conscious choice: to deepen awareness, and be consciously present, through the breath and the vital body. Deepening awareness breaks down the illusions the ego identifies with, and this may temporarily bring feelings of abandonment and being totally alone. This is why the egocentric mind does not want to experience the sustained consciousness we call enlightenment but prefers to think and talk about being spiritual, and makes a spiritualized ego identity by aligning itself with a group or individual. People will often attend meetings, workshops and courses simply to reinforce this spiritual ego identity, and may become agitated or angry before the stillness or silence of spiritual consciousness and its source, Being.

To see life clearly and accept and understand that the physical and psychological worlds are in a continual flux of change is not easy. Being able to see and cope with the death of a loved one or the loss of a home, the breakup of a relationship or whole communities, nations, and all the things that we believe to be permanent causes a breakdown of the ego, which will either facilitate or impede our awakening, depending on how we respond. We may enter a depression that we cannot see the way out of, which can also lead to destructive and life negating behavior. If we then look for revenge against life, it can turn us into a miscreant.

To hold to the position that John represents means to stand in stillness, witness the light of our Being, and speak and act from there. Wherever we are and whatever the circumstances, we can meet them with consciousness, lucid awareness, and an acceptance of what is. When we accept what is, we awaken the ability to move or change within the patterns of creative life.

In verse eight, we read that "this John is not the light itself, but a witness to it." As we have seen, one of the biggest problems in spiritual work is that the mind through ego identification seeks to spiritualize itself. But mind is only a tool created by consciousness; the Soul too, is a created vehicle that enables consciousness to move within the universes of form and matter. The awakened Soul is self-aware; subject and object diminish into the unity of presence. John holds steadfast to the birth of greater consciousness, and experiences the illumination of Being within the Soul; he experiences the light of consciousness as it manifests in the physical body and universe. This sustained awareness draws creative life force into the physical universe, which brings the possibility of real, rather than superficial, change.

John is the conscious witness in the unconscious psychological wilderness. This is achieved when you begin to act consciously in your daily life, a process that has to be held to in the face of skepticism, indifference and ignorance, not only in other people, but more importantly, in your thinking mind. In the mind, are the traits of apathy, laziness, distractedness, and busyness, which keep you from experiencing consciousness. In the language of the Bible, the achievement of greater consciousness comes through release from psychological and physical bondage, symbolized by slavery in Egypt, to a state of freedom through a series of psychological deaths and rebirths. John represents that process within each of us that, through the wilderness years of psychological renewal, prepares the Soul for contact with the creative Spirit and Being, symbolized by entry into the promised land of spiritual consciousness.

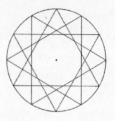

Meditation

The poem is asking you to become aware of what John represents within you, through observing your psychosomatic natural energies, and bringing them under conscious, focused, attention. Your natural energies are not negative in any way, they are a part of life; they only become negative when the ego uses them to gain a greater sense of power for itself, separating them from the flow of life. In their negative form they manifest as fear, guilt, greed, anger and hatred, and the lust for power in all its forms; all the illusions that separate you from the conscious presence of Being.

John stands at the inner Sun, *Tipheret — absolute life held in balance; consciously held space, presence, never ceasing to be, never holding onto form (crystallizing).* To awaken John within, is to learn to be, and move from this point of stillness. To awaken spiritually is to become conscious that you are connected to all of life, nothing in existence is separate; all is One. Life on Earth, the solar system and the Cosmos can all be experienced through deepening our awareness, because we hold the same patterns within us.

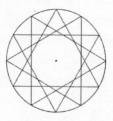

To start the meditation, first create a sacred space. You do this through breathing consciously. Conscious breathing becomes your foundation,

deepening your awareness and sensitivity. When you are conscious, when you connect with the breath in this way, you are able to watch all your moods and desires, the schemes and mind games of the ego without being subject to them, and see your true motives. You can then act and speak honestly.

To do this meditation sit comfortably with the spine erect, and breathe with a nice deep easy rhythm, aware of the abdomen rising and falling. Once sufficiently relaxed, bring conscious awareness to your physical frame. Focus especially on the spinal cord from the cranium to the coccyx, and then feel the life force within your whole frame — from the top of the skull, in your face, your eyes, ears, lips, and nose, down through the neck and shoulders, through the rib cage, the bones in your arms and hands, and down the spinal cord to the pelvis and hips, the legs and feet. Be aware of the finger and toe bones, the palms of your hands and the souls of your feet. With each breath, you are connecting with the spinal cord and becoming aware of the subtle energies within it. When you breathe consciously, you allow space between the joints and free up the movements of all your bones.

Next feel your flesh, the muscles, tendons and ligaments, make sure they are relaxed and not contracting your posture, or restricting the internal organs. Be aware of the blood coursing through your veins, and the air in your lungs, carried on the rhythm of the breath.

Now become aware of the sensation of your aura. Feel the aura as your vital body from a point deep within you, and coming out from your center. Don't become fixated on where this is, as a position in the body. It may appear to be at different places at different times, such as the naval, solar plexus, heart, throat, or third eye; just feel it, and allow it to be. What is important is that you feel a radiant point within you, coming out through the skin, connecting you with the space about you. Feel the life force of the body as a circle or sphere about you.

Be aware of the in-breath rising up the spinal cord from the coccyx to the top of the head, and the exhalation pouring out like a fountain, going down around the body into the Earth, to be drawn back up the spine again. Create a comfortable rhythm and feel the breath entering the blood stream and into the cells in the body — into the bones, allowing spaces between the joints, especially the vertebrae. Let the breath find its own rhythm like water washing on the shore of a great lake or sea.

The rhythm of the breath also pulses from your center out to the periphery of the aura; the spine is like the trunk of a great tree that draws nourishment from the Earth below your feet, and from the Spirit above the crown of your head. Allow its life pulse to support and nourish you. The spine is rooted deep within the Earth; that which we take from the Earth we return to the Earth. The spine through the crown of the head is also rooted deep in space; that which we draw in from Spirit we return to Spirit; Earth and Spirit are One. The center of the circle is continually creating life, the periphery continually dissolving form and matter. The continual flow of creative ideas become forms that solidify, before dissolving and returning to the formless center.

Observe your mind; watch any thoughts that come up, and release them on the out breath, bring your attention back to your inner center, awaken, and breathe from there. Be present in the form of your body and to the forms of life about you, enjoying them whilst they last, and know that you are not the body, nor the mind, nor the ego: you are consciousness, which allows the experience of the free flow of abundant life to pass through you; cease to fear the dissolving of form; accept life as always changing, always creating new form.

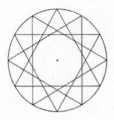

Because you can observe your thoughts and emotions, you are not your thoughts or emotions; you exist beyond mind; at your very core is consciousness. There is space between your thoughts, stillness and silence, holding creative potential.

When you finish the visualization, close the sacred space as before. It is important not to leave yourself open, until you can realize space beyond the unconscious thoughts and emotions of others.

Chapter Four

The Revelation of Divinity in Matter

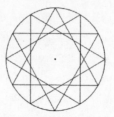

1:9 The Divine light is the true radiance, which illuminates every human being coming into the Cosmos.
Verse nine, describes Logos as the perfect, true light, which is the spiritual illumination — the enlightenment — of every human being who enters into the Cosmos. The Greek word *Phos* translated as light, means Divine presence, *Being*, and the illumination of the mind — a spiritual awakening. As humans, we take on form and physical substance, but at our core, our essence, we are formless *Being*. It is our inherent potential to realize this.

The Cosmos is the vastness of the material universe, countless galaxies each containing perhaps two hundred billion stars: our Sun is a single cell in a single galaxy. What we observe in the sky on a clear day from the Earth's surface is the core of the Sun. The Earth is not only within the aura of the Sun, but is itself made from the Sun's energy we observe as light. Sun or Stellar light is consciousness expressed through form into matter. This conscious light energy is within the cells that make up your physical body, and is the substance of all life forms. We live in this vast macrocosmic expression of Divine Being, yet all that appears in the Cosmos as so vast and external is also contained within us, through the creative patterns of life. We are each a microcosmic reflection, of that seemingly endless expanse of the

44

patterns and rhythms of life, contained in the stars.

The poem also uses Cosmos to describe the mind and universe of forms; a vast and seemingly endless psychological world, where ideas take on color, sound, texture, feeling and emotion in our dreams and thoughts, until they begin to take on material substance, a field of gravity, that becomes what the ordinary everyday mind experiences as solid.

When we begin to understand that nothing is separate, that all is linked in one interconnected whole, we begin to experience the unity of life through the Cosmos. As soon as an idea takes form, it is already dissolving. The day you are born, the moment you take your first breath, carries the imprint of your death as an ego and physical body. All form and matter is in a constant flux of change, and to try to hold on to form, identify with form, and accumulate form as possessions, is the cause of much of our suffering, and the root of much of our collective madness.

Logos is our source, from where we are continually created, and this same source is sustaining us now whether we are conscious of it or not. Even in the darkest psychological hell or purgatory we make, humanity is still sustained by the light of Logos. Nothing that exists, that is created, is separate from the One. All separation is ultimately a mind made illusion.

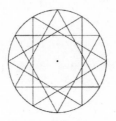

1:10 The Divine light was in the Cosmos and the Cosmos came into created existence through the Divine light, but the Cosmos did not perceive this Divine light.

Logos is *eternal presence* in the Cosmos from its very conception. Logos continually gives birth to created existence — all life governed by time unfolding in space. The Cosmos, all that is form and matter, exists on account of the timeless Being of Logos and its creative space. The source of all life is stillness; holding all movement in the eternal now, beginning and end, life and death. The poem says that the Cosmos cannot, of itself, perceive its origins. This is a very significant statement, which focuses the term Cosmos on humanity. Reflect on the following for a moment.

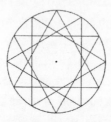

All creatures outside of humanity hold their own perceptions of life in their own unique and individual way — each creature lives and moves as an expression of Divine light, forming and reforming through the unveiling of creation into form and matter, sustaining the vast web of life. All creatures are aware of both objects (forms) and creative space (the formless) without knowing that they are awake, it is their natural state. They await our awakening, where we join with them in the conscious communion of life that takes place at each moment, through the diverse expressions of the One.

Every creature has a specific function within the created whole, and we humans are not an exception, or a special creature. Humanity differs from all other creatures in that we have become so identified with form and matter (the Cosmos) that we are no longer able to perceive creative space (the formless light of Logos). Unless we choose to awaken, we are not capable of comprehending Logos, that is, of having direct knowledge of *Being*. This means that we are not able to be actively involved in the creative unfolding of life, nor understand the sacredness of life in the Cosmos. We are at best passengers unaware of our connection with the landscape we are journeying through. At worst, we act like a parasite, carried by life, draining its resources without giving anything back, without any true creativity. The creatures that manifest the animal, vegetable and mineral kingdoms naturally create life on Earth, through a complex ecosystem that gives humanity a physical life in which we can evolve spiritually. Whilst we remain unconscious, we repay them by destroying their habitats and driving them to the point of extinction. Through this collective insanity, we are cutting ourselves off from eternal life, which is bad enough when we can honestly say that we do not know what we are doing. But if we begin to awaken, and in awakening merely seek the illusion of power, we corrupt the creative life force that flows through us, commit the felony of willful ignorance, and the light — consciousness recedes from us.

As the observing consciousness — or the witness — John represents a departure from the old, unconscious way of life. Instead of only being aware of objects (form – the Cosmos), John is the awakening to the eternal presence and creative space in which all objects are able *to be*. Logos, the illumination of creation, is present in humanity here and now, watching, on the Earth. In the teaching stories of the Bible this full realization of humanities *Being*, is called Enoch, which means "the initiated, the awakened," *who walked with God and was no more*. This human being became transformed into Metatron: the presence of *Jahveh — Elohim*, and is said to appear in history as Melkitzadek, "the King of Righteousness." Known by different names in different cultures, such as Kidur in the Sufi tradition and the Green Man in the Celtic, it is said that she or he appears at crucial times to aid human awakening. *Enoch — Metatron is simply the presence of Being we awaken within us.*

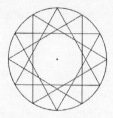

1:11 The Divine light came to its rightful dwelling place and its own kin did not admit it.

1:12 But as many as received (gave hospitality to) the Divine light, those it empowered to become descendants of God, for they put their trust in the Divine name.

1:13 Who came into created existence not by blood, nor of the will of the flesh, nor of the will of man, but of God.

The language of verse eleven is intimate as it describes humanity as "the rightful dwelling place," and "own kin" of Logos. Yet we choose to remain largely unconscious of our inner connection with Being and true creativity. It may be occasionally perceived through our work, even if only for brief moments, before we become distracted by old, established patterns of thought, and emotional reactions, or the ego reasserts itself, becoming inflated by what we do, claiming what is created or made as its own. We have not yet learnt how to sustain conscious presence; we still believe that creativity is "mine," rather than the fountain that we drink from freely.

Awareness of Logos — conscious presence — may happen during profound life events: the birth of a child or death of a deeply loved partner, relative or friend, when the ego's hold on our thought processes is temporarily interrupted or reduced. When we are in shock or terrible grief, it is possible to be awakened by the pressure put on the ego. This pressure comes from our own spiritual body and *Being*, through the circumstances of life. If this pressure fails to rouse us into consciousness, our psychological blocks can manifest through the body as illness, and illness can bring us to a point of stillness, moments of lucidity, a space that enables us to begin to release and transform our negative thought forms. The energy released is then used to bring us towards the reality of our true Being.

When you are inspired through realizing the beauty of the natural world around you, through the work of another artist, or by a spiritual practice or yoga, realize that the beauty you see, hear or feel, is within you. If this can be sustained, it brings a change in our perception of life — and the outer world of appearances reciprocates. In other words, life meets our new state of consciousness by reflecting back to us what has moved or shifted in our perception. To bring about a permanent change requires determined effort and courage, because it is easy to fall back into old habitual patterns of thinking and compulsive behavior. It is essential that each of us realize the conscious presence within us *now*, use the life given to us creatively in all our actions and words, fulfill our spiritual potential and allow *Being* its rightful dwelling place or inheritance — *To Be* — *to live in presence and perceive the unity of life.*

The opening of verse twelve is usually translated as "But as many as received him... ." The word translated as "received" has a Greek root *elabon*, which literally means "to receive as a guest" and also "to accept in the sense of hospitality". This is the meaning of the Hebrew word "Kabbalah:" that is, to be receptive and open to the presence of Divine Being, and to the teaching that is given to us through life. To be receptive is an active state — it requires that we become alert, observing life without a constant stream of thinking or anxious feelings obscuring clarity of presence.

Those who receive Logos as a guest (give hospitality), simply means anyone who makes the effort to be spiritually conscious. Such people often have no conventional religious calling, and some may describe themselves as agnostic, as they may have rejected all the usual forms of traditional spiritual thought and practice, and all human made forms of God. Instead, they have a developed compassion for their fellow humanity, and a sense of wonder at the beauty, complexity, diversity and interconnectedness of life.

When we are conscious, we notice more. Things seem more alive and vibrant to us, because they *are* more alive and vibrant than we normally allow ourselves to experience. When we dull our senses and perception, we block out life. When we raise our consciousness, we begin to remember the interconnectedness of life and experience its reality. People cannot hide from us, nor we from them, and we see and feel both their, and our own, true thoughts and feelings. The spirits of places, animal, plant and mineral life also speak to us, and seek to commune with us because they find a receptive being who can take in what they give to *the World* — *Cosmos*. As we become more alive, so life is attracted to us and flows through us in greater measure.

It is through this awakening that we are, as the RSV translation says, "given the power to become children of God." What the Greek word *ezousian*, ("power" in the RSV), means, when taken in the context of the verse, is that by choosing to interact with Logos — *your own inner source of Being* — our subtler organs of perception and communication are opened up and integrated with those of the physical body. A deeper meaning of this Greek word is therefore "empower" and "authority." If we are empowered, then we are focused, and by being focused we concentrate our energy to work consciously on ourselves, and in the world, because we stand on our own inner authority; this is Gnosis or experiential knowledge.

To open up these largely dormant faculties of higher awareness, is to awaken to the eternal presence within you now, to become a descendent of *the Elohim*. The root of the word *tekna*, usually translated as "son," includes both female and male, and means "a descendant" or "offspring." In Hebrew, this is "the beni Elohim," *the progeny of the Divine name of God*. Until we chose to awaken the creative Spirit remains largely latent within us. Once we truly acknowledge Logos — the eternal essence within ourselves, we are in the process of re-membering, of putting back together our dormant faculties and abilities.

The end of the verse speaks of believing in the Divine name. Two words are important here. The first, translated as "believing," comes from a root *pisteuo,* which means, "to be convinced" and also "faith." Real faith can only come through knowledge that has been gained through experience, not through blindly taking on what someone else has said. The second word is translated as "name," which is the Hebrew term *Ha Shem* "The Name," used to address the Divine presence of God. A Kabbalistic teaching says, if you wish to know *Ha Shem,* first put yourself under discipline. This means inner silence — to still the mind. Then you are able to take the next step on the journey, which is listening, and means being receptive. Once in a state of receptivity then learning can take place. Real knowledge is gained through one's conscious interaction with life, and this the poem calls "putting one's trust in the name" — which in the Greek text is Logos.

Logos holds within it the whole of life, and the whole of humanity. Consciousness of Logos, comes into the Soul through as many as are capable or willing to receive it. It is our individual response to life, conscious receptivity that brings *Gnosis,* knowledge through experience. Once we begin to live in knowledge, we can impart that knowledge to those who are receptive, through example — by living as consciously as we can. To live as daughters or sons of Elohim, is to become consciously synchronized with the flow of life, aware of *Being.* This is to live under grace, to be creative in all that we do.

Verse 13 states that conscious realization of the Logos is not dependent on purity of bloodlines or racial origin. Neither is it dependent upon physical intention — the will of the flesh; nor the will of man, that is to say, human design, the political scheming of the ego. The revelation of Logos — Divine Being, comes through choosing to be consciously present, and sustaining conscious presence.

It is one of the great human fallacies to feel special because of our racial origin or religious affiliation, to think of ourselves as "God's people" or God's representative on Earth, from a line of the prophets or apostles, a lineage holder, etcetera, the list is endless. Such claims are a major illusion and the cause of psychological and pseudo-spiritual hubris, which leads to the persecution and demonizing of others, to cries of heresy and blasphemer, and to hatred, wars, and division among ourselves.

God, Divinity, Logos — or any name we give to *the One* source of life, can never be the property of a particular race or religion, of a priesthood or lineage of teachers; it is universal and totally free. For a man or woman to think that only through belonging to a particular religion or spiritual group will they be given salvation is psychologically immature, but such a belief has dominated much of human history. Believing in the Name does not mean being religious, or even taking up what might be considered as overt spiritual practice. It simply means living life as consciously as possible, in whatever we choose to do.

Spiritual practices were developed for the purpose of helping us to awaken and to acknowledge the Divine presence in all that we do creatively. But if we perform such practices as an unconscious routine, they have the opposite effect, simply reinforcing the unconscious mind and strengthening the ego.

Conscious presence gives us the *ability*, to be *beni Elohim*, descendants of *Absolute life* — *Being*. There is no-one, no-thing, between you and the possibility of total presence: no form, image, or sense of separation. The beginning of creation is here, now, containing the end of all time, all past and future. The past is there to be redeemed, the future to be realized in the eternal present. All the Gospel is asking us to do is become a human who has realized awareness of Being.

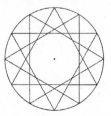

Walking Meditation

When you are out walking, wherever you are, but especially in the countryside or a place of beauty, in the mountains and valleys, in a forest, and next to the ocean, a lake, river or stream; be conscious of your breath, the air in your lungs, and of the blood coursing through your body, as the life that breathes and courses through the World around you.

As you take each step, be aware of the energy in your feet and in the spinal cord, connecting you to the Earth, allowing the Earth to support you.

As you take each step, be present — you are walking, moving, out of stillness. Be the still point, so that it feels as if each footstep is pushing the Earth backwards, the landscape moves past you: the mind moves, but you are the observer, the witness, the Stillness out of which all movement occurs.

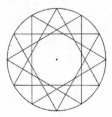

Why do you need to be present? Because, everything that has ever happened, or will ever happen, does so in the present moment. Physicality is the appearance of *Being* that is stretched out and slowed down through the different time and space continuums of idea, form and making, so that the mind perceives things appearing to it sequentially. Yet, all that you are, all life, is here with you now.

Chapter Five

Stilling the mind: The Realization of Sacred Space

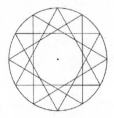

1:14 And the Logos became flesh and dwelt in us, and we beheld its glorious manifestation, like unto the splendor of that unique issue of the Father, perfected grace and truth.

Logos is the essence of all life, which through the creative process becomes diversifying form and physical substance; the One becomes the many. For humanity, this means that our flesh and bone is the dwelling place, the tabernacle, of Logos. The Greek word *skenoo* translated as "dwelt," means "a temporary dwelling place," "*a tabernacle* for the Divine presence." It is also a metaphor for our physical body, the temporary dwelling, which the Soul, through the mind, constructs and inhabits, the ephemeral, physical, garment of the spiritual, and Divine bodies that give it life.

In the teaching story of Exodus, the tabernacle is the temple design given by the Divine attribute of God, JHVH, to Moses, who instructs the children of Israel in its construction. JHVH means *"to be Being,"* and Moses *"to draw out."* Moses, like John in the poem, represents awakened higher consciousness, and JHVH is the revelation of *Being.* In Exodus, the tabernacle is set up in the midst of a nomadic people, as they move from place to place through the wilderness — a psychological landscape which depicts the unconscious mind, and its awakening. The tabernacle is not the permanent structure of a fixed temple, but a temporary habitation; ephemeral and mobile, assembled out of animal skins and woven cloth sewn together and hung as curtains on a timber frame. It is structured to symbolize the four universes of existence; the curtains dyed different colors to make us aware of each level as we move from the realm of the physical, scarlet outer court, through to the purple inner court of the psyche and Soul, into the blue sanctuary of formless Spirit. In the sanctuary is the pure white holy of holies, within which lies the Ark of the presence, the seat of the *Shekinah* — *the Divine presence*. The entire temple is held together by links of pure gold, which symbolize the Divine presence diffused throughout, and sustaining the fabric of life in all the universes. In the sanctuary is a solid Gold Menorah, which represents the unity of the Tree of Life.

As the people moved on their lifelong journey through the wilderness, they dismantled the tabernacle and carried it to their next resting place, and assembled it again in a different time and place. This movement through ever changing form is also an analogy of our own life, the changes we go through in our present physical body, and through the cycles of life and death. We move on, find a new place to settle; yet, all form must die because the constant renewal of creative life — our Spirit — demands it. The presence of Divine Being is always here — now. What is temporary, is the dwelling place or tabernacle, the physical body, and the mental forms we hold onto. The mental forms may last longer than the body, but they too, must fade and dissolve under the pressure of emerging creative life. When we are still and present we enter our inner sanctuary, and there we touch upon the eternal abiding presence of Divine Being.

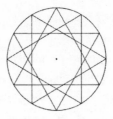

Take a conscious breath, and be as present as you can.

The Hebrew for "Spirit" is Ruwach, which can be translated as "expansive creative space," and "the movement of the breath or the wind." It is within you now, giving you life.

The temples and sacred sites we build, or the features in the landscape, and the trees we hold as sacred, are external focal points where we meet what is already present within us. They are reflectors, which mirror back to us the presence of Being and the creative outpouring within us. In reality, the whole of what we experience through mind and body, as the outer natural world, is sacred, and a mirror of inner life. When the delicate, sensory system of the physical body engages with higher consciousness, we begin to experience moments of the unity of life: all is One in our tent of meeting.

We need to be present to the life force flowing through our physical body, and at the same time detached from psychological forms, and we do this by creating inner space. The creation of inner space is a freeing up and dissolving, of all thought forms that block creativity, and our ability *To Be — Being*. We experience it as life force within every fiber of our body and Soul. At first subtly, occasionally dramatically, we realize space — make space around thoughts and emotions — detach from and witness the mind. Holding a conscious awareness of space is natural to us, but because we have collectively lapsed into unconscious patterns of ego identification, it must be re-awakened, and worked on through attention and focus, so that consciousness begins to flow more freely. This is what is now popularly understood in the West as Karma, and which was known, in the language of the Gospels, by the phrase *"as you sow, so shall you reap."*

We influence our future by our thoughts and actions, and if we hold onto past patterns, we will project them into the future, continually re-creating the same circumstances. Prolonged unconscious thoughts and actions eventually bring about physical or mental imbalance and illness, and this is true for us both as individuals and in our collective responsibility to the world around us. When we realize that we contain sacred space, we experience more clearly the sacredness of the natural world, the solar system and the stars in the cosmos, to which we are intimately connected. In our towns and cities, in the mountains, forests and wild places, and on the seas, wherever we are, we can connect the inner and outer beauty, and experience them as one. *"And the Logos became flesh and dwelt (as in a tabernacle) within us."*

The experience of the presence of Logos in the form of flesh and bone, and all the creatures of the Cosmos, is called *"a glorious manifestation; like unto the splendor of that unique issue (Logos) of the Father, perfected grace and truth."* The Greek term *Pater*, means Father, and is used metaphorically to mean the originator, generator or transmitter of anything — there is no gender. It is applied as an attribute to the will of God the Absolute: no-thing and all.

Logos, as the reflection of the Absolute, is One, and is therefore called *monogenous*, a word often translated into English as "the only begotten son," but which can also be translated as "that unique issue," meaning, the only one of its kind. For this reason, Logos is called perfected grace and truth: *Being* — Unity, a still center, out of which creation continually unfolds. What we perceive as inner and outer are known as One; the cells in the human body and the stars in the Cosmos are acutely felt as One. There is no separation, Logos is all and in all, continually creating every living thing from out of the eternal now.

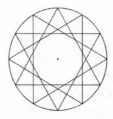

1:15 John witnesses concerning the glory of Logos, and cries out saying, "This is of whom I said, 'the One who comes after me has come into created existence before me because the One precedes me.'"

The One who comes after John was in created existence before him, because the One precedes him. This means that the One is always present outside of time. John witnesses the Glory of Logos, and cries out. This does not mean to shout aloud but to rise up in consciousness to experience his spiritual body. The words that he speaks are drawn from the *Book of Numbers 27:16-23*, and refer to future and past consciously witnessed in eternal presence through the Spiritual Body — all movement experienced as the continual outpouring of creation; radiating from the center; present within you and within all life, here and now. In the Hebrew text, the Spiritual Body is personified through the figure of Joshua son of Nun, who enters and returns before the congregation of Israel (the Soul) into and out of the tabernacle (form and matter). What this represents is the continual creative pulse of life, which is within you now. *Become present for a moment with all your attention, and listen; listen for the silence containing every sound.*

Whilst we remain unconsciously identified with our ego, we are unable to experience conscious presence. We live attached to the forms that populate the unobserved mind, experiencing life through time unfolding in space only as fragmented, disconnected movement. What we think of as future and past, is the flow of life continuously involving itself into form and matter, and the return — the dissolving of form into a state of total presence — stillness. *"The One who comes after me has come into created existence before me because the One precedes me."* The flow of future and past happen simultaneously in the eternal present.

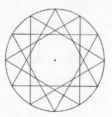

Take a few conscious breaths and consider the following.

Sacred space holds the eternal stillness at its center. By becoming still within, realizing space, we can begin to consciously experience eternal presence within all life, the Glory of Logos. It is into this still center that the past is flowing, and it is into this still center that the future flows to meet it.

By focused attention, breathing consciously, we realize that the present moment is all there is, all there ever has been and all there ever will be. This is held in the Spiritual Body as creative potential and released as created life, in the same way that we breathe. All form and matter is limited, which is set the moment we enter into it, and lose ourselves in it through unconscious identification.

Whatever you are doing, and wherever you are, you can choose to be present. The present is as it is; when you acknowledge this, you can act and speak with lucid awareness. If you need to change a situation or make something happen, first find inner stillness and silence, then you can begin to receive life fully, and join with the rest of life in creation. This is what is meant by, *first enter the Kingdom of Heaven:* become still, be present, *be* prepared to receive life without resistance to change — accepting continuous creation; allowing creative movement to be. When you observe or witness the flow of life into form without identifying with any of its forms, you move with the creative flow without becoming lost in form that is, attached to form.

The Kingdom of Heaven is here now: It is the creative dynamic of presence within you, un-obscured by attachment to form. Through the witness, you are able to begin to see beyond "my life" and move with the freedom of conscious life. Creative life demands that you move, physically, psychologically and spiritually, if you do not, then life will move you because not one thing that exists within time in space is static.

Creation is the continual flow of life from the eternal present. In the Genesis story humanity is the last creature born into the creative outpouring as a Spiritual and androgynous being at the end of the sixth cycle. It is the sixth cycle, which is the connector of all life, the center and periphery beheld as a unity.

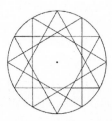

Be still; and know that you are creatively connected to the great circle of life.

From your position in the relative universe, future and past are in movement towards the still point of "Being — I Am."

When "I Am" realizes itself there is total presence.

In Hebrew this is understood through the mantra of the conscious breath,

Ehieh asher Ehieh — I Am that I Am.

Ehieh can be heard through the rhythm of the breath cycle, in the sound of the ocean waves, the unheard music of stars and planets in space; this takes us into silence behind sound, into stillness behind movement.

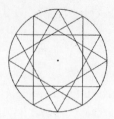

1:16 Because out of the perfection of the Divine we all receive, grace on top of grace.

From the unity of total presence, we all receive abundant life. The Greek word translated as received is *elabomen*, which also means, "to have admitted, acknowledged, or taken to our side." Divine presence is described as perfect because it is One: life without separation, eternal presence. The Greek for grace is *charis* meaning "beneficial opportunity" or "benevolence." Grace on top of grace connotes that beneficial opportunity is a continuous flow of abundance: *Creation is always giving life to new forms, always dissolving old forms.* We all receive creative existence whether we are aware of it or not, but when we acknowledge, realize, that we live by this grace, then it flows through us in abundance because we consciously engage with it. We are always given what we need to accomplish our work, our life, but this may not come in the form our mind expects or wants. And as beneficial opportunity implies, we cannot just sit back and wait for something to happen to us, we need to be consciously present.

We enter the Kingdom of Heaven through conscious presence, giving up attachment to form, and outcomes. If we live with a lover, wife — husband, children, we don't become distant or unfeeling, but we allow inner and outer space. We do our job, raise children, enjoy our recreation, but without attaining a sense of identity from it. By being conscious we connect with life's forms directly; without subject — object separation, we experience the creative pulse out of which form emerges.

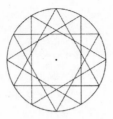

1:17 Because the Torah is given through Moses, grace and truth come through the Anointed Jesus.

Most translators and commentators on this verse have contrasted the law given through Moses, with grace and truth that now come through Jesus Christ. This engendered the belief that the Judaic tradition had been superseded by grace and truth in Jesus Christ, now embodied by the Church; and that the Teaching of Moses — Torah — had been made obsolete because of the new covenant with Jesus Christ. Most would add that Jesus Christ is the only true savior. It is, to say the least, unfortunate that teachings designed to free us from dominance of the ego should end up reinforcing unconscious ego positions. As soon as we begin to awaken consciousness, the ego will try, often successfully, to regain its power by turning spiritual and mystical teachings into dogmas and beliefs. Our God supersedes your God, our version of God, our religion, is better than yours, the only truth. These are extreme forms, and good illustrations, of the unconscious, and spiritualized ego of the religious mind. In order to understand this verse properly, we must put aside all the dogma, doctrine and Christology of the Church, which has been superimposed over the original mystical teaching.

Quite simply, the verse tells us that the Torah of Moses gives us the awareness to receive the grace and truth that comes through the Anointed Savior. We must remember that the Torah is *not* a set of dry laws or written regulations, but the universal, perennial teaching, which is not found in the pages of a book or scroll. The noun Torah comes from a Hebrew root which means, "to teach," and also "to shoot:" that is, to shoot straight and hit a target. The Torah as *living tradition* is primarily oral, containing teachings about the patterns through which life expresses itself.

This short verse gives us an overview of the esoteric teaching story that runs through the books of the Torah, and culminates in the book of Joshua, which was given a new form in this poem. On the surface, these books tell the story of Moses and the liberation of the Israelites from bondage in Egypt, their journey to the Promised Land, and the Anointing of Joshua as a new king and spiritual leader. To understand what all this means we need to look more fully at the symbolism used in the text.

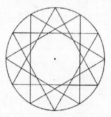

Remember, all the characters and the places in the story are archetypes, aspects of your own psyche, Soul, Spirit, and Being, in your own inner landscape.

After fleeing Egypt — our familiar but stifling unconscious psychological surroundings, Moses awakens to meet life in a new way. He meets and is trained by a Holy man called Jethro — *"abundance,"* and under his tuition passes a series of important initiations, which lead to his marriage with one of his teacher's daughters, Zipporah. Her name means "Bird," a creature of the air (Spirit), and "to turn, dance in a circle, to turn oneself about (a spiritual rising)." For Moses, this union signifies greater contact with the Soul and Spirit. By "turning about," Moses experiences the presence of Jahveh *(To Be Being),* and through this communion he is given the task of returning to Egypt to face Pharaoh — the egocentric and materialistic human unconscious. Pharaoh thinks of himself as a divinity or god, as important, and powerful, the ego-dominated mind that seeks to accumulate physical possessions and psychological control, to cover up feelings of emptiness, that life is meaningless without "me" as its center.

Their confrontation leads to Moses taking the children of Israel out of an ego dominated state into a higher awareness where, during forty years of wandering in the desert — a synonym for transformation through psychological and spiritual work — the old generations die out and are replaced by a new generation that has not known the slave mentality that comes from domination by the unconscious thinking mind, and its compulsive use of the drives of the body.

Moses is our awakened connection with Spirit and Being; as such we make the symbolic ascent of the spiritual mountain where we are given the essence of the Torah, the codes that govern life — the laws of existence. Our inner Moses holds the Torah and imparts it to the Israelites at the foot of the spiritual path of ascent — Mount Sinai. There are rebellions, anger and divisions, by the immature aspects of the persona, failures and setbacks, but eventual sustained conscious awareness. Experiential knowledge of the Torah brings the Spiritual Body into the conscious awareness: this is personified through the figure of Joshua, which, when translated into the Greek of the Gospel poem, becomes Jesus.

As a self-aware human being, working from the Soul, we begin to perceive our own spiritual consciousness, personified by Joshua. When he first appears in the text, Joshua is called Hosea son of Nun. In Hebrew, Hosea means "to be" or "to exist," while Nun means "the fish" which was a symbol of inner and outer fertility. These two energies symbolize potent forces for transformation within us. Moses, directed by Divine Being, initiates Hosea who is given the name of Joshua. The Hebrew name Joshua means "JHVH (*To Be Being*) is salvation," and salvation means "safe passage home." Joshua is the personification of our own salvation: which brings us home, integrates us with our Spiritual Body, and *Being*.

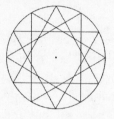

Joshua is the name for the Spiritual Body of every human being; it is the part of us that creates life; that embodies the codes of life as living Torah.

In the narrative, Moses, under direction from JHVH –"*To Be Being,*" lays his hands on Joshua and anoints him: the Anointed Joshua represents the full realization of our Being: to be a Human with Being, whilst in a physical body: In Hebrew, Joshua the anointed: In Greek, Jesus the Christ.

When Moses dies, he is buried beyond the Jordan, which, in the symbolism of the story, means to be outside of the Holy Land of the human spirit. Thereafter, he represents the link between the Soul, and the psyche and body, with the spiritual universe. The Anointed Joshua leads the psychologically mature people of Israel into the land flowing with milk and honey — continual creative abundance of life, the spiritual universe. Here Joshua dwells as the spiritual consciousness of Israel (the Soul), and when he dies, is buried in the Promised Land to become synonymous with our Spiritual Body.

Spirituality can never be owned, or be the preserve of any one, particular ethnic or religious group. To be one of the people of Israel means to live from the awakened Soul, and to live by spiritual principle — our own, inner Joshua. The teaching has found its expression in modern Judaism, and in Christianity, and the Islamic tradition. Yet we have not been able to hold to living purely by spiritual principle: instead of seeing each other as members of a common humanity, we twist the words of the teaching to justify our hatred and division. We commit physical and psychological murder, and in doing so, lose our connection with the Soul and Spirit, and remove ourselves from Being. In the symbolism of the story, we have become slaves in Egypt again. When the unconscious ego reigns, our religious institutions become images of the ego using its tricks of lies, hatred, fear, sexual repression, abuse of power, control, and collective ego-identity through belonging to an unconscious group mind.

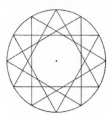

The Anointed, which means messiah, *is not* an individual personality, or an ego: it is *Being* made known through fully conscious human beings. It belongs to no one and is the potential of everyone. Joshua/Jesus personifies the Spiritual Body within each of us, and cannot be confined to a single point in time or history. This is why in a Sephardic synagogue in the mountains of Galilee there is an inscription on the ceiling, which reads, "Joshua draws near" which means "Salvation from JHVH draws near:" It is a statement of spiritual principle, the realization of Being. This is the meaning of Jesus' saying; *"I Am the way, the truth, and the spirit of life; no one can come unto the face of the generator of all life (Father) except through what I have."* Ch14 v6. *This is the I Am of total consciousness, experiencing the whole of created existence.*

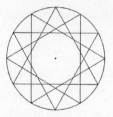

1:18 No one has ever gazed upon the Absolute at any time: the unique issue, who lies in the heart of the Father, is revealed through the Christ.

The Divine Image is called the unique issue, who lies in the heart of the Father. The Greek word Kolpos translated as "heart" is a feminine noun, which also means "bosom," "lap," and "garment." Here we are reminded of the many images of the Goddess with the Divine infant in her lap, or held to her breast. The use of the term Father is of its time, and simply means generator or originator: it could equally be expressed as Mother. However, Father was also used to denote the active dynamic, and Mother the passive dynamic universal Creator. Father and Mother, God and Goddess are images applied to the formless unity of Being, which is beyond image or gender.

The Divine Son or generation in the heart of the Father means *To Be At — One* with the will of God the Absolute: No-thing that we can say is anything.

Being (the Son) is called *the unique issue,* and comes from a combination of two Greek words *monos*, alone, and *genos*, to come into existence. Monogeny is used in English to denote an organism that has produced itself from a single cell. In itself, the word "alone" is a combination of "all" and "one." The term "unique issue" refers to the unity of Divine Being or Logos as the single source of existence and all that is created, formed, and made.

The verse says that *no one has seen the Father at any time; it is the Christ that reveals him.* To understand this we have to remember that in the mystical tradition God does not exist in terms that we understand as existence. God is Absolute — cannot be contained by existence, cannot be known by the mind. The will of the Absolute is symbolized by light, the light of the Absolute is *Being*. It is through *Being* — *Christos in Greek* — that the Absolute as Divine originator is revealed.

In one of the teaching stories, the disciples of Jesus ask him, "show us the Father," Jesus says, "When you have seen the Son, (unique issue), you have seen the Father." Whilst we exist within the great circle of life, to experience the consciousness of Being is to experience the Originator of eternal presence — the Father. It is through *Being* that we experience the essence of all life; called the will of the Absolute.

Chapter Six

Witnessing the Ego and Psyche

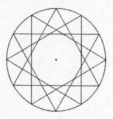

1:19 And this is the witness of John when the Jews of Jerusalem sent envoys, Priests and Levites, that they might ask, "Who are you?"

The power of perennial teaching stories is that they present psychological and spiritual archetypes that exist within your inner landscape, your inner world — beyond thinking, outside of time. They are designed to bring you to a point of awakening, from identification with the unconscious ego, to a lucid awareness of conscious presence. Ultimately, this is *Being*, which can only be experienced by your focused presence, here and now.

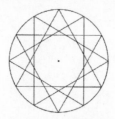

The text is addressing you directly, asking you to stand with John, still the mind, be silent within. Breathe consciously, and bring peace into your inner world.

In the still silence beyond all thought and emotion, stands your witnessing presence that asks, who Am I? Who are you beyond the temporary dwelling place of the body? Who is it that looks out with deepening vision through the eyes? Who are you when all the images that you identify with dissolve, as they must? When all that is held within the vessel of the Soul passes away into formless Spirit: Who are you?

In the symbolism of the story, the Jews of Jerusalem represent the egocentric positions of religious and political authority. Their envoys, the Priests, represent the functions of practice, passion, and devotion, and the Levites, the learning of theory, and dissemination of information, and codes of law. They equate with the Hebrew concepts Netzach and Hod, which only become negative when we identify with them as possessive powers in the egocentric unconscious mind. "As priests we have special powers, stand between the people and God," and "I/we alone can interpret sacred texts and disseminate God's laws." The workings of the ego are very basic; I take what I want, and make it mine. If I am not a powerful leader then I will follow one who is, and my sense of ego identity will come from being allied with them. Serving them faithfully, or the great cause faithfully, gives me a sense of power, and meaning. This feeling of external power, covering an inner emptiness, is then made into a graven image, a thought form that the ego worships as God — in reality, as an image of itself.

The term "the Jews" in the Gospel has been used fallaciously over the centuries to denigrate and demonize the Jewish people. The Aramaic text of the Gospel gives *"the Judeans"* in the equivalent passages as a critique of the political elite controlled by King Herod, and of the zealots who violently opposed them. They therefore illustrate strong egocentric positions. It was Herod as Rome's regent, who appointed the Priests and Levites, mostly from the Greek communities of the Diaspora, to run the Temple and the city of Jerusalem, and through it Palestine as a province of Rome. It is for this reason that various groups of Pharisees, the Essenes, and others, sought to distance themselves from Jerusalem and the Temple, either physically or spiritually. This inevitably brought with it much Jewish self-criticism, which was expressed in some of the writings of the period.

By the end of the fourth century, Christianity, through the Church, was established as the official religion of the Roman Empire. Having severed its roots in Judaism, it began to see the Synagogue as a rival to its influence over the population. It is during this period that we begin to see polemics by Church leaders explicitly condemning the Jews as the murderers of Christ, the ones who have rejected the new covenant. This has been the shadow side of the Church ever since, where it is acceptable to demonize others — not just the Jewish people, but also Muslims, Pagans, "heretical" Christians, "non believers," and women. This has brought out the worst aspects of unconscious human nature with terrible consequences, in the Crusades, the Inquisition, witch trials, persecutions and expulsions, and the concentration camps of the Second World War.

This history is very poignant, precisely because the teaching in these verses is concerned with the need to confront our own demons, which simply means witnessing our own unconscious ego identities, our own shadow, and denying them power over us. Problems of ego inflation persist as long as we are susceptible to the belief that we exist as a separate form, disconnected from the creative, abundant life of existence. We become fearful of not being good enough, lacking what "successful" people have and believe that we are powerless in a world full of danger, and threatened by enemies. We seek to make ourselves bigger and stronger, to have power and status in the world; authority and control over other people, and over nature; all of which attempts to cover an inner emptiness. It has nothing to do with being creative, learning to better our lives, and help others become spiritually conscious, which has no status.

John represents sustained conscious connection with the Soul, which is why he is confronted by the ego. Spiritual consciousness diminishes ego identity, and is therefore seen as an opportunity by the diminished ego, to regain its place of importance. The temptation is that the ego will turn spiritual awakening into "a game," or "an experience" that becomes a new ego identity. As heightened awareness allows us to feel more alive, more connected with life, the clever ego wants to claim this as "something" for "me," a "bigger, better, wiser me." Old mental and emotional patterns reassert themselves, with a greater energy that we believe to be part of an awakened state. Seduced back into unconscious behavior, we say to ourselves "I am spiritually conscious, my knowledge is more than theirs," "I know God's laws, what God wants for us."

We may begin to see ourselves as an authority or as belonging to a collective authority, administering judgment and mercy — in Hebrew, Gevurah and Hesed. Without our conscious presence, these neutral functions become unbalanced psychological — pseudo-spiritual distorted lenses, through which we view ourselves, and the world. Gevurah's discernment and precision become judgments and obsession with detail (rules and regulations). Hesed's mercy and benevolence become overbearing interference or a smothering possessiveness. If we seek to use these powers for outer status *then we have our reward*, but the heightened awareness of the Soul is diminished.

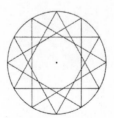

To move beyond this, still the mind allowing no thought to distract you. Be the witness, as if you are looking out from the back of the head, which increases your peripheral vision and sensitivity. Become conscious of the vital energy flowing through your body, connecting you with the

Earth, allowing it to support you. Use the breath to become aware of your center deep within, the still point, from out of which all movement occurs.

If you begin to live consciously, with lucid attention and awareness, you learn to be; if you allow yourself to be; you allow others to be. Your sense of inner space gives others the opportunity to feel their own space and freedom. When you begin to disengage from unconscious patterns of thought and emotion, and their use as tools of egocentric power, you realize you have no external adversary.

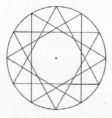

To stand with John, is to observe the ego identities that seek to draw you away from your witnessing presence: Through awakened observation, you no longer fall prey to them, nor allow them to take control. You begin to experience space between your Self and emotionally charged thought patterns.

The points of intersection between the three circles and the upper half circle in the diagram below, mark places of energy transition or transformation. These points are represented in Biblical Hebrew letter formations such as Keter, or Malkut, or are personified in John or Jesus, or represented through place names such as Bethhabara or Jordan (place of stillness, peace) etc.

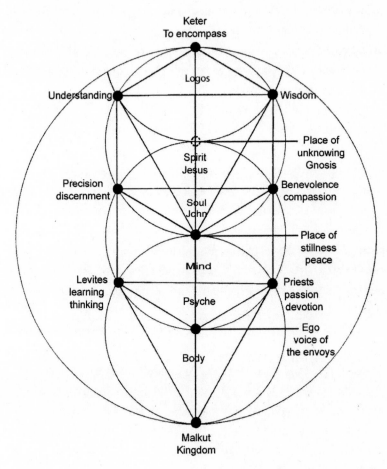

The diagram shows the archetypal principles personified in the text laid out on the Tree of Life. John holds Tipheret and thus realizes Jesus — Joshua within him.

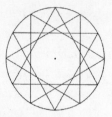

1:20 And he acknowledged, he did not deny, but acknowledged that "I am not the Christ."
1:21 So they asked him, "What then, are you Elijah?" and he said, "I am not." "Are you a prophet?" and he answered, "No."
In Bible stories and Jewish folklore, the human shadow of ego identification is triggered by *the Satan*, which in Hebrew means "the adversary" or "tester." We must forget all images of horned devils with cloven hoofs. The old Greek god Pan, who represented fertility and the burgeoning life of the natural world, was made into an image of a devil as a way of gaining power over us — to control our sexuality, through fear and guilt, and disconnect us from the body and the life of the natural world. This has engendered demonic projections onto certain animals, and fear of the "wild" natural world, which we need to "tame." These have become deep-seated collective human pathologies we need to consciously address.

All evil comes from within the unconscious human mind. We are seduced and tempted by our fantasies and illusions of worldly power, the ego's greed to accumulate more wealth, and the need of status in the eyes of the egocentric human world. In itself, the ego is not wholly negative: it is simply an ephemeral mechanism, a mirror, which reflects the Soul's connection between our inner world and the outer world. It is only through identification with accumulated thought forms, that the ego becomes a problem. The more we identify with it, the more we energize it, and believe it to be all that we are. We make these thought forms into symbols of *separate* power, that become "me," or in the collective "us" — enabling them to become evil, that is, destructive and life negating.

The voice of the tester asks John, "Are you the Anointed of God?" But he remains centered in stillness, and consciously answers "No." Consciousness is the creative essence of the whole of life; the ego sees itself as separate entity, and identifies with limitation or lack, and unlimited accumulation. If John were to claim, "I am the Christ," he would lose his ability to be conscious by identifying with an ego image. He would lose his connection with true creativity and *Being*, become a slave to the illusion of existing as a separate power from the *Unity of life.*

A human being may take up the role of a spiritual teacher, or a social leader, there is nothing wrong with this, but with it come the projections of being "a master," or "special," a Mother or Father figure. Projections are inevitable, they are a part of our psychological life and it is only when we identify ourselves with them, that problems occur. As with any political, religious, or business leader who sets themselves up as an authority, or statesman, we become slaves to these thought forms, which seek to use us to maintain themselves. The unconscious ego is monotonous because it is repetitive, taking on one form after another, but underneath always the same. Awakening consciousness alerts the ego to the possibility of regaining its position with greater power. The temptation is to become a magnetic personality for others to follow. Although we may not say, "I am the Christ," we may still identify with the image of Christ's or God's messenger, servant, or minister. We might believe that we represent "Christ or God" who "speaks through me or our institution."

To fall into the illusion of these needs and projections is to become a slave to greater forces in the human collective unconscious, which eventually take over and block the internal connection with spiritual consciousness. The leader or institution then becomes more and more reliant on the energy of their followers, who become beguiled by their own projections; this is what is meant by — "the blind leading the blind."

The collective energy of unconscious thought forms take on a life of their own, but having no root in either Body or Spirit, they must feed themselves to continue to exist, and increase their power. To get food, these thought forms engender feelings and emotions of belonging and exclusivity within their human hosts. To draw more energy, they create a climate of fear, hatred and greed. They aid this by promoting the cult of status, big business, the prostituting of sexual energy and the widespread use of drugs and excessive amounts of alcohol, and of course the need for war.

When we are unconscious we give our energy away to these thought forms. To deny them energy, we simply need to disengage from them by observing the games the ego plays. We hold to the consciousness of the witness, the observer or watcher that dwells in the body, and utilizes the mind, but is beyond them — our creative Spirit, the breath of Logos.

Questioning through negation, as depicted here, is the gradual stripping away of the illusions and misconceptions we have about ourselves — saying I am not this, not that — we may begin to know the limits of our individual psyche and become conscious of *Being*. John makes no claim to be Elijah, (*In Hebrew; My El* — *God, is JHVH* — *to be Being,*) and the name of one of the greater prophets — teachers of humanity. Nor does he claim to be one of the lesser prophets. He stands firm; consciousness drawing the psychosomatic energies into a focused unity. To witness the personality for what it truly is, an ephemeral mechanism, enables the awakened Soul to be the meeting place of psycho-somatic and spiritual-Divine energies. We move from living unconsciously — motivated by our physical and psychological drives and needs — to living in the greater state of awareness, experiencing consciousness beyond form, creative life continually emerging from *Being*.

It is for this reason that conscious awareness, or Tipheret, is called walking the path of honesty. Honesty and truth, goodness and beauty, describe your sustained ability for greater awareness, and to witness the ego playing its mind games, without being drawn into them through judgment, fear, or intellectual superiority. Through focused attention and non-attachment, you make a space around thoughts, feelings and emotions, before they become your identity. John represents our ability to utilize Hod — clear intellect and communication, Netzach — vitality and pleasure, Gevurah — precision and attention, and Hesed — benevolence and compassion, in conscious balance, without being seduced into identifying with a role or an image, whether inner or outer.

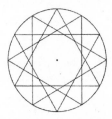

1:22 Then addressing John they said, "Who are you, that we may give an answer to those who have sent us, what do you say about yourself?"
1:23 "I [am] a voice crying in the wilderness, 'Make straight the way of the Lord,' as the prophet Isaiah said."
Now John is challenged to give his *own* account of himself. This has a powerful effect on the process of awakening; we gather all our energies, all our attention, into a single focal point, beyond the thinking mind. John's answer paraphrases Isaiah 40:3: "A voice cries: 'In the wilderness prepare the way of Jahveh, make straight in the desert a highway for our Elohim.'"

The Hebrew word *kora*, which is translated as "crying," more accurately means "the call" or "to proclaim." It is linked to an Arabic root from which the noun Koran is derived. This "call" comes as a resonance from deep within the Soul, felt like the note of a bell or singing bowl in the sacrum; consciousness, the voice of the Soul, rising out of the Solar plexus, where it radiates out as a song, as your true voice reverberating within, felt as echoes of stillness and silence within.

The spiritual path through the psychological wilderness is called, "the way," of Jahveh — *"To Be Being."* The Hebrew root *derek*, means "the journey or way," "to press out spiritual essence as in a wine press," and "to adopt an attitude of behavior, a way of *Being*." The song of your Soul is your way or journey "To Be Being."

The Hebrew word *yasher*, which is translated as "make straight," literally means, "to make the sight of the eyes straight." This means so much more than physical sight. If we are unconscious, our sight is refracted through the unobserved ego — we cannot see straight, we need to defend our position, or attack the positions of others, real or imagined. The root also means to be "upright in the heart," which is not referring to the organ pumping blood around your body, but to the source of your psychological and physical life. John (the awakened Soul) is calling himself into presence: deep interior stilling, holding integrity and honesty — an inner knowledge.

Make straight the inner sight (honesty) in the lower, dead regions (the desert), an exalted way for our Elohim: Absolute life: Being of beings. The Hebrew word *salal* translated as "exalted way," means "to connect," "knit together," "to lift up" as a song. It connotes a resonance with higher awareness. To translate John's answer in another way we might say: *"I am the call, the resonance, of spiritual knowledge(consciousness) laid out through the wilderness (the unconscious), make straight the sight — become conscious of Being."*

If we sustain consciousness, we create a visible way in a terrain where it is hard to see a straight path. Only by following the path of the Sun or a Star do we avoid getting lost or trapped in the psychological wilderness of the repetitive unconscious mind. Spiritual consciousness puts the ego under pressure, and brings about real change in our lives. But since the ego does not want consciousness or real change, it *thinks* its way out of experiencing consciousness by going around in psychological circles, replacing one thought form with another.

To make this way straight means to begin to live from Tipheret, with action and intellect, discernment and benevolence held in balance. From Tipheret we draw physical and psychological energies into consciousness and unify them into a whole. In biblical terminology, it is referred to as raising the serpent energy in the desert; the focusing of the natural energies that aid us in sustaining consciousness.

We need to inhabit our physical bodies consciously; to be present on the Earth with the full circle of life. We may be a fit athlete or totally absorbed in amassing material wealth, power and sexual gratification, but this does not mean we are present in the physical body. Often it means that we only touch the Earth to take what we want or need. To live consciously in the body means being present in all our actions, being aware of the subtle centers sustaining the body and psyche, and becoming sensitive to the interface between the physical and psychological and Spiritual creative life, not only in ourselves, but in the whole of life. When we sustain an awakened state we come into the presence of the Spiritual Body, and the essence of life; Being; the Logos.

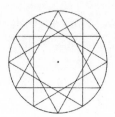

Breathe consciously, focusing all your attention into the present, allowing no thought to distract you. Breathe from the Solar plexus, allowing the heart to open out, feeling the vital energy giving life to the

body. Listen to the silence behind all sound; become aware of the stillness supporting you, the timeless presence supporting all life. Ask; Who Am I? Be still, silent, and listen.

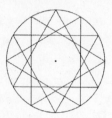

1:24 Note that these people were envoys from a school of Pharisees.

1:25 And they questioned him closely, and said to John, "Then why do you baptize if you are not the Christ, nor Elijah, nor a prophet?"

1:26 John answered them saying, "I baptize in water, but at your very heart is a permanent presence of which you have no experience."

1:27 "This One who is coming after me, the latchet of whose sandal I am not worthy to untie."

In the Gospel, first John, and then Jesus are shown confronting groups of Pharisees, yet Jesus, is also portrayed in the Gospels as teaching in the style of a Pharisee, walking from town to village to instruct people, using parables, and training disciples. The name Pharisee means "to break bread" and "to distribute," and there were many schools, with widely differing interpretations of the teaching. However, many who called themselves Pharisees were clearly not capable teachers. The Talmud, which emerged out of the oral teaching of Judaism, states that of the nine schools of Pharisees only one was righteous.

This confrontation with John dramatizes the conflict between an esoteric knowledge of spiritual teachings, and that of a politicized religious authority. The awakened state of consciousness shares — breaks bread and distributes — the teaching freely. The unconscious authoritarian mind wants, and needs outer status. This can come in the form of the need to be seen as an expert, and show how knowledgeable we are. Egocentric questioning seeks to undermine the confidence and credibility of others: what right has she/he to baptize if she/he does not have the status of a prophet? The voice that asks, "Who do you think you are? What right do you have to be here?" comes from an ego that feels the threat that someone else might have more or be greater than "me."

Verse twenty-six is usually translated as "John answered them, 'I baptize with water; but among you stands one whom you do not know.'" This translation masks some very important teachings: The Greek word meaning, "to baptize" comes from the root *bapto*, meaning, "to dip" with obvious connotations of water, but also "to dye," that is, to mark by a change of color or state. Baptism is not only immersion in water, but also a change of state through dyeing — an awakening. In modern psychological language, John would say; "I initiate psychological change," a transformation from ego identification, dominated by unobserved thoughts and emotions, to being consciously present. But the mind alone cannot heal itself; a greater awareness is needed.

The Greek root, *mesos* commonly translated as "among you," literally reads "at your very heart or core," and "to mediate or reconcile," which implies a point of balance. The following Greek word *histemi*, translated in the RSV as "stands," also means, "to endure permanently." This permanence is the presence of *Logos* — *Being*, the eternal source of life within you. An alternative translation to the verse might read, *"At your heart there is an enduring permanence about which you have no knowledge."* The Greek verb for knowing, *oidate*, means knowledge gained through experience, which encompasses much more than refining the intellect. The root also means "to perceive" or to "recognize" which implies a sense of reconnecting, or awakening spiritual insight into conscious union with the Logos.

To the ordinary mind John says, *"If only you knew it, Divine presence is your permanent core of creative life."* But to know that we must be present, as illustrated by John, with knowledge of the wilderness, both internal and external, beyond the mental activity that keeps us away from the present.

To our inner authority figures, consciousness is an unknown quantity. Why is he behaving like this? Who is he, exactly? Consciousness dissolves the foundation of our old world, as the old ways of living, acting and behaving no longer work for us. But still the ego fights to remain as the center of our life, no matter how painful this has become. Often it is only through such pain that the illusions are finally shattered, and we are able to let go and move on through accepting death. It is only through experiencing this inner death that we experience rebirth, and to do this takes great courage.

In verse twenty-seven John says, *"This One who is coming after me, the latchet of whose sandal I am not worthy to untie."* The beginning partially repeats verse fifteen, significantly, as it follows the questioning in which he has stripped away false ideas about himself. The second half of the verse is paraphrased from Joshua 5:15 where Joshua is instructed to take off his sandals and realize the place where he stands is holy — he becomes sensitive to Divine presence as the source of all life. John is the Soul that receives this presence of spiritual creativity and Divine Being, pressing upon him, seeking to be consciously known within.

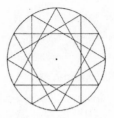

1:28 These things occurred at Bethabara beyond the Jordan where John was baptizing.

There are two place names associated with this verse. The first is Bethabara, the one I have used above, due to its geographical location on the river Jordan itself, opposite the city of Jericho. The second, found in most of the extent manuscripts of the Gospel, is Bethany, located up in the hills near to Jerusalem. Bethany is of Aramaic origin meaning, "the place of answer" or "response." Like Delphi in Greece, it is a place of oracle. It can also mean "to humble oneself" or "to be troubled by something," indicating a point of response or change, due to the pressures that build in our psychological world when we earnestly seek spiritual knowledge — Gnosis; to be conscious of consciousness in yourself.

Bethabara, which is Greek for Beth ha Abara, the Hebrew name meaning "the place of the ford," indicates a point of transition or transformation. It is linked with the name "Jordan," which means "the downward flowing waters," the creative waters of life, flowing into form and matter. In Bible stories, the Jordan is synonymous with the process of death and transformation through rebirth. In the *book of Kings*, it is used by *Elijah* for purification and healing, to wash away sin, that is, to bring clarity, to let go of old thought patterns, and painful memories we repeat to ourselves. John's meeting with the envoys from Jerusalem occurs at this place of spiritual revelation. In Biblical symbolism this is Tipheret, the place where the physical body, the psyche, Soul, and Spiritual Body are realized as One; this is to experience what is called in Hebrew, *Malkut Ha Shamaim — the*

Kingdom of the creative or heavenly universe.

When we step into these waters, we become aware of the many currents of time. On the surface physical time appears to us as fixed, yet it bends and expands and contracts; is multi-layered. When we experience this, we are moving deeper into the universe of forms, because psychological time is mutable, stretches and contracts like elastic. Each frame of time is like an eddying swirl in a great flowing river, some swirls lasting longer than others, moving against each other, transforming, dissolving and reforming. An hour may feel like a day; days can flash by like minutes or seconds, the quality of our focused attention affecting our experience; time in the fixed physical sense has little meaning. When we step into *Malkut Ha Shamaim* — the Kingdom of Heaven we experience creation — sequential movement on the edge of stillness. Inner and outer spatial movement merging, synchronizing and dissolving time. The quality of awakening to the present moment stays with us beyond the mind's understanding of our physical and psychological world. We realize that our Spiritual Body contains all time unfolding in space, movement from the central stillness of Logos.

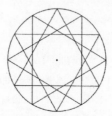

Breathe from the Solar Plexus, finding your center, and still the mind. Allow no thought to distract you from the present. Beyond and behind every movement and every sound is the presence of stillness and silence. As you breathe feel it supporting you.

In the symbolism of the story, to be "beyond the Jordan," means to dwell in the psychosomatic universes of mind and body, whilst the Holy Land of the Soul and Spirit is referred to as "the *land* beyond the Jordan." John's arrival at Bethabara or Bethany marks the point of crossing from the lesser into the greater state of consciousness.

In the book of Deuteronomy, Joshua, having been anointed by Moses, crosses the Jordan with the Ark of the Covenant, the dais on which the presence of God descends. It is carried before the Israelites, who symbolize the awakened Soul; it is the Divine presence that guides them on their journey back to their Symbolic spiritual home, which lies in the heart of every human being. Having reached their promised land (*become spiritually conscious*), the people of Israel (*the awakened Soul*), set up a circle of twelve stones, taken from the dry bed of the river Jordan at Gilgal. The name Gilgal comes from a Hebrew root which means "to turn" or "a circle or wheel." It represents the wheel of the Zodiac, which Joshua and the twelve tribes of Israel, and Jesus and the twelve disciples symbolize: the great circle of life.

In the biblical narrative the warriors of Israel — the Soul, go before the people to fight and clear the land. In Hebrew the meaning of "a warrior" is to be "strong" and "organized," and does not necessitate killing; the use of physical violence, to invade another peoples ancestral land, to steal and murder is pathological. This needs to be properly understood, because so many have used these stories — and continue to do so today — as an excuse to carry out wars against a projected evil adversary. The belief that God requires us to make war or carry out killings is the result of the pathologies and desires of the unconscious mind, and when we are caught up in these ways of thinking and their emotions, we cut ourselves off from consciousness. Anyone who dies through an act of violence for God, or carries out an act of violence for God, has made violence their god.

We must be absolutely clear that this is not a physical landscape and there is no violent action. The warriors of the Soul go to the City of *Jericho*, which comes from a Hebrew root meaning, "Moon," and the measure of time through the lunar cycles. It also means idolatry, the worship of images, not just of God, but also of ourselves and our past, all the forms of ephemeral possessions, and the personal and collective memories and unconscious patterns, which imprison us through ego identification. They all need to be dissolved and the energy set free.

The fight for the land beyond the Jordan and the battles depicted in the book of Joshua are allegories of the internal struggle, which ensues within the Soul when we begin to receive spiritual consciousness. All the walls and structures crumble as we dissolve the phantoms possessing the city of Jericho.

The images and forms held within the Soul cannot be maintained within the formless Spiritual Body. This may make us uncomfortable and frighten us, but any form of God, any form of self will dissolve under the pressure of the creative spiritual life force: all separation dissolves into unity.

Joshua tells the Israelites that within three days they will have taken possession of the Land of the Spiritual Body, "which JHVH your Elohim gives you to possess." To understand what is meant by these three days of transformation we will look very carefully at the process that unfolds in the next three chapters.

Chapter Seven

The First Day of Transformation

The use of a period of three days as a symbol of profound trans-formation is not unique to the Gospel of John. It appears many times elsewhere in the Bible, and is also common to different cultures and spiritual traditions around the world. It was known to the initiates of the Greek and Egyptian mysteries as well as those of the East, and represented the period in which the initiate underwent a death and rebirth.

Although the transformation is presented in the Gospel story over a three-day period, it is not physical time as counted in days or years that is significant. Rather, they represent three stages or cycles, in which the old ego-dominated personality with its mental habits and emotional possessions dissolves, and a new consciousness emerges. This lucid state may last for some time, before the old habits and traits reappear to be faced by the new consciousness.

Often we think we have changed, but we merely end up replacing one form with another, one ego identity with another. But if we are able to retain enough conscious presence to continue observing the mind, we can see the outlines of our ego's traits and engrained emotional patterns clearly. We no longer rely on them for our sense of self, as if an actor identified with their part. As they present themselves through life's circum-stances, they can be acknowledged, released and transformed by our increased consciousness. In this way we begin to engage in the work of creation; we engage with life fully in a creative way.

Rituals and initiations are valuable markers of transitions and crucial points of psychological and spiritual growth that are sadly lacking in western culture today. But, true initiations happen naturally whenever we are ready to meet life consciously, however unready the everyday mind may feel. Life itself becomes our initiator and our teacher. Inner transformation is marked by consciously facing death; without understanding death there is no increased awareness of life, no dying to all that is separate. This is .neither pessimistic nor morbid: death is integral to life. It is a profound transformation initiated by clarity and honesty without fear. The repetition of this theme of death and re-birth, winding through the text like the ascending loops of a spiral, is the most fundamental, underlying structure of the Gospel. At the last meeting with his disciples, before the cruci-fixion, Jesus tells them *"Truly, truly, I say to you, unless a grain of wheat falls into the ground and dies it abides alone. But if it dies, it brings forth an abundance of fruit." 12.24.*

What follows now is one interpretation of that archetypal process. As the story unfolds over the next three chapters, remember that the masculine names used for John, Jesus, and the disciples represent archetypal patterns and states of consciousness that are inner aspects of all women and men.

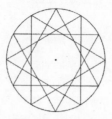

1:29 The next day John perceives Jesus coming towards him; and says, "Behold! the lamb of God removing the sins of the Cosmos."

The words "the next day" signify the beginning of something radically new. If, like John, we sustain consciousness through the awakened Soul, observe the processes of the mind, and increase awareness of the vital life force within the body, we create space for new life to emerge. What the Soul experiences through this inner awakening is greater awareness of life beyond the thinking mind: intellect is of little use; there are no theological or philosophical concepts to be discussed and argued over: it is real.

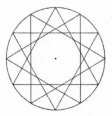

Stop for a moment, breathe consciously, and still the mind. The Earth is spinning through space on the outer arm of a spiraling galaxy containing perhaps two hundred billion Stars or Suns, held in space at the edge of form and matter. Our own Sun continually breathes life into the Solar system; sustaining all life, each moment of each day at the edge of form and matter. What John now perceives as the vision of the figure of Jesus coming towards him, is at the edge of form and matter. This place of meeting exists within you now.

In chapter six, we saw that Joshua led the Israelites into the Holy Land, symbolic of the Spiritual Body. When Joshua dies he is buried in this land, becoming synonymous with the spiritual body — the created universe Beriah. Joshua, translated as Jesus in the Greek texts of the Bible, means salvation is from Jahveh — *To Be Being*. And salvation is safe passage home, which means realizing who you are, *Being* who you are; beyond mind, beyond form, beyond the physical body.

The RSV translates the first part of the verse as "John sees Jesus coming toward him," but the Greek verb *blepo*, means, "to exercise the faculty of sight," which has the connotations of conscious discernment, of beholding with inner perception in a lucid state. Here, now, John (your Soul) perceives Jesus, (your Spiritual Body): That which is without form becomes a tangible perception in the consciously awakened Soul. What we call a mystical experience is beyond form, as you return into form the mind clothes the "experience" in imagery; the formless is perceived in a form; this is to touch the hem of the spiritual garment.

The Greek root *erchomai*, translated as "to come" in the RSV signifies something much deeper than physical movement: rather, "to come toward" in the spiritual sense, a "return." It is used in scripture of the appearance or return of the Divine image of God. This is sometimes referred to as the Paraclete, (which means "the Comforter,") and although associated with concepts of the Holy Spirit or the risen Christ, simply means, the inner peace that comes to us through conscious presence.

This greater awareness is the result of the new-found clarity of perception that enables us to go beyond the mind. Unhindered by habitual thinking we consciously observe and connect with life from a deeper sense of ourselves. What we experience as moments of illumination from the Spiritual Body have a deepening effect on our lives; we become aware of our path in life manifesting in the outer world. This changes the way we live our lives, which becomes our art as we apply greater conscious, focused attention, to whatever we do.

We may ask, and feel we need to know, what is the purpose of my life? What is my destiny? This can come from a desire to be seen and heard, acknowledged by the world in some way however small. The answer is neither glamorous nor exciting, but brings inner peace; our destiny is to learn *To Be*. If we become consciously present to life, then answers in terms of the detail of "my life" and "my purpose," become unnecessary. Life is; I am; there is unity, which is the meaning of at-one-ment with God. Spiritual consciousness realizes that there is no separation between ourselves, and Divine presence: between ourselves, and the continual unfolding of creation that is present within us, and what we perceive as the outer world. Such sensitivity of perception cannot be understood intellectually, nor taught by a spiritual teacher, no matter how much knowledge she or he may have. A teacher can only guide us, helping us to realize the consciousness that is already within, *calling us To Be.*

John's spiritual eyes open, he exclaims, "Behold!" In Hebrew "Shema!" which means "Awaken! Become conscious! Be present now!" There is no mention of anyone else with him; John is alone. The command *awaken* comes from within; we are alone in order to focus all our energy into a single conscious point, *Tipheret.*

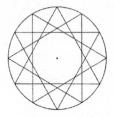

Breathe consciously from the solar plexus, allowing the heart to open, connecting through your spine and legs with the soles of the feet, and again through the spine with the heart and lungs, the arms and hands; look through the eyes with focused attention, but as if you are observing from the back of your head, from deep within; be present to all that is about you. Listen to the silence behind all the sounds, within and about you, feel the stillness out of which all movement arises.

From here John says, "Behold! The Lamb of God removing the sins of the Cosmos." This ancient symbol has been distorted into a mental concept that has lost much of its meaning. The phrase has connotations of restoring wholeness, setting things straight, and infusing new life, and could be translated as *"removing imperfection from the lower human mind."* An alternative would be *"restoring the integrity of the Cosmos."* The Cosmos that is in need of restoration is not what we perceive as the external universe. The natural world and the angelic ideas and forms, which give it life, shape and substance, are without *sin; there is no lack of integrity.* Only humanity has lost its integrity, through egocentric unconscious thoughts and actions that bring imperfection, adulterate and compromise life. As we awaken, we realize that all of creation awaits our conscious participation in life; that our responsibility is to restore the integrity we have lost individually and collectively.

The symbol of the Lamb of God has roots in Egyptian and other mythologies of antiquity. In the Judaic tradition, it is depicted in the sacrifice of the Passover lamb. An old Jewish proverb says, "*this is the lamb slain from the foundation of the World.*" Logos — Being, becomes created life, evolving into form and matter.

It is also a symbol of spiritual awakening, freedom from slavery to our psychological, emotionally charged illusions, the mind weighed down by painful memories, future projections, mental distractions, and identities. When the Israelites were wandering in their psychological desert, the first-born lamb was sacrificed each year as a token, to take away the sins that they had committed. The Hebrew word for sin simply means, "to miss the mark," and all of us at some point in our lives act unconsciously, and compromise our integrity. The lamb is the symbolic focal point of the internal transformation, which leads to a change of perception of life, through our conscious awakening.

We cannot become conscious without observing the ego, and illuminating our shadow. This teaching is depicted in the Bible through the concept of the reviled and persecuted suffering servant, drawn chiefly from the imagery of the Book of Isaiah in Chapters 52:13 to 53:12 and, especially Chapter 53:4–7, which speaks of one who has endured all of humanities disease, carried our pains, has been pierced for our sins: "*through his wounds we ourselves are healed ... He was led as a lamb to the slaughter... .*" When we give up long-cherished ideas about ourselves, not just the ones we experience as painful and negative, but also ideas of status, and being special, unconscious energy is released and transformed into new life.

At Passover, thousands of lambs were sacrificed at the Temple in Jerusalem. Its citizens and visitors went to the Temple to buy lamb for their Passover meal. John's Gospel differs from the other Gospels in that Jesus does not eat a Passover meal, but has a last meal a few days before and is crucified at Passover, the day on which the sacrificial lamb is eaten. The Anointed Jesus personifies the lamb that will release the sins of the past, and on a universal level, initiate entry into a new cosmic age; here, from Aries into the age of Pisces; a new way of Being.

We partake of this feast whenever we practice forgiveness. In forgiveness, we release ourselves, and therefore others, from illusions in form. When we release any memory, pain, or fear, we loosen the bonds on all those associated with it.

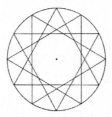

Breathe consciously, be present with all your attention, touching the Earth through your physical body, and aware of the creative Spirit of life flowing through you. Through forgiveness of unconscious thoughts words and deeds, you redeem and release the shadows that bind you; trapped memories, psychological and emotional pain, transgressions against fellow humans and the diversity of life on the Earth. This is redemption, and working consciously with others, including our fellow creatures in the animal, plant, and mineral kingdoms magnifies the effect. This is the sacrifice you make to know peace.

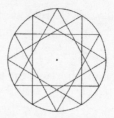

1:30 This is the One about whom I said, "After me comes a man who has come into created existence before me, because he has preceded me."
1:31 "And I did not know him. But in order that he be revealed to Israel, I came baptizing in water."
The stillness of Being, holding all past and future in the eternal present, (first introduced in verse 15, and reiterated in verse 27), is referred to again as the realization of spiritual illumination in the figure of Jesus emerging out of the formless, deep within. Jesus — at the doorway to *Malkut Ha Shamaim* — the Kingdom of Heaven — faces John across the Jordan, the river of creative life, flowing into form and matter from the abundance of the spiritual "land" flowing with milk and honey. John says retrospectively, *"And I did not know him,"* now able to understand and recognize, what he has been searching for and known intuitively.

John says, *"In order that he (creative Spirit) be revealed to Israel (Soul) I came baptizing in water,"* an initiation, where the Soul — *Israel* — is awakened through concentrated presence, stilling the mind. Spiritual awakening is a revelation of internal union, marked by conscious integration with the vital energy centers within the body and grounding through the physical body. Without the stilling of the mind, the Soul is not able to sustain contact with spiritual and Divine consciousness. First encounters may be brief and tenuous, but through conscious attention, you begin to open up longer periods of awareness.

The figure of John has a lunar quality in relation to the solar quality of Joshua/Jesus. In ancient cosmology, the Sun represented Divine and spiritual consciousness that sustains the psychological and physical worlds, whilst to be under the sphere of the Moon was to be under the unconscious influence of the ever-changing and ephemeral worlds of the body and psyche. This is voiced in chapter 3:30 of the Gospel when John says, *"That One must increase, but I must decrease."* The Greek verbs *auxano* and *elatto* translated, as "increase" and "decrease" also mean "to gain strength" or "increase in power," and "to decline in importance" or "dwindle in influence." As spiritual consciousness increases in power within the Soul, the psychosomatic energies are consciously unified — realized as creative spiritual energy. That which "declines in importance" or "dwindles in influence" are the unconscious use of bodily drives, and ego identification with thought forms. These energies no longer bind us in a state of illusion, and deprive us of our freedom. John recognizes spiritual consciousness, and gladly relinquishes his sense of separation; there is no resistance to his death, which is illustrated in the story of his imprisonment and beheading.

Biblical texts only give a précis of the myths and legends found in the folklore — the oral tradition — on the death of the Baptist. John's Gospel simply states that, *"he was not yet put into prison."* In the full version of the story, we are at the court of King Herod, a figure of totally corrupt power and tyranny, who represents John's shadow — total identification with the ego. Salome is present as the feminine counterpart of John, and she tricks Herod, through appealing to his lust, into giving her John's head on a platter. In reality, Salome dances, not for Herod, but for John, and her sacrifice is to perform the sacred dance of the Seven Veils, a ritual, which came from the cult of Isis in which the Goddess was slowly unveiled. For the participants, this dance represented their inner transformation: the stripping away of the outer layers of form that hid their essence. The dance consciously performed is the enactment of the revelation of the Spiritual Body and Divine Being.

The symbol of the severed head is widespread in world

mythology: it can be found in the Celtic legends of Bran's head, and in Hindu mythology as a symbol for the union of the Sun and the Moon. In the ancient world, the human head symbolized the place where the Spirit entered and sustained the body. The severing of the head from the body represented the raising of these energies. Many of the old Orthodox icons of John the Baptist illustrate this teaching very clearly, showing him as a spiritually enlightened, winged figure, standing next to his severed head on a platter. The spilling of the blood of a holy man was said to render the land infertile, so Herod tries to stop this, by ordering the head to be put on a platter. But the blood begins to boil over onto the land and a new sacrifice was required to restore fertility. In the folklore, it is John's father, who symbolizes the Christos that must be sacrificed.

In the Icon below, the resurrected John is illustrated as a winged (spiritually enlightened) figure; he lifts the veil from the severed head of the old unenlightened human, placed in the receptacle at his feet.

After John's death, Herod realizes the consequences, and understanding Salome has tricked him, orders his men to kill her. This symbolizes the desperate bid by the shadow for retribution as it faces its own inevitable demise, and its illusory power becomes meaningless. John's death initiates our death to all that is separate to total consciousness.

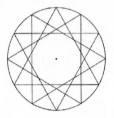

1:32 And John witnessed, saying that, "I have discerned the Spirit coming down as a dove out of the Heavens and it indwells him."

Within every human is *Being*; total presence. Absolute consciousness, stillness, silence, and peace can all be used to describe that which is: Unity, the One, source of all life, beginning and end held in the here and now. The more words, the further the mind will take us from that which is. John — the awakened Soul, witnesses that which *is*, through being totally present — no mind, no separation. As put succinctly by Rabbi Hillel, a spiritual teacher who taught at the Temple in Jerusalem in the first century BCE, *"If I am not for myself then who is for me? And if not now, when?"*

The Greek *theaomai*, is usually translated into English as "beheld," I have translated it as "discerned" because it helps to give a fuller sense of the apprehending of a person or event with the inner eye, a heightened awareness that brings together psychological and spiritual perception with physical sight. As we awaken to the Spiritual Body, we open up the five physical senses in order to experience life fully, which includes engaging with the natural world consciously. The physical senses are the manifestation of organs of perception, which exist in our psychological and Spiritual Bodies — our eyes, ears, taste, smell, and touch, so to speak, in those worlds. Their source rests in Divine Being, and through experiencing them spiritually, we realize that they constitute one conduit of consciousness that begin to differentiate and separate out in the universe of form.

As we become consciously present, our ability to alter the frequency of perception enables us to experience different realities simultaneously. It is our perception that changes, through the increased awareness that John describes. It is from this Greek root *theaomai* that we derive the English word and concept of "theatre," a place where, at its best, one may be lifted out of the ordinary thinking mind, through a dramatic portrayal in a Greek tragedy or a Shakespearean play, into deeper psychological awareness, and a universal understanding of life.

The second Greek word to examine more closely is *emeinen*, which is usually rendered into English as "rested upon" or "abode on," sometimes depicted as an image of two mating doves or tender lovers, but which also means to "indwell" and to be "permanent." A more literal translation of its root *meno* might read; "to be in close settled union." We may understand this through the mandala of the Star of David: the awakened Soul receives the consciousness of our Spiritual Body, and *Being;* unity, fully realized within the vital and physical bodies.

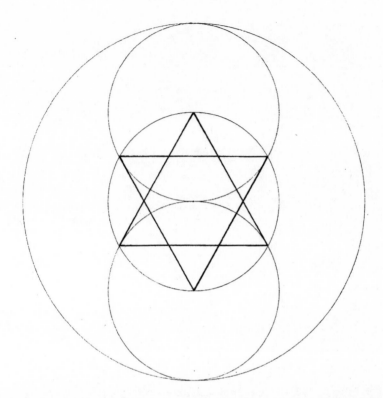

The Star of David representing the sacred heart or innermost center of every woman and man.

For our minds, this may seem a long way off, whilst we experience spiritual presence as a fleeting illumination, a mystical experience that fades and seems to leave us. Spiritual consciousness takes focus and attention on our part. To put our hand to the plough and not look back needs courage. Whatever happens to us and wherever we find ourselves, we can choose to awaken, and be conscious to the best of our ability.

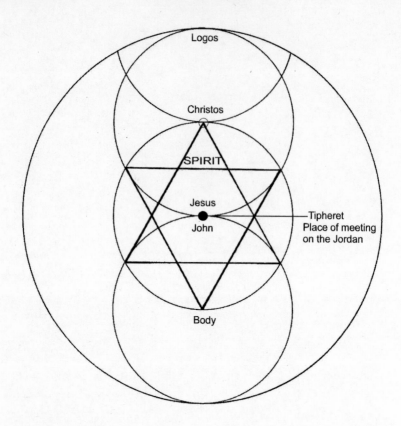

John, the awakened Soul, stands as a permanent presence consciously realizing his own Spirit and Divine Being, at the place of the downward flowing waters. This is the meeting place of formless Spirit and Being, with the psychosomatic bodies of form and matter, in unification. The Soul, conscious of Being, lives in the universes of form and matter without identifying with any form or outer appearance.

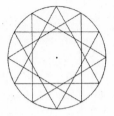

1:33 "But the One sending me to baptize in water, that One says to me, 'On whomever you see the Spirit descend and indwell, this is the One baptizing in the Holy Spirit.'"
1:34 "And I have beheld and I have witnessed that this one is the Son of God."

These two verses illustrate the anointing, the full realization of Divine Being, the full realization of Logos in the human body. The Baptism of the Holy Spirit was sometimes called the Baptism of Divine Fire, initiating the realization that consciousness illuminates every cell in the body, all life within the aura of the Sun, and every Star in the Cosmos.

The usual translation of the opening of verse 34 is "I have seen," from the verb *horao*. A common Greek word derived from the root is *heoraka*: Eureka literally means, "to see with knowledge," and to intuit something, the inner vision of a seer. It is the exclamation on realizing for oneself that something is true and was used in biblical Greek to describe being admitted into the immediate presence of Divinity. John says that he has borne witness that "this One" is the Son of God, the Divine Image: the unity of existence, the full reflection of God the Absolute.

In the Jewish tradition of the time, Son of God was the title given to a human who had fully realized her or his Divine Being. As a Son of God, the Christ is said to have come into the Cosmos through a virgin birth. This draws on the symbolism of the Isis — Horus myth of Ancient Egypt, and the Isis cult was very popular throughout the Greco-Roman world of the time. It relates to the cosmology on the re-birth of the Sun on the 25th of

December, aligned to the house of Virgo, Latin for virgin. In Women's mysteries of Isis, the pregnant virgin was a title given to someone who had conceived, that is, understood and recognized her Soul as a dwelling place for Divine Being. *In the fulfillment of that realization, Consciousness gives birth to itself.*

Total consciousness continually renews life, and is what is meant by a new covenant with God; we experience the constant creative renewal of life. Jesus is depicted as saying to those he had helped to heal or transform, *"Do not thank me, but go into your innermost room — your core — realize Being, commune with God in secret."* There is no separation, no other, between you, and the source of creative life. We do not identify Jesus or anyone else with consciousness or Being: it is an open conduit within, bringing healing, transformation, and Gnosis. A true healer or enlightened teacher acts as an experienced midwife would at the birth of a child, helping to facilitate change, to bring out the knowledge that exists within us.

The Gospel story asks you to awaken now, and be present, be a conscious Soul — a receptive vessel. *To Be Being* is your origin and the origin of all creation: *To Be Being* is to realize unification.

Chapter Eight

The Second Day of Transformation

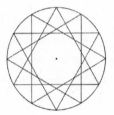

1:35 On the next day, again John was confirmed with two of his disciples.

The next phase of inner transformation is indicated by the words "On the next day." The Greek text uses the word *histemi* to describe John's inner state, which I have translated as "confirmed," and which also means "to stand firm" and "to be proven," indicating the sustaining of conscious presence at the point where Soul and Spirit meet. It is inner stillness, in which we experience clarity.

This is a deeper experience of *Tipheret*, as the conscious presence holding the continuous outpouring of creative life. The pressure of life held in balance by its resistance; beginning and end, the alternating pulse of life and death, which enables prodigious diversity in form and matter.

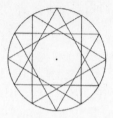

Be still, take a few conscious breaths and be aware of your inner space expanding out from your center, deep within you. Be aware of that stillness in the world about you, behind all movement and sound.

In this deepening consciousness, two of John's disciples are stood with him. Symbolically, this tells us that the dualities of the psychological body are brought into equilibrium through the light of consciousness illuminating the Soul. This dynamic balance occurs through our increased ability to remain conscious, integrating Soul and Spirit, in the realization of Divine presence.

We might imagine John as a central presence, his two disciples, one on either side of him, looking at Jesus. John acts as the central column of consciousness, and the disciples as the right and left hand pillars of active and passive dynamic energy. These two pillars can be understood through many different symbols. On the Tree of Life, they stand as the outer columns of Mercy (benevolence) and Judgment (discernment), with John holding them in conscious balance through Tipheret, at your inner core or center. The two disciples can be understood further in the astrological sign of Gemini, which was originally depicted by two bound pillars of wisdom, linking Divinity, the Spirit, Soul, and Cosmos. The dual aspects were later anthropomorphized as twins, and sometimes as an angel and devil that sit on opposite shoulders whispering in the mind. Mercy and Judgment, good and evil inclinations: Through the light of consciousness they are now brought into silence and stillness by John.

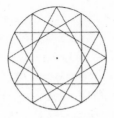

To not speak, yet to keep up a continual stream of thought, especially when charged with emotions such as fear, anger, or sadness is not silence. Nor is meditation silent, if the mind continues to run a commentary in your head. To be motionless, and yet continually think or daydream about what you need to do, or have done, is not stillness.

To be silent and still means no mind, no thinking, no distraction from presence.

This silent, still point, brings a new and deeper clarity as you observe the mind without being caught up in thought. When the mind is clear, thought and intellect can be utilized creatively when needed; you then return to the still, silent, awareness that bears witness. When you awaken to the eternal presence within your Soul, even fleetingly, you begin to reveal a treasure house of knowledge held in memory, which you utilize in the present. You are then able to apply this knowledge to life in the now. This brings about the ending of time as the mind "thinks it."

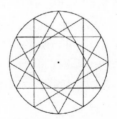

1:36 And observing keenly how Jesus was conducting himself, says, "Behold! the lamb of God."
The Greek word *emblepo*, usually translated as "looking," is better understood as, "to look attentively or searchingly," and more significantly, "to see clearly." This inner sight manifested

on the first day, now takes on greater depth because it is established. In order to realize this, we harness our latent intuitive, or mystical insight, our greater state of consciousness, so that physical and inner sight become one. We learn to do this with all our senses, so that we may live in the presence of the greater consciousness that permeates and sustains life.

The RSV translation says that John sees Jesus walking. The Greek word used here is *peripateo*, which equates with the Hebrew *Halakah*. The inner meaning of *peripateo* and *Halakah* refers to a way of consciously conducting one's life: Jesus is literally walking the Torah. It was said that one who practiced Halakah was following in the footsteps of Solomon, imitating him in life and manners. When we speak of Solomon, it is not the man, but what he symbolizes that is meant. His name is derived from the Hebrew root *shalom* meaning "peace," and "a sense of completion." He symbolizes Knowledge, wisdom, and understanding of Torah, internalized and lived.

When we conduct ourselves consciously, we live in harmony with the laws of life; the laws, which govern the unfolding of created existence from formless ideas, into patterns of ever diversifying beautiful form, taking on gravity, into matter. We experience all life as an interconnected whole. To be spiritually conscious is to embody the Torah: the matrix of living patterns of created life. This has nothing to do with reading texts, and referring to them blindly or even learnedly. We become present to life, so that each step we take connects us with the creative patterns of life, and their expression in the physical universe.

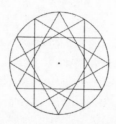

The Torah is the unfolding of life, which is continually being written through the life of all creation. Everything we meet, and experience as outer, is a symbol of its inner quality, expressing itself in form and matter.

Because we live in a world where we are identified with form, when we begin to awaken, it appears to us that the Divine light grows stronger or weaker across points of time. In the current human collective, this is relatively true. But, Divine Being is always present; it is we who move away from it, and it is we who must reawaken from the "outer darkness," the mental illusion of its absence and otherness. *Logos is closer to you than own your breath and the blood coursing through your veins, it is in the cells of your flesh and bones. You breathe consciously to remember this: that all things come from the One and are sustained by the One.*

In bringing this teaching to humanity, Jesus — your spiritual essence — is depicted as instructing those who can "see" and "hear," to find the source within themselves. This is the Spirit of *Torah*, which contains the seeds that seek fertile ground within the human Soul.

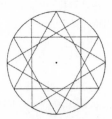

1:37 And the two disciples understood exactly what was said, and accompanied Jesus.

The RSV reads, "The two disciples heard him say this, and they followed Jesus." The word that has been translated as "heard" is the Greek verb *akouo* meaning "to take heed." This means "to take in," "to understand exactly," and "to admit." By admitting something, we are accepting and acknowledging a greater level of awareness in ourselves. It is a deep resonance that goes beyond the ordinary hearing of physical sounds.

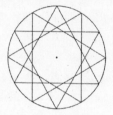

To hear the sound of the universe, the Sun and planets, to feel their presence, become still, silence the mind. Use the conscious breath to increase your awareness of the vital energy centers sustaining the body. To perceive the heralding of the Divine birth within your Soul, become conscious of the silence behind all sound.

The disciples of John respond by accompanying Jesus; the Greek *akoloutheo* has a root meaning, "to follow as a disciple," "to accompany," and also "to imitate or follow the example that has been set." Quite literally, it means "to follow step by step:" Jesus is conducting himself consciously, the disciples, having understood the instruction, have also started to maintain this state of Being. To walk in an awakened state step by step, means to live in the eternal present; each moment of time dissolves into the now, and the Torah lives in you.

Expanding consciousness from Tipheret, the seat of the Soul, you "move," always remembering the still point, deep within. To walk, or to ride in the chariot, are both symbolic of moving in time with the creative patterns of life, whilst becoming more conscious of the point of stillness within. This is an internal shift from being with John, the awakened Soul in the universe of forms; to being with Jesus, the formless Spirit, and *Eternal Presence*. Having reached the limit of his influence, John now starts to relinquish his powers to his greater consciousness (Jesus). The realization of *Being* comes, in part, through the transference of energy that we have invested in staying in a lesser state of unconsciousness. This energy is redeemed, released to the greater state of consciousness. The lesser state that dies, becomes the greater state.

This can be understood in a text attributed to St Paul, where the metaphor of leaving childhood and becoming an adult is used. In the Greek *nepios*, the child is the untaught, and unskilled unconscious state, without knowledge and understanding. The adult, *aner*, is a term used to mean psychological maturity. I have written the following translation in such a way to bring out the nuances in the Greek text.

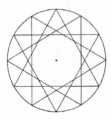

"When I was a child, I spoke without knowledge, I lacked under-standing, I reasoned without knowledge or wisdom; when I became an adult, I deprived those childish ways of their power and influence over me. For now we discern as in a darkened mirror, but then in immediate presence (face to face). Now my Gnosis is partial, but then I will know, as I Am known." 1Cor 13:11–12.

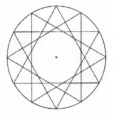

1:38 And Jesus turned to examine closely the nature of their conduct as they followed him, and said to them, "What do you seek?" And they said to him, "Rabbi", which means teacher, "Where do you dwell?"
1:39 He says to them, "Come and see for yourselves." They

went and saw where he dwelt in close settled union. And they abode with him that day. It was about the tenth hour.

The RSV tells us that "Jesus turned, and saw them following ... ." The Greek root *strepho*, "turned" also means "to make a change of substance" and an "inner conversion." Here the act of turning indicates an act of self-transformation, reminiscent of the sacred dance of the whirling Dervishes who, through turning, die; transform to a higher consciousness. In the steps of this spiraling dance, Divine presence turns, and pours into the consciously receptive Soul and awakened physical body. In this meeting face to face, consciousness beholds consciousness: in *Eternal Presence*, all is known as One.

The text says that Jesus "examines closely" the two disciples accompanying him step by step. Again, the Greek root is *theaomai: A* "to visit" and "to expose as in a theatre." Jesus asks them "What do you seek?" "Seek" is the translation of the word *zetew*, which could also be translated as "What are you trying to uncover?" or "What are you enquiring after?" It is a deep internal questioning, stripping away all of our deceptions to uncover the essence of who we are. There is nowhere to hide, and nothing to hide from, we cannot turn away into the mind and pretend or lie to ourselves.

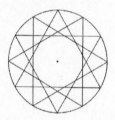

These, the first words spoken by Jesus, mark a deep internal change through drawing out the meaning of who you are as a conscious human being.

The disciples' response is to say, "Rabbi (teacher), where is it that you dwell?" The Greek verb *meno* is the same as that used to describe the dove coming down out of heaven, and means "to indwell," "to be permanent" and "to abide in close settled union." Another way of interpreting their question would be *"Where is your permanent dwelling place?"* To be "in close settled union" is to be in the presence of total consciousness, the realization of Logos.

Jesus replies, "Come and see for yourselves." We have seen the Greek verb *horao* before: it means "to behold" and "to be admitted to witness,'" "to perceive more deeply." Therefore the opening of the verse can also be translated as *"Come, and experience in yourself the revelation of Divine Being."* The text says, "they abode with him that day." In biblical symbolism, this simply means a complete cycle; seconds, hours, days or years have no meaning. It is a moment of illumination, which is timeless presence.

The text says that it was the tenth hour. On the Zodiac, which has twelve houses or hours, the tenth hour is the mid-heaven, the highest point or most visible area of the sky, the pinnacle of the vertical axis on the equal armed cross, the crown on the tree of life. Cosmically it relates to our direction in life, our calling *to be,* the fulfillment of our life. At mid-heaven the inner Sun radiates the Divine presence in the depths of the Soul.

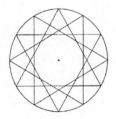

1:40 One of the two who understood John and accompanied him was Andrew, the brother of Simon Peter.
1:41 This Andrew first seeks out his own brother, Simon, and tells him, "We have found the Messiah," which, when translated, means Christ.

The RSV translation reads, "One of the two who heard John speak was Andrew ... ." The Greek root *akouo*, commonly translated as "hearing" also means "to understand," and "to obey." To obey without understanding can be disastrous, not only for ourselves, but also for others. Blind obedience is to act without intelligence or awareness, and it is useless in spiritual practice, only causing harmful tendencies and actions.

The name Andrew means a fully-grown human being — a psychological adult, who lives with a sense of unity from the Soul, hence he is described as "one of the two." All our mental concepts of duality are now brought into equilibrium, all that is still psychologically infantile or adolescent, within a fragmented sense of Self, is brought into conscious unity where we are able to observe the fluctuation between our different psychological ages. Andrew is the first of the disciples to be named, which marks the illumination of the mind. The Soul has ascended with Jesus to dwell with the Christ — our inner Being: to observe our life beyond time, to witness the unfolding of life as beauty. The Soul becomes the new focal point of the psychosomatic bodies, drawing their aspects together to act as one. The Christ now directs the Soul to consciously integrate the twelve divisions or aspects of our humanity.

In this gathering into the center, felt deep within you, *Andrew first seeks out Simon, his brother.* Translated from the Greek *adelphon*, which means "from out of the same womb" or "birth process." Andrew and Simon are brothers born from the same awakening. Andrew illuminates the mind — stills the mind — and consciously reconnects with Simon. The name Simon comes from the Hebrew root from which the command Shema! (awaken) is derived, and means "to obey with understanding," and also "to hear with inner ear," *"to listen — awaken."*

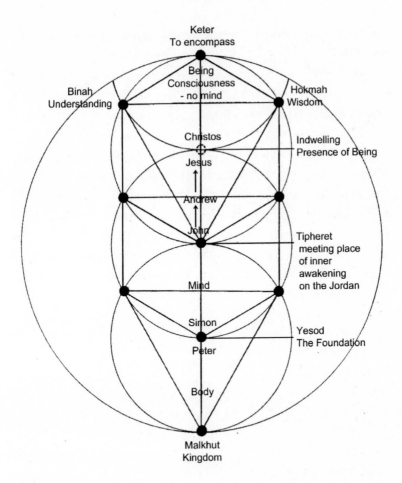

The meeting of John and Jesus on the Jordan, and the movement of Andrew to the place of the indwelling Presence of Being. In ascending to be with Jesus at the place of indwelling, Andrew is the Chariot Rider, raising consciousness from the Soul to the Spirit, and the eternal Presence of Divine Being.

When Andrew tells his brother that he has found the Messiah, he communicates a sense of presence beyond language. Simon represents the energies of the mind and body, as his name — to obey with understanding — suggests, he no longer acts unconsciously as a slave to the ego and physical drives, but can function under the greater awareness of the unified Soul and Spirit.

When we have a spiritual insight, our new consciousness seeks to earth itself. This isn't often acknowledged by the mind, especially when we misunderstand spiritual practice, thinking it will take us away from what we believe to be a mundane or painful life. It is we that need to change, not the World. It is our perception of what we thought of as mundane or painful, that is transformed into an appreciation that life is extraordinary. We acknowledge inner and outer space and see and feel the beauty of life. Andrew personifies our ability to consciously direct the mind as an awakened Soul, rather than being swept on the tides of emotion, *distracted thinking* about past and future, beyond and the egos endlessly chatter and attachments to images.

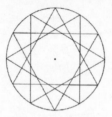

1:42 He led him on to Jesus, and observing him clearly, Jesus says, "You are Simon, the son of John, you shall be called Cephas," which when translated, means Peter.

The Greek word *egagen* begins the verse and is translated as "to lead on," it also means, "to guide" and "entice" which gives us a clue to the new relationship between the Soul, and the mind and body. The Soul is now the focal point for the conscious union between the Spirit and the mind and body in place of the ego. The Soul does not identify itself with any form, but focuses on the spiritual presence within.

Jesus looks upon Simon searchingly, and seeing him clearly, says, *"So you are Simon, the son of John."* Spiritual consciousness acknowledges Simon as the son of John, which means that mind and body are generated by the Soul. It is out of the Soul that mind and body emerge, and when the body dies all that we experienced in the body returns to the Soul; the Soul is animated by the creative Spirit, which has at its core, Being.

This recognition — and recognition means; *to know again that which is* — is depicted through Jesus meeting with the disciples, and they in turn recognize what he is. Jesus initiates Simon saying, "You shall be called Cephas," which in Greek is Peter. Both mean "the rock," and, "the building block." The act of naming him Cephas gathers the psychosomatic bodies into a new foundation. The awakened Soul is *the new foundation* in the universe of forms on which to build, a receptive vessel in which we can *Be at-one* with life. Simon Peter anchors this greater awareness in the body.

As the flow of creative life increases, energies locked in the unconscious psyche release, and are met by spiritual life force permeating our whole Being. To obey with understanding is Simon Peter's potential; however, the Gospels depict him as passionate, emotionally underdeveloped and even violent. He still has to overcome his passions to fulfill the potential of his name. The capacity to obey with understanding depends entirely on our ability to live through consciousness held in the Soul, the still center, depicted in the meetings of Andrew, John and Jesus.

When the mind is engaged consciously with the Soul, our unconscious patterns are brought out to be enlightened, rather than acted out unconsciously. The body acts as a filter through which the psyche may be cleansed. Simon Peter as the keystone of the inner Temple, aligned in harmony with Andrew, acts as a conduit of consciousness for Divine Being all the way into the cells of the physical body. This can sometimes be perceived as a burning sensation in which the cells literally glow with what feels like fire. If we consciously connect with the body, the vital energy brings us into the present.

The awakened Soul as the new foundation, gives you a new-found freedom, *space to be.* What you do in life, how and when you speak becomes aligned with creativity, because you are connecting with the whole of life through the Spirit and the eternal I Am — Being. The mind now becomes the servant of greater consciousness, thought becomes clear, no longer burdened by habitual thinking and unobserved emotions. Your physical body also becomes lighter, more vibrant and alive, when you are present in the spiritual sense, because you no longer weigh it down with fears, depression, or anger. Above all your words and actions are no longer competitive or exclusive, no longer serving the individual and collective ego. The creative presence of the Spirit makes you aware that life in all its forms is sacred: an expression of the One consciousness the Gospel calls Logos.

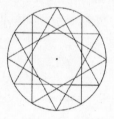

The Awakening Soul

The Soul is the seat of Divine Being in formation and matter, and for this reason was referred to as the chariot, and the ark of the Divine presence in the written accounts of the Merkabah mystics. The wheels of the chariot symbolize the energies of the natural human, and the natural world. The natural world is not only the life on Earth around us, but also the Solar system and the Cosmos. The awakening of the Soul (The chariot) acts as a conscious vessel, which journeys through life driven by the creative Spirit to meet with the essence of life in Logos. The awakened Soul, as the Ark of the Covenant, unites the four universes of existence. The Gospel depicts the unification of the four universes through John realizing the presence of the

Anointed Jesus. The teachings allow each of us to understand the journey into eternal presence, in our own way.

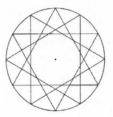

Preparation

If you are working on your own, familiarize yourself with the text of the meditation before performing it as an interior journey. Or you can simply read and contemplate it as an archetypal story. What is important is to put yourself into an awakened state by practicing the breathing exercises given earlier. If it is performed in a group, it should not be read in a fixed format. If you are guiding the meditation, allow your own imagination to speak and the collective imagination of the group to work with the Soul and Spirit. By imagination, I do not mean fantasy, which is a dispersion of concentrated thought or will. The art of imagination allows a connection to be made with the world of forms, which is a living reality in which the Soul exists. The images we create are filled by the greater awareness of the Soul, so that formless spiritual ideas may be experienced directly.

Our intention is of paramount importance and the meditation should always be preceded by creating a sacred space; this means becoming conscious, focusing your attention without the distractions of the thinking mind. Use a favorite prayer, or an invocation to awaken you to the presence of God. Similarly, when you conclude any exercise it is also important to finish with a closing prayer or statement of intention, and ground yourself consciously in your body. Most important, is that you breathe consciously from the base of the spine into the Solar Plexus and heart.

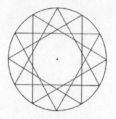

Meditation: Crossing the Wilderness

You are walking across a desert landscape. Look at the terrain about you. The climate is hot and dry under the midday sun. You look at your hands, and then down at your feet; note the color of your skin and the structure of your bones, are they thick set or fine? Are you a Woman or a Man? Notice how you are dressed.

Looking about, you see that you are with a group of companions on this journey. What has brought you to this point? You remember your first step on the path. You remember some of the significant turning points throughout your life on this journey, and the deaths and births of those who started out with you. How many remain of those who started out, and how have they changed?

You are following an ancient track across the desert, and ahead of you in the distance, you see an oasis. You can make out a figure coming slowly towards you from the oasis. As you approach each other you see them more clearly, how is he or she dressed? You look at the features and into the eyes of a wise one or guardian.

The wise one greets you, welcoming you to the oasis, and tells you the name of this place. What is it and what does the name mean to you? As you draw near you see that many others have gathered here. All, like you, have journeyed from afar. You can see the smoke from their campfires and their circles of tents. You and your company are led to a particular place at the oasis, down by the water's edge.

Your company makes camp. Some mark out the circle and put up the twelve tents. Others chop wood, make and light the fire in the center of the circle, fetch water, and cook food. Another group of you look after the young children and tend to the animals that have carried you here. All the generations work at their own pace and level; together you are able to make camp as the Sun begins to set and the Moon rises in the night sky.

You see the Stars appearing in the heavens, and as darkness falls, you see the Cosmos in all her glory. You listen carefully, what can you hear? Some of the constellations stand out to you, take note of them, and feel what they might mean to you. Sirius is especially bright standing before the three stars of Orion's belt.

You pick up a large pitcher to fetch water from the Oasis. From the center of the circle of tents with its fire now glowing brightly, illuminating the whole camp, you walk out into the darkness and down to the water's edge. Here you can see the moon and the depths of space reflecting in the water, the reflection is clear in the black crystal of the pool. You kneel down and dip your hand into the still water, sending ripples out across the surface. You scoop some of the water up in your hand and bring it to your mouth. As the water touches your lips, you experience the stars in the cosmos all about you, as well as the campfires burning around the oasis. You feel the cells in your body alight with fire. All are a reflection of the one life force that flows through existence, and that is flowing through you. As if in the blinking of an eye, you are aware of physical time once more and taste the water at your lips.

You fill the pitcher with water and carry it back to the camp, pondering what you have just experienced. You go to your own tent and lie down on your bed. Soon you fall asleep and dream. What do you dream?

In the morning you awaken, the Sun is just coming up, rising over the rim of the Earth. Its first rays greet you. The guardian who met you on the way enters your camp and tells you that today you must go on a journey alone. You pack a bag, taking with you things you think you might need for your journey. Each item that you take represents a particular skill of the tribe. What do you take? The guardian leads you through the many camps at the oasis. You see the faces of the different peoples who have journeyed here from all over the world. You are taken to a place of meeting where one person from each group of travelers waits to be instructed about the journey. You are told that you must travel for three days, totally alone. All that you are given is the direction in which you must walk. The guardian asks, "Are you ready for this journey, or do you wish to turn back?" This has been the purpose of your long journey to this place and of the sacrifices that you have made on the way. What do you chose to do?

You set out on your own. Only the sound of your footsteps and your breath can be heard. After a while, you look back at the camp in the distance. After a brief pause, you turn around again and walk on across a flat plain stretching out before you, beyond your own sounds, you become aware of the sounds and movements of life all about you. At length you reach a ridge, which reveals a wide sweeping valley. On the other side, you can see a range of great hills or mountains. You know that you must reach them by nightfall. You set out. It takes all day to cross the valley and climb up the other side. By the time you reach the top, night is falling and you are exhausted from the day's travel. You make camp for the night as best you can, and take from the provisions that you have carried in your bag. You see the Moon and Stars above you illuminating a landscape that seems to go on forever. Drink in the atmosphere of this place. After a while, you lie down and fall asleep, and dream. What is the dream?

The next day you are awakened by the sunrise. You get up and see before you a fertile valley. You make yourself ready and climb down the ridge into this lush green valley, taking in all its fragrances. You walk for some hours until you hear the sound of running water. You can smell it in the air. Following this scent, you walk on until you see before you a great river. You go down to the bank. The river is deep and strong as it flows down to some great distant sea. You can feel the great and varied currents of time as you walk along its bank.

Eventually you see a place where there is a ford, a crossing point. Look at the land on the other side of the river. Focus on it. It shimmers in the brilliant sunlight, seeming to be more vibrant than the land upon which you now stand. The Sun faces you, dazzling on the water; you look at the beams of light dancing on the eddying waters. It is as if the light is connecting with your heart and Solar plexus.

You step out into the waters and begin to cross the river, wading into its strong flowing currents. Allow yourself to feel these different forms of time within you. The waters become deeper and deeper until they swirl about your chest. Suddenly you go under the water and, then, you see the sunshine glimmering on the surface above you. At that same moment, your foot touches a large stone on the bottom of the river and you push upward.

You break surface and realize that you are able to walk on the bottom as it slopes up to the other side. As you look ahead of you into the Sun, you immediately see the outline of a figure.

The figure is moving towards you from within this land that you are crossing the river to reach. Come up out of the water and meet the figure face to face. The figure speaks to you in your own voice saying, "walk with me step by step."

As you take each step, you breathe consciously, the rhythm of your breath deepening as you move into the rising sunlight, which infuses you with life; moving with the rhythms and cycles that govern all of life, all forms, and all manifestations of those forms.

You step further and further into the land, feeling it flowing with the rays of the Sun, feeling your own being flowing with the source of all life and blending with it. The Sun burns brighter and brighter until you become aware in the midst of the light of a point of stillness; the place where the Divine indwells.

Breathe consciously out of the stillness; realize all that lives and moves is One and is sustained by the One: This is Logos.

Come back out of the brilliant light, until you feel as if the sky is moving through you, see and feel its clear blue color. See and feel the land about you and in you once more. Come back to the water's edge. Feel the current pulling you back. You turn and cross the river until you feel once more the ground of the fertile valley beneath your feet. You look back across the waters to the land of the Spiritual Body.

Then you leave this place, retracing your steps through the fertile valley back up to the top of the mountain where you find the place where you slept the night before. It is now evening and the light is fading, once again, the Moon is rising and the Stars begin to burn brightly in the night sky drawing in about you. The night is very clear and the starry heavens seem deep and vast, and at the same time close enough to touch with your outstretched hand. Feel yourself within the Unity of all life, both in the heavens above, and in the land below you that sweeps away to either side. You lie down and drift into an awakened dream in which you feel the touch of the World and the universe; what do you see and experience?

Next day you wake at dawn, and after rising, take some more of your provisions from the bag to sustain yourself for the journey ahead. You stand up, look across the fertile valley and then turn and walk back through the great valley, up over the ridge and across the plain until you see the oasis once more.

Soon you reach its edge, and to your surprise, your companions are coming out to greet you. They look at you differently somehow, and you also see them differently after your experience. How have they changed? You speak for a while and they point out some changes in you. Then you walk back to the camp. The fire is lit and everything seems as it was before you left, yet all is different in some way, and can never be the same again. All that you now see, hear, feel and touch is somehow sharper and clearer, and you see the people around you with more depth.

That night you dream about your journey of the last three days and you realize that the wise one is no longer at the oasis, but living within your own Soul. The next day you break camp and leave the oasis. You continue on your journey and you find yourself coming back into the physical place that you left, back into your body. Feel its life force, feel the blood pulsing through your veins, the air in your lungs, and the soles of your feet upon the floor. Open your eyes and stamp your feet upon the floor, coming back fully into the body.

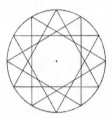

The most important part of meditation is to be in an awakened state, and this can be done without visualizations and visions wherever we are. But remember to give yourself space from the unconscious of the collective and individual ego (including your own), which seeks to run your life and the human world.

Chapter Nine

Day Three of Transformation

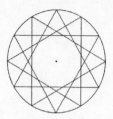

1:43 The next day Jesus purposed to go out into Galilee. And he seeks out Philip, and Jesus says to him, "Walk with me step by step."

The purpose of Jesus going out into the Galilee is to bring the power of Divine Being, through the receptive vessel of the awakened Soul, into the Cosmos and what appears to the mind as the outer world. Being shining through the Soul into the Cosmos is met by its full reflection; the experience of unity which is the reality that we hide from in our separation. The whole of the outer world is suffused with Divine consciousness, there is no other.

We need to remember that in this symbolic story the consciousness of Christ is the stillness out of which Jesus moves, going forth and coming back. In the same way, when you take a conscious breath, the lungs move, but the observing consciousness remains still. Spiritual consciousness represented by Jesus is the continual outpouring of creation from Divinity at the center, which never moves.

The Greek word translated as "purposed" comes from the root *thelo*, which means, "to exercise the will properly or clearly, without attachment." This alludes to the spiritual illumination of our will, and needs to be carefully understood. Spiritual consciousness has a purpose or aim, primarily to be present: in the moment; to bring the light of consciousness to bear on whatever we do through focus and attention, supported by the creative space of presence. In the light of intense awareness, subject and object dissolve into unity.

You may begin to experience something of this when you are enjoying yourself in a creative activity, when you are so present in what you do that the mind is silenced through giving full attention to the activity. You become at one with the moment and gain a sense of freedom; time disappears, the sense of subject and object diminishes, as you are absorbed in the present, without stress, anxiety or struggle. If higher awareness is sustained, you may begin to experience what is meant by non-attachment; there is no attachment to an outcome, which means you are not distracted by expectations of past failures or successes, and future promises or possibilities. This brings greater clarity and purpose to all that you do, because you are aligned with the creative patterns of life that continually emerge out of unity.

When you walk in the countryside, and give all your attention to the natural world, you can experience it as an interconnected creative pattern of life. Birth and death are continually present as the creative pattern of life continually unfolds, but behind this, there is unity, harmony and balance, experienced in the beauty, all of which is also present within you. This brings a sense of inner peace, and when you engage with life in an awakened state, you bring peace into all that you do.

Every creature that exists has a purpose within the circle of life, and carries it out. This is instinctual and requires no thinking. Humans are more than instinctual creatures, so we have to rise above the distractions and fragmentations of the thinking mind and find the presence of purpose within ourselves. Spiritual consciousness is like a laser beam, without distraction, beyond the minds understanding of time, so our purpose is to be in the moment, to be as present as we can in our daily lives.

The Hebrew root of Galilee means, *"a wheel,"* *"a circle of stones,"* and *"circle of eternity,"* as well as *"a calm or tranquil sea."* We have seen this Hebrew root before when we looked at the place name Gilgal. Both it and Galilee connote sacred space, and the Cosmic wheel symbolized by the twelve tribes of Israel, the twelve disciples, or the twelve signs of the zodiac.

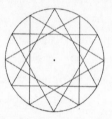

Pause for a moment and imagine a tranquil sea. When your inner psychological world is still and calm you witness life with greater depth and clarity. In biblical imagery the Soul is depicted as a boat on a sea or lake, the Christ — Being — dwells within, riding the waves of the psychological watery universe, with the spiritual wind driving the boat onward. Divinity shines upon the sea bringing stillness to the waters. The sea or lake of Galilee is the great circle of life on which the Divine Sun realizes itself.

I once witnessed this at dawn, on the shores of the Sea of Galilee facing the eastern horizon. As the Sun came up over the Jordanian hills, it cast a path of brilliance; dazzling sparks of light danced in the air across the waters. As my awareness deepened, I felt the Sun to be a cell in the physical manifestation of *Being*: the Cosmos as the manifestation of consciousness. From this still point, I knew that this is the Son of God spoken of in the Gospel, walking across the water, on a pathway leading into my heart. It does this within us every moment of each day, whether we are aware of it or not.

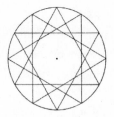

Such realizations are for each one of us to understand in our own way; Human consciousness and Solar energy are One: At your core is the light of the world; just as the Sun illuminates the life of the solar system so too a conscious human being illuminates all that they do, all that they touch.

Allow the rhythm of life to breathe through you. In stillness, the beauty of life speaks to you through its many voices, which merge into a single voice. This is silence.

A circle of stones is the demarcation of sacred space, made to focus awareness and bring body and psyche into balance and harmony with the Spirit, and ultimately with Being. The wheel of the Cosmos spinning on the Divine axis and the Sun witnessed within the movement of the Cosmic wheel — its 12 companions — tells you, *that at your core you are spiritual consciousness, that your essence is Being.* When you are consciously present, you bring out the illumination that is within you; this is to *know* the source of life within you; the Cosmos as a sacred or sanctified place, the Earth, and all natural life forms as manifestations of Divine Being.

When Jesus ventures into Galilee his purpose is also to "seek out" Philip, whose name means "lover of horses." Horses symbolize your inner vital body, the vital energy that manifests the physical body. At a deeper level, it is at one with the continuous flow of creation from the eternal presence of God. The horse body — your inner vital life force — is vibrant, alert, eyes noticing every movement, ears every sound. It smells and tastes other creatures and elements on the air, and the skin senses every gust of wind, and the gentlest touch. As you breathe into this vital energy that sustains your physical body, you are engaging in, and with life through and beyond the senses. *It is that expansive quality of greater life that moves as the wind across the Earth, yet always remains aware of the still center out of which all movement arises.*

Love of horses represents the rider who achieves balance and harmony with these vital forces. The rider neither holds her horse too tightly in check, nor allows the horse's energies to race out of control. Instead, she gathers them together into a heightened state of poise and harmonious balance. As the love, or consciousness, deepens she becomes aware of the creative energies, which continually unfold out of stillness. In the classical literature of ancient Greece, the perfect rider was the one who allowed the horse to freely unfold all its potential for beauty and movement. *"Those are the horses on which gods and heroes ride,"* wrote Xenophon.

In classical horsemanship, the art of riding a *perfect circle* demonstrated that horse and rider had united in balance and harmony. In Hebrew this is Tipheret, the fulcrum of life; to hold right and left, what is before and behind, above and below you in perfect — which means conscious — harmonious balance; the circle, the center, and the six directions.

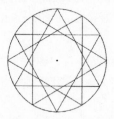

Become aware of this balance and harmony within you now; breathe from out of your center. Be aware of the space within you radiating before and behind you, through the spine above and below you, to the left and right of you. Be aware of this vital energy from the soles of your feet to the top of your skull, through your arms and hands, radiating the

great circle of life, your dwelling place of meeting.

On meeting Philip, Jesus says, "walk with me" — accompany me as a companion, keep pace with me, step by step.

To walk step by step in Being, is to be at One with the creative rhythms in life, and remain aware of the still center at your core. Love of horses is to know exactly what you have to do, and to choose to do it consciously, with creativity, and enjoyment. Whatever you do becomes an art in which the Soul expresses Spirit, and Being. This is illustrated in the creation story of Genesis, where humanity is directed by the Elohim to be fruitful and multiply (creativity), fill the earth (to be consciously present) and till its soil (cultivation of burgeoning life). The doing, the action is at one with Being.

Awakening the vital body also reveals the raw energy of emotion that we have held on to from the past. It is by remaining aware and observing the mind that we release the thoughts and emotions that the mind presents. Breathing consciously, aware of the vital energy field within the body, will help you to do this. As an emotionally charged thought comes up, your presence creates space around it before the mind turns it into a shadow, an ego identity. As an awakened human being, your responsibility is to acknowledge the emotion or thought without becoming attached to it, without projecting it outwards onto the world or people around you. In this way, you redeem all that is unconscious within you, which increases your ability to stay consciously present.

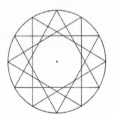

1:44 Now Philip was from Bethsaida, the city of Andrew and Peter.

Philip is said to come from Bethsaida, a place name made up of two Hebrew root words, *beth* which means "a house or dwelling place," and *saida* meaning, "to hunt" or "supply oneself with provisions," to "provide sustenance for a journey." In other words, it is a dwelling place of self-sustenance, and is also the city of Andrew (the full grown human) and Peter (the new foundation).

The inner meaning of the verse is that the awakened Soul knows that it is provided for on its journey. You are no longer seeking outside yourself for something to make you whole, or your life complete. The Soul is your new foundation allowing you to be in form but not of it, anchoring you into the vital body and giving you a love of abundant life. Being becomes your source of inner strength. From here, you experience freedom; fear of loss and dependency on outer circumstances for happiness no longer dictate your life. You are no longer drawn into old negative thought forms, nor dominated by the thought forms of the collective, whether they are social, religious, nationalistic, racial, or any other of the myriad dogmas and doctrines that the ego makes, and uses to strengthen itself.

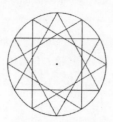

Become centered within, using the breath to help you; allow it to flow in and out of you with ease. Be aware of the energy field within you; your inner Being is the sustaining presence of life, connecting you with the whole of life, receiving and giving in equal measure.

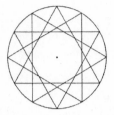

1:45 Philip seeks out Nathanael, and says to him, "We have discovered the One whom Moses wrote about in the Torah, and of whom the prophets have written; Jesus, the son of Joseph, from Nazareth."
1:46 And Nathanael says to him, "Can anything good come out of Nazareth?" Philip says to him, "Come and see."
1:47 Jesus beheld Nathanael coming towards him, and said of him, "Behold! Truly an Israelite without deception."

The name Nathanael is normally translated as "whom God gave," that is, grace. Through its Hebrew letters it has the deeper meaning of the generation of life, its resistance and death, out of which comes the generation of new life; cycles of life as a constant rhythmic movement animated by the changeless presence of Absolute life. This can only be understood as you begin to experience it as a reality within you. As you realize presence, you are creating space for new life.

Philip's seeking Nathanael is the vital energy opening out through the deepening awareness of the unity of life. Jesus is *the One* whom Moses wrote about in the Torah, and of whom the prophets have written: Joshua son of Nun, messianic consciousness; "I AM," the realization of the unity of *Being*. Jesus is the son of Joseph, whose name means, "to increase or be plentiful." He is from Nazareth, which comes from a Hebrew root meaning "to watch, observe and to guard, to be vigilant." The term Nazarite is also found in texts from the Dead Sea scrolls, where it was taken to mean the Soul of a righteous (honest) human being.

Nathanael's response is to say, "Can anything good come out of Nazareth?" At one level, this is an example of the Jewish irony that is often found in the Bible, but that can easily be missed or taken with deadly seriousness. The Greek *dunamai*, translated as "can anything," also means "to be able" and "to manifest power as a king." The word was used to imply omnipotence, and the enabling of spiritual powers to manifest. Nazareth is situated in the Galilee, a place that attracted mystics, because of the quality of light there. It also attracted those who wished to distance themselves from the politically intense atmosphere of Jerusalem. Galilee therefore had a reputation for defiance of religious authority and dangerous ideas. It represents a state of awareness where one begins to live and act from a point of Gnosis within oneself. Philip answers Nathanael with, "see for yourself" — an invitation to experience the source of life.

Jesus greets Nathanael with "behold!" (Observe and know for yourself), "here is an Israelite in whom there is no deception." Israel, the symbolic name given to the Soul, has two components, *Sarah* "to rise in splendor as the Sun," and *El* "strength through presence." Divine presence causes the splendor of the Sun to rise on the Galilee, illuminating all that is unconscious in humanity. The Greek *dolos* means "deceit, fraud, corruption, adulteration, and insidious artifice." To be free of this is honesty, to be clear of self-deception and all that is false and destructive in the egocentric mind. In Divine presence and the creative spiritual consciousness, the Soul becomes free from identification with physical and psychological forms.

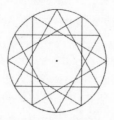

1:48 Nathanael says to him, "From where do you know about me?" Jesus answered and said to him, "Before Philip called

you, I perceived you under your fig tree."

1:49 Nathanael answered, "Rabbi, you are the son of God, you are the King of Israel."

The Greek word *pothen* means "from where," in the sense of place or origin. It is used to denote a state of being, for example, "what is your cause or source?" Nathanael is asking, "How do you know my place of origin, my internal cause or source?" When you acknowledge the depth of observing consciousness within you, beyond your thinking mind, who is it looking through your eyes? Can you feel the eternal presence that exists within you now? Are you aware of that same presence in all the life around you? *Be still and breathe from there.*

Jesus replies, "Before Philip called you, I saw you," literally, "I knew you." This refers to two different levels of conscious perception. Philip *called* to Nathanael: the voice is the symbol of creative movement out of stillness passing through time in space, but Jesus has already *seen* him: this is inner knowing, beyond time in the eternal now: Logos. Jesus says, "I perceived you under the fig tree:" Literally, "under its influence." This is a very important biblical motif; like the vine, the fig tree is a symbol of the Spiritual Body. An example is given in the first book of Kings 4:25:

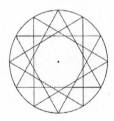

"And Judah and Israel dwelt (to be still) in confidence, every individual under his vine, and under his fig tree, from Dan (to master) even to Beersheba (the seven springs/wells) all the days of Solomon (peace)."

To be still under one's fig tree is said of those who are balanced, tranquil and happy, at ease with life, knowing peace and spiritual prosperity. The fig tree symbolizes your Spiritual Body, which carries the seeds of both male and female genders. Whilst certain fig trees are self-fructifying, both the masculine and feminine aspects incorporated in the same tree — others live in symbiotic relationship with a tiny wasp for pollination. The fruit of the tree is really a container of both seed and flower, likened to a secret garden full of tiny white flowers emitting a delicate perfume that attracts the wasp that enters through a small opening, symbolically the narrow gate into paradise, our turning within to grow in the inner world. The Hebrew *te'enah*, from which fig tree is derived is also used of auspicious meeting; what you meet is the eternal creative presence that *is* within you now.

On being made aware of Divine presence, Nathanael calls Jesus, the Son of God, and the King of Israel. To be a Son of God (the Hebrew for son also means a generation) is the realization of conscious union. The King of Israel continually draws, the awakened Soul (Israel) to the inner source of Being. As titles, they are meaningless, and have nothing to do with earthly power, psychological power over others, or any projections and beliefs that dissipate our life force through the unconscious mind, and the external seeking of salvation.

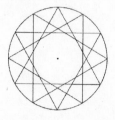

1:50 Jesus says to him, "Because I told you that I saw you under the influence of the fig tree, you believe this!? You will be admitted to witness far greater things than these."
1:51 And he says to him, "Truly, truly, I say to you, from this moment you will be admitted to witness the heavens opened

and the angels ascending and descending on the Son of Humanity."

This response is often interpreted as Jesus' astonishment at the faith of Nathanael, which again misses the important use of Jewish irony. Taken in this light, Jesus is actually gently chiding Nathanael. Jesus' response is to bring Nathanael back into focus and ground the experience. "Stay awake! Just because I told you that I saw you under the fig tree you call me the son of God, the king of Israel?!" He continues by telling Nathanael that from *now* he will see far greater things than these.

The Greek root translated as "see" is the verb *opsei*, which means, "to witness for yourself," and was used by Hellenistic Jews to denote the first watch after the Sabbath. Essentially this is the space we create within ourselves for communion with God, to experience Unity of Being. The Sabbath itself is a time for conscious re-creation and reflection, and to hold the first watch after Sabbath is to view the everyday world in a conscious state. This space gives you the opportunity to view your familiar surroundings with new eyes. This is an important meditation, which awakens the higher faculties of awareness. You then begin to experience that the ordinary everyday world you inhabit, is full of the extraordinary, and that physical form is an ephemeral mist, mostly space, beyond which other universes or dimensions exist. All that the mind thinks of as permanent and solid is continually appearing and dissolving, held in temporary form by consciousness.

The phrase "truly, truly" is "amen, amen" in the Greek; it is a transliteration of the Hebrew *amen*, meaning "most certainly" and *"so be it," that is, be aware of the space that allows everything to be; be aware of the eternal presence that is. From here, the Soul witnesses the heavens open and the angels ascending and descending on the son of humanity. All forms arise out of stillness, and return to that same stillness, the source of all that is. This is the fountain of living water experienced through the conscious breath.*

The description of the visionary experience given here is

based on Genesis 28:11-12, which reads:

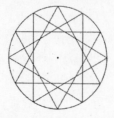

And he (Jacob) came to a still place, and dwelt there, because the Sun (Brilliance) was set there (Stillness). And he took from the stone (strength) of that still place, and set it at his head (source or place of origin) and lay down (to die) in that established place of The Name (Being). And he grew in vital strength and beheld (knew with clarity) a ladder (a state of exaltation) is established on the Earth (the seedbed of Absolute life), and its source pierced through the heavens (creative universe); and he saw with clarity, the angel (creative movement) of Elohim (Absolute life) ascending and descending within it. (My translation.)

Breathe and feel the vitality that sustains the physical body. Be present, allowing no thought to distract you. Become conscious of the eternal presence sustaining all life. In this moment, in this space, forms are appearing and disappearing. In this moment and space, creative life is descending and ascending into and out of form and matter. In this moment and space, is life in fullness, nothing is separate. At all times and all places, whatever the circumstances of your life, you can awaken to the eternal presence of Absolute life to the best of your ability. Be present now so that you may know Peace.

Chapter Ten

The Conscious Realization of Divinity in Earth

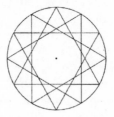

And on the third day there was a wedding in Cana of Galilee, and the mother of Jesus was there. Jesus and his disciples were also called to be present at the wedding. 2:1–2

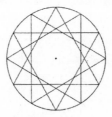

First, take a few moments to bring your full attention to your center; take a few moments to become present, and be aware of the vital energy within the body, from the top of the head, down the spinal cord, to the soles of the feet. Feel your connection with the Earth. Breathe consciously. Awareness of your vital energy and the breath, acts as a door to a deeper level of consciousness within you.

Now become aware of the space within the body; the space between the cells, holding the form of your body; within that space, cells are continually, dying, and being born. Recognition of space frees you, allows movement to flow without restriction. Breathe deeply and clearly, allowing no thought to distract you; feel the life energy within you, in the air in your lungs, flowing into your blood, flowing though your veins into every part of your body. Be present, here, now, to the life force sustaining your body, as fully as you can.

You are now asked to be present at a wedding in Cana, which brings to a resolution, the three phases of transformation you have just witnessed. It is a marriage that takes place deep within you. Now we are going to explore the deeper meaning of the symbols that are presented in the text.

The Wedding

At the wedding at Cana, consciousness marries consciousness; *Divine Being is realized by your witnessing consciousness as the sustaining presence of all life within you, and in what the mind perceives as the outer universe.* The Greek text literally says, that the wedding has *"come into created existence"* at Cana, which means that it is an act of spiritual renewal, of continuous creation, the conjunction of Heaven and Earth, creative power and its realization. This conjunction is happening now — within you and in all of life's forms. You bear witness to it through stilling the mind, by giving this stillness all of your attention.

Cana — the Place of Reeds

The name Cana, in Hebrew *Kanah,* means "the place of reeds," is associated with the Ark woven out of reeds by the Mother of Moses, to bear him up on the waters of the river of psychological forms. "The place of reeds," is where she hid Moses from the Pharaoh (the ego), who sought to drown the newborn sons of the Hebrews in these waters; symbolically this means to overwhelm the birth of new consciousness by plunging it back into identification with form. The place of reeds is where Moses was revealed to the daughter of Pharaoh as she bathed in the river. She is the aspect of the Goddess (the vital body) who draws out the awakening consciousness from the psychological unconscious, dominated by the ego, into an awareness of the spiritual universe. This teaching story of the birth of higher consciousness (Moses) is much older than the biblical version in the Exodus, with origins in Akkadian — Mesopotamian, and Ancient Egyptian Mythology. The Egyptian reed fields are the heavenly paradise where Osiris, the consort of Isis, dwells, a place of rebirth, and renewal from out of darkness and death. It is the union of Osiris and Isis that brings about the birth of their only begotten Divine Son, Horus.

Here in the Gospel of John, Cana is linked with Galilee, the great circle of life, the sacred or sanctified place. The marriage ceremony takes place within sacred space, which means a spiritually awakened state. To consciously experience the Unity of life is the end of the illusion that the death of your body is the end of your life; that you are an ego, a separate entity, disconnected from the rest of life. Every death is also a rebirth and renewal.

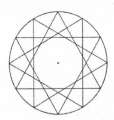

This spiritual awakening is to experience *Heaven and Earth as "One,"* as here now; to live consciously as the spiritual essence of who you are. It is the marriage of inner and outer universes, of male and female, of the "One" with its reflection. You begin to remember all that you have ever been, and all that you will ever be, in *"One"* consciousness that flows through you, that flows through the entire circle of life, in abundance, an abundance that is always present.

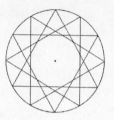

The Mother Goddess

The Mother of Jesus holds the space in which the marriage ceremony takes place. This is the first point in the text, where the Logos is explicitly represented in feminine form. In the Old Testament stories, Joshua (Jesus) is called the Son of Nun, "Fish," "abundant fertile life." Nun -נון in Hebrew is the sign of generation; of generations and their connections with their unfolding forms, universes within universes, worlds within worlds.

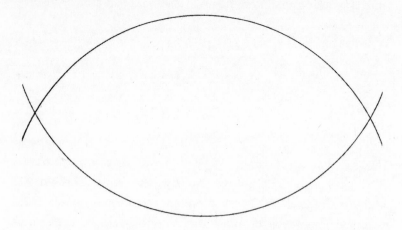

The space in which the wedding ceremony takes place is represented through the image of the Vesica Pisces, the symbol of the Fish, in Hebrew Nun, the sign of abundant and fertile life. Joshua (Jesus) is called the Son of Nun, the Son of the creator or generator of the abundant patterns of life and its connections.

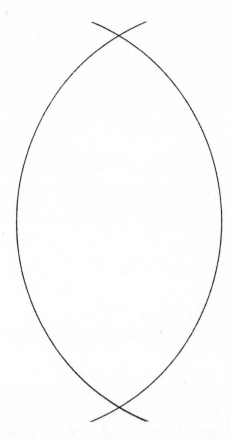

In Judaism, the Divine Feminine is also called the Shekinah, from a root meaning, "to be present." She is the unifying Divine presence that continually gives birth to and sustains all created existence, all diversity of form, all physical life. The diagrams above illustrate Logos as the One source of all life, and the unifying presence which continually gives birth to created existence. From the polar tensions of active and passive dynamic within creation, comes the flow of life in ever-increasing diversity and complexity in the universes of formation and making.

In the New Testament the Mother of Jesus is called Mary — Miriam, one of the forms of Isis, the Great Goddess of Antiquity. The Divine Mother is Unity, Space, in which creation unfolds out of the eternal formless, timeless present. The Unity of the eternal present is the space in which diversity, and its resultant multiple possibilities takes place. The formless takes on life in the play of forms, life expresses itself though the patterns of emerging diversification.

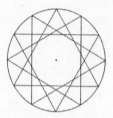

The Hebrew name Miriam (Mary) can be translated in various ways, but the letters — מרים taken as ciphers mean; the flow of creative mutable power, containing as principles, the seeds of absolute life; creative presence in Space, giving life to forms, to all that we experience as matter.

Miriam is the great sea of *prima materia* — the formless source of all matter — she is the initiator of change, through the constant pressure of movement from one state of existence to another, what we experience as birth, conjunction, and death. All these states, so to speak, are one. That is, they form a continuous flow, beneath and behind which, is the presence of the watcher that never changes.

When you are able to witness the flow of passing life forms, your attachment to them diminishes. This is not to deny any emotional response, but an acknowledgment that the passing of forms initiates a greater awareness of life.

Throughout this book, I have explained that the masculine names used in the texts express that which is beyond gender, and contain the potential of both. Why then, is it necessary for us to acknowledge the Divine feminine? God is nothing that we can say is anything; all images, and all names are only psychological forms that cannot contain, and ultimately limit your perception and understanding, of that which is beyond all form, and gives life to all form.

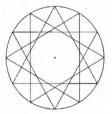

God — Divine Being, is neither feminine nor masculine, but expresses life through both in equal measure.

The expression of life through both feminine and masculine in equal measure is the essential point. To become spiritually conscious is to hold feminine and masculine in balance. We cannot know this balance without being spiritually conscious, and we cannot be spiritually conscious without knowing this balance. From this still point, we naturally acknowledge and address the imbalances that have been so much a part of human suffering, and that have spread as pollution from psychological form into the natural world. A great deal of our collective sickness, and pathological behavior, is a result of the marginalization, deliberate suppression, and ultimately the demonization of the feminine.

This suppression is intimately allied to our loss of inner stillness, silence, and space; and with it our connectedness, and knowledge of the sacredness of life in all the forms that manifest as the natural world. We now have a stark choice: to continue to poison and destroy the web of life — the path we are currently taking — or, to embrace life as the unity of diversity into which we are intimately woven. We can choose to awaken *now*, this very moment, and consciously participate in creation.

The Greek text in verse two, tells us that we are "summoned," or "called into the presence" of the wedding, as Jesus and his disciples. This "summoning" is true for all time, it is always now, it exists outside of time. As we have already seen, the twelve disciples, or the twelve tribes of Israel, are representations of the signs of the zodiac that form the great cosmic wheel: the sacred circle of all life. At the center stands, Divine Being — total consciousness — whose radiance unites all created existence through your spiritual awakening.

As a guest at your own inner wedding, you are called to draw the universal aspects of humanity into conscious union with the source of all of creation. This is Logos. Within you is the life represented by Jesus and the twelve disciples, the center and its complete reflection in the great circle of all life.

The dialogue between the Divine Mother and the Divine Son that follows, initiates this realization of creative power within the Cosmos.

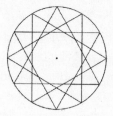

And there being no wine, the mother of Jesus says to him, "They have no wine." Jesus says to her, "What has that to do with you and me, madam? My hour is not yet come." So his mother says to the servants, "Do whatever he says to you." 2:3–5 Again, remember that this is your inner landscape, and that all of the characters presented in these verses are universal, archetypal, aspects of consciousness.

Mary's address to Jesus is drawing *your* attention to the fact that the wine is lacking. This does not simply mean there is no wine left: the Greek root *usteros*, translated as "there being no", also means "to fall short of," "to be inferior" and also "to be late." The overall sense is "to make good or complete that which is lacking in the world," in both your individual interior world, and the external Cosmos.

Like the vine, wine is a symbol of the creative spiritual universe and spiritual awareness. The wine that is lacking or inferior, symbolizes the human descent into unconscious and fragmented thinking that is dominated by the ego. What is lacking in the world is the conscious presence of humanity. Every time we lose spiritual consciousness, we lose our connection with true creativity; we are no longer present to the life within and around us.

In reply, Jesus says, *"Madam, what does that have to do with you and me? My apportioned time has not yet come,"* or in a more literal translation, *"the moment I possess is not present." "The moment I possess"* is the eternal present; and this is what the guests at the wedding feast are unaware of. The unconscious collective mind of humanity is not able to *realize* or *be* with the full presence of life.

Mary now bestows the powers of which she is the custodian — the powers of the Goddess-creator, the giver of life, the healer — on Jesus (realized conscious presence). The literal Greek, although cryptic, reads more as a command, "Whatever he says to you, do." The word translated as "do" comes from the Greek root *poieo*, meaning "to make," "construct," "to bring to pass," "to accomplish," "fulfill" or "put into execution." It connotes far more than the carrying out of a series of instructions. Another translation of the verse might be, "Act in accordance with his will." This is spiritual will emerging out of conscious presence. It is the conscious performance of a creative action, in synchronicity with its environment, resonating with the whole of life.

The Mother's servants become the Son's servants; teaching and healing through deep understanding and knowledge of the laws of the Cosmos and created existence, so that all that has become disconnected and fragmented, can be realized as whole again. This is neither special nor exclusive; it is the potential within any awakened women or man, and is open to anyone who is prepared to work to become spiritually conscious.

This is in complete contrast to how the ego functions, manipulating life for its own ends and treating it as if it were a commodity. The creative power of the spiritual universe cannot be owned or manipulated and its fruit, is never life negating nor destructive. The truly creative use of will is perfectly aligned with the flow of life, in balance and harmony, continually sustaining all form and matter. Creative power acts with understanding and knowledge that every living thing is related to our inner Being. Subject and object diminish, we become at-one with life. This is Logos.

When we are conscious of the unity of life, we do not commit adultery, which means, we do not poison the land, rivers and oceans. We do not rape the land and sea of the beauty and diversity that sustains life. We do not murder, that is, we end our destructive behavior. We do not destroy and plunder that which sustains our presence here on this planet, and which is inseparable from our own vitality and life. We do not bare false witness, that is lie to ourselves, and others in order to amass personal wealth and power, at the expense of our fellow humanity and our fellow creatures.

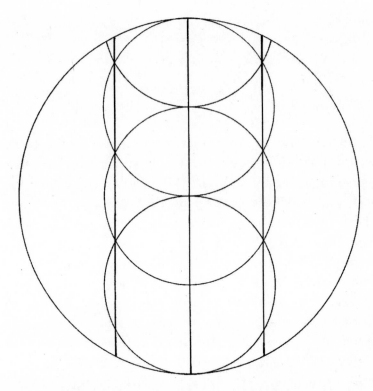

In Jewish mysticism, the Feminine voice of Divine Being is often equated with the word "Binah;" meaning, "the gestation and generation of life," and "to come to an understanding." Translated from its four Hebrew letters, בינה – Binah can be interpreted as: The containing power of the seed of Absolute life, and its generations, held and released on the universal rhythmic breath; cycles of birth and death. Binah expresses feminine power as the passive dynamic holding principle, the essential compliment of the active dynamic principle Hokmah - "revelation" and "Wisdom." She personifies the power of space to receive pure unstructured energy — Hokmah, so that it can gestate, germinate and take on creative pattern and form.

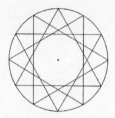

And there were six stone water-pots set out for the Jewish purification ceremonies, each containing two of three measures. Jesus says to them, "Fill the water-pots with water," and they filled them up to the top. 2:6–7

The Greek word *lithinos*, means stone, and it was used figuratively of Christ — *Divine Being* — at the core of manifest existence. *Being* is constant presence, the permanent, the real, within created existence. The physical universe is the most ephemeral level within existence, called by the mystics, the blossom of the tree. In the physical universe, stone is the manifestation of consciousness, the densest level of its material expression. Yet each atom of solid matter is mostly space, the space that allows matter to be. The magma at the core of the planet Earth, is the foundation upon which physical life takes place, and we live on the thin solidified crust of this dynamic abundant outpouring; the continual remaking of the building blocks of physical life. Planet Earth is in continual flux, and continually re-cycles the material that all life forms use for their physical appearance.

The six stone vessels represent the outer appearance of the inner creative pressure that comes from the power of eternal Divine presence. The text says that these six vessels are "set out," in the sense of an interrelated dynamic pattern, in proportion, for the purification ceremonies. It is your presence, your higher awareness that allows universal creative energy to flow through you.

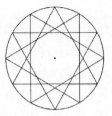

Be aware, as you breathe, of the dynamic space within and around you; the multi-dimensional space that sustains you connecting you with the circle of life.

The six stone jars at the wedding feast, set out around the central circle of un-manifest Being, are represented here in geometric pattern. Unity in diversity, and diversity held in Unity. The six circles can be seen as the six directions of space. The points at which the six circles intersect, and where they touch the outer circle represent the twelve segments of the Zodiac or Cosmic wheel of life.

The Greek root of the word translated as "purification" is *katharos,* which means, "to be unsoiled, clean from guilt, virtuous and void of evil." The vessels therefore represent our conscious participation in life, our "wholeness" through conscious presence and living knowledge of the sacredness of life.

The number six is significant in Jewish mysticism, and is represented by the letter *Vav* – ו — in the Hebrew alphabet, which means *hook, nail,* or *peg; the fertilizing agent; that which impregnates, and joins.* It is the number of perfection or completion, symbolized by the six pointed Star of David. It is on the sixth day in Genesis that creation is completed, and on which humanity first appears. This means that humanity is intimately connected with every living thing that has been created.

The letter Vav appears in the first line of the creation story of Genesis, which in the familiar translation reads, "In the beginning God created the Heavens *and (Vav)* the Earth." *Vav* is the Divine conjunction, *"and."* It is the Divine hook that binds all Heaven and Earth; the spiritual creative universe, the formless, with the Cosmos; form and matter. *Vav* is therefore said to be the creative connection between all 22 Hebrew letter numbers. In the Torah scroll, used in the synagogues, the scribes emphasize a letter *Vav* to mark the midpoint of the text. Vav or six therefore symbolizes the central point out of which the Torah emerges; the staff thrust into the Earth to mark the center of the sacred circle of life.

The six-pointed star represents unification, Divinity in Matter, the formless holding the patterns ratio and connections of all that is form. It is the realization of Heaven and Earth as One, here and now, and is one of the geometric depictions of the Hebrew concept of Tipheret; Goodness, Beauty and Truth.

In Verse seven, Jesus instructs the servants — his creative awareness — to fill the six stone pots to the brim with living waters; this represents the awakening of the vital subtle energy centers. The awakening of the crown (Keter) within the physical body opens the way to the heart of the psychological body, connecting us with the creative Spirit at Tipheret, the place of the ford, where we meet the continual pressure of the downward flowing waters.

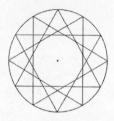

This can be experienced as a sensation of vital energy flowing down through crown of the head into the body, through the skin on the forehead and face, piercing down through the throat into the heart center and the internal organs, and through the spinal cord into the pelvis; expanding as you breathe into it, so that you become aware of the energy in the sacrum, coccyx, legs and feet, connecting you with the Earth. Allow your awareness to expand outward in the six directions, be aware that you are supported by the energy centers in Earth and in the space about you and within you in balance and harmony. As you bring consciousness into the body you meet the life in the spine rising up like a fountain from deep within the earth; consciousness meets consciousness in the body.

This image of the six stone jars represents the brimming of the physical body with creative life force, and the integration of these vital energies into a unified whole. The senses are heightened, so that we can feel, hear, see, taste and smell far more acutely. When we consciously inhabit our physical body this, in turn, activates what is often referred to as the sixth sense, psychic ability, intuition, or the gifts of the Spirit. The physical senses are the terminals of conduits of consciousness that run from Divine Being, through creative pattern and form, into your physical body, and Cosmos. They become dulled and disconnected through our unconscious drives, desires and emotions, or our need to hide from greater awareness of life.

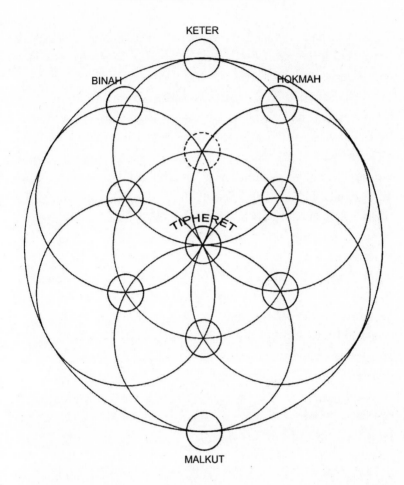

As the mother of the Divine son — Joshua/Jesus — the Divine feminine is a vessel in which conscious union occurs. She holds the axis of consciousness, between the Hebrew concept of Keter — "to encompass, and contain absolute life as existence," (the circumference of the circle,) and that of Tipheret — "the unfolding of Absolute Life as existence, held in balance through its resistance," (the center of the circle.) She is the presence, the space, which allows the passing of creative life from the formless, into its expressions in form; total consciousness, continually giving birth to itself as creative pattern, and diversifying form.

All of us have moments of illumination: flashes of vision and heightened perception. Some of us will be able to have sustained periods of illumination, but what is depicted here is the complete fulfillment of these latent abilities. We can only achieve this through sustained work, that is, sustained presence.

When the greater state of awareness is truly engaged, then we become aware of the mythical Eden, and enter the Kingdom of Heaven, without departing from our everyday physical world, although our perception of it is altered immeasurably. Our perception of life in all its forms changes and deepens as we realize that *Being* is always present, and that different realities exist within the same space that we think of as solid and permanent.

Through this realization, we are presented with more possibilities and opportunities to live our lives to the full, in balance and harmony within the greater awareness of all life. Whether our physical body is healthy or sick is not an issue, we can be still, and experience the fullness of life in the present moment. We do this through focusing the lenses of our inner bodies into One consciousness: then it is possible to perceive what, in the symbolic language of the Bible, is called the New Jerusalem, the New Heaven and the new Earth.

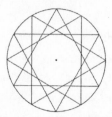

And he says to them, "Draw out now and bring forth to the master of the feast," and they brought forth. But as the master of the feast experienced the water which had been created wine without knowing its origin — but the servants who had drawn the water knew — the master of the feast calls the bridegroom. And he says to him, "Every human being sets out the good

wine, and when they have become intoxicated, sets out the
inferior: You have kept the good until the present." 2:8–10
Jesus instructs the servants "to draw out *now* and bring forth,"
from the six stone water-pots to the master of the feast. The
transformation of water into wine occurs *now* in the eternal
present moment. Spiritual, creative, transformation is always
present.

The Greek root translated as "to bring forth," *phero*, also
means "to conduct," and "to bear or be borne." It was used of a
ship's progress across the ocean, driven at speed by the winds,
and depicts an active, dynamic movement, a progression from
one place to another, which has to be carefully and deliberately
carried out. This comes from our ability to be present, and the
sense of "bearing something," suggests that the process requires
our focused attention, strength, and commitment.

To become conscious does not mean that life is easy for us. It
brings an acceptance of situations, to be at peace with what is,
whatever place or situation we might be in. It does not necessitate that we experience hardship or suffering, but gives us the
ability to accept the passing of life, in the universe of form, as it
is in each moment. Peace comes to us when we accept a situation
and are able to meet it consciously; to act consciously arises out
of stillness, and this gives our actions purpose, without fear or
distraction.

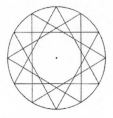

All conscious movement arises out of stillness and returns to stillness.
All creativity arises out of stillness; all life arises out of stillness to take
on form, and when the form dies, its essence withdraws into stillness.

The Gospel of John tells of the woman of Samaria, meeting Jesus at Jacob's well where she has come to draw water, and Jesus says to her, *"Whoever receives into the Soul, the waters that I shall give them, will never suffer thirst unto eternity; the water that I shall give them will come into being in them as a spring of waters welling up to eternal life." (John 4:14). (My translation).*

When you awaken spiritually, you are the spring of life, and you do not need to draw the living waters, because they flow through you in abundant grace — the eternal renewal of life. These abundant waters flow through all life, sustain all life, connect all life, and they are welling up in you now, your own source and connection with all of created existence.

In verse nine, the usual translation is that the Master of the Feast "tasted" the water that had become wine, but the Greek word *gignomai* "tasted", also means "to have experience," and "the inner perception of" a given thing. The other significant Greek word is *ginomai*, which is usually translated in this verse as "turned" or "became." A more accurate translation might read, "to exist by an act of creation." The transformation of the water into wine has been achieved through an act of creation, a change of substance through bringing spiritual consciousness (wine), through form (water), into physical existence (stone jars), which we call a miracle. This "miracle" is always present in life, because life is that miracle.

This miracle, performed by the anointed Jesus, was said to have occurred on the 6th of January, the day of epiphany — the manifestation of *Being — Life that is.* This date was celebrated in the ancient world through the festival of the Dionysian wine miracle, when it was said that water drawn from the Nile was turned into wine. This was a great celebration, the people decorated themselves with vines, a plant that draws up water from the Earth to produce a fruit full of juice, which with human creativity, working in harmony with the natural world, becomes wine. In the Bible, the vine and wine signify the creative Spirit of life, under which every awakened human being is said to dwell.

The master of the feast represents the old spiritually unconscious personality who is undergoing something outside of his previous experience, because he does not know where the wine comes from. The Greek word for this person — architriklinoi, means a supervisor of a dining room in which three couches are set around a central table.

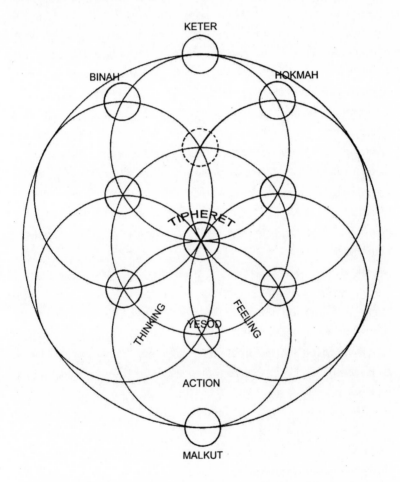

In Kabbalistic terminology and ancient mystical teachings, these are the three functions of thinking, feeling, and action set around Yesod, the persona or ego. Yesod "foundation," can be understood as a mirror,

which reflects our inner life to the outer world and vice versa, and acts
as a filter through which things may pass or be held back through our
discernment. If we are spiritually unconscious then our awareness is
mostly limited to the ego and we become dominated by thoughts and
feelings, which determine our actions.

The Master of the feast is becoming connected to greater
awareness through the servants of Mary and Jesus who *do* know
the wine's origin, because they are acting under *spiritual*
awareness and presence of Being. This means that when you observe
your mind, your feelings and emotions, you then act or move
from the stillness and silence of *Being.*

Jesus is the bridegroom the master of the feast calls to and
says, *"Every (anthropos) Human Being, sets out the good and the*
beautiful wine, (consciousness)." This signifies Tipheret, our inner
Sun or center, the source of presence, from where we experience
the continuous outpouring of life. *"And when they have become*
intoxicated (unconscious) sets out the inferior nature (dominance by the
ego): You have kept the good and the beautiful to the present."
(Tipheret).

The Greek word *arti* often translated as "last," means the
eternal present moment, which never leaves us. It is we who
leave the present when we become identified with the time
bound mind. The good and the beautiful is kept present, through
our awakening to the inner marriage with Being in the eternal
now. This is to be in the eternal present, in the moment; this is
Logos.

The six stone water pots are brimming with wine, and as they
are poured out to the wedding guests, a joyous celebration
begins, in which the whole of humanity is invited to participate
in the new creation, that is, *To Be, Now.*

The Goddess Bride

The bride, who is not mentioned, is the second aspect of the Great

Goddess. In the Gospel, she is depicted through the figure of Mary Magdalene. The Aramaic root of her name *Migdal* can be translated as *"a strong, tower,"* or *"fortified city."* This comes from a Hebrew root meaning *"to grow great,"* and *"to be magnified."* The bride is the feminine aspect of Jesus united in the spiritual marriage, the androgynous Spiritual Body of the human being, crowned through the anointing of Divine realization.

In John 3:29-30, drawing on Old Testament teachings John the Baptist says, *"The One who is joined to the bride is the bridegroom: but the friend of the bridegroom that stands still in understanding rejoices greatly because of the bridegroom's clear voice; this my joy is now fulfilled (filled to the brim). This One must increase but I must decrease."* (My translation.)

The bride is not mentioned in the text because she personifies the intangible and elusive Spirit and Divine presence that we yearn for and seek to find in ourselves. The mind tells us we must spend more time searching for this *"other,"* maybe lifetimes, because it knows that in finding *her* it is *the end of time as we think it*. With the end of time as a mental concept, comes the end of the ego as a dominant, controlling shadow, which sees all of life as a series of separate objects, which it can acquire or discard.

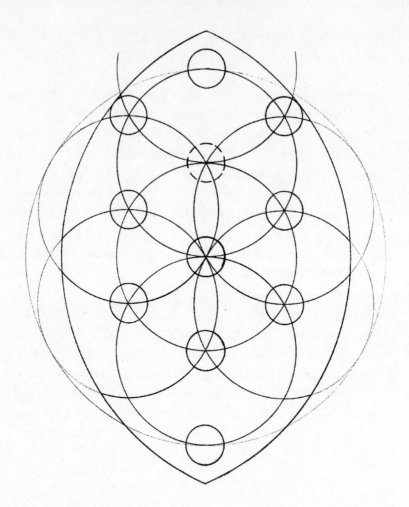

You are a tree of life, a living vine, connected to all that is unfolding in the natural world, the solar system, and stars. You have within you the water and the wine, and beyond these symbols of form and Spirit, the light of consciousness that continually gives birth to and sustains creation. In the beginning, the Logos was, and the Logos was next to God and the Logos was Divine. The Perfect reflection of the Absolute expressed in diagram above as the creative universe held within the eternal presence of the Logos. Logos is both the timeless One and the creative pattern of life.

Meditation

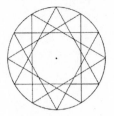

How can we cut ourselves off from the Earth that sustains our physical life? How can we cut ourselves off from space, the solar system and the stars, that sustain our life, and through which we journey when we leave our physical body, and return to our spiritual home that is not built of matter but of what we experience through the physical senses as light?

Many years ago, I began to experience the Divine Feminine, just as my life opened out, and I moved to the beautiful mountainous area of North Wales on the edge of the Snowdonia national park. In this elemental place, Her presence grew stronger in me. I lived where mountains sloped down to meet the sea, and the constant changing light and sunsets melted into the open horizon. There I began to experience the essence of life behind the thin veil of physicality, in the living rock, in the woodlands and forests with their flora and foliage, and in the rivers and waterfalls swelling the abundance of life. I began to feel how all physical existence comes out of light, and how light shapes and holds all the diverse beauty of the natural world. Light is consciousness of Being made manifest in the Cosmos. It lives and breathes the rhythms and cycles of planets and stars, and they give life to the Earth in all its diversifying forms. Constant movement and change held by the still silence, that is the essence of life.

The life span of a physical body is short, like the cycle of one breath on our journey, so who is it that breathes the breath? Who is it that plants one foot then another on the Earth? The footprints dissolve behind us as we make our way, taking with us all that we can ever have: Conscious presence.

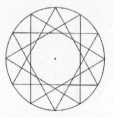

Take a few moments to relax, and practice the conscious breathing exercise as before. Empty your mind of the day's thoughts and concerns, using the breath to help you become present. Whenever you notice your mind wander, use the breath to bring yourself back to the present.

Now imagine that you are standing amongst fields of ripened wheat due for harvest. Above you is a clear blue sky, the Sun burns brightly above the wooded mountains as the evening draws in; you hear insects and birdsong. About you, in the foothills, are vineyards; you can smell the aromas of herbs and flowers, and the scent of the rich soil beneath your feet, carried to you on a cool breeze coming off the mountains in the distance ahead of you.

As the Sun sets and the sky darkens the Moon rises into view, full, clear, and silver-white. You feel it drawing upon you and the abundant life of the Earth about you like a great magnet. You can feel the depths of the Earth beneath your feet going down through layers of rock to the core of the planet. You feel pressure within welling up like a great fountain. Hold this image and feeling as you breathe, keeping to a balanced rhythm. On each in-breath see and feel the waters rising up from beneath your feet, up your spinal column, higher and higher, until they well up out of the crown of your head. On the out-breath, they pour out around you, coming to rest down in the Earth under your feet. As you breathe feel the sensation, of the waters of life pouring out through you, from the crown of your head and down into the

Earth beneath you, to be drawn up from beneath your feet and back up the spinal column on each in-breath. It is your conscious presence that turns the waters into spiritual wine.

Feel the Earth, the fruits of the earth, vegetation — trees, plant life, and then the animals, fish and sea creatures, and the creatures of the air, as a part of this great outpouring. The bread and wine are the fruits of the Earth and Spirit, expressions of the One life force that is all and in all. They are the manifest expressions of the pressure of life that flow through and sustain every created thing. Like you, the Earth is intimately connected to the Solar system and the Stars, and through them to the universes of form and creation.

Once again, feel the breath, now in golden light, coming up the spinal cord on the in-breath and pouring out around you like a great fountain, which has its source at the very core of Being. Now feel your consciousness expanding from the Solar Plexus down into your feet into the Earth allowing it to support you, and up the spine and above the skull. Feel your whole body suffused with the rays of your inner Sun and know that, All is One.

Feel the Sun burning brightly at the very core of your being and as you do this, become aware of the planets in the Solar system, of Mercury orbiting the Sun, then Venus, the Earth with its moon, and Mars, Jupiter, and the outer planets of Saturn, Uranus, Neptune, and Pluto. See all the planets held within the aura of the Sun. See the light as you focus on the core of the Sun. Bring your full attention to the center of the Sun. Feel the rhythm of the breath and the pulse of life that is flowing out of this center.

Now feel yourself expanding out beyond the Sun into the Cosmos, which burns with billions and billions of stars. See their light becoming ever brighter, until they merge into one light — feel it now within you and all about you. You stand now at the Cosmic Axis, the center of the universe that constructs and sustains all life, the pupil in the ever — open eye of the cosmic wheel, around which the great creative dance takes place and through which all life is continually blessed.

Become present now; give your full attention to the life flowing through you, just as it is flowing through the universe of Galaxies and Stars. Be aware of your inner space connecting you with what the mind perceives as outer space, the outer world. Be still, (still the mind), focus on the breath of life, and listen with your complete attention, to the silence containing every sound.

Concentrate on your breath once more and slowly allow the light to fade. Be aware of space — the great body of the Solar system. Feel the air in your lungs and the blood flowing through your veins. Feel your physical body, the solidity of the skeletal structure and your feet upon the solid Earth. Come back fully into the present time and space, and open your eyes to the external world about you, where the seasons revolve to the pattern set by the Moon and Sun. Be aware of your feet upon the floor, and make sure you are fully grounded in your body.

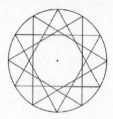

This marked the beginning of the signs of Jesus in Cana of Galilee, and it revealed his Glory, and his disciples believed in him. After this, he went down to Capernaum, and his mother, and his kindred spirits, and his disciples went with him, and they dwelt there for a while. 2:11-12

It was said by the first-century mystic Johannan ben Zakkia that the mystical tradition can only be taught to someone who already knows. This means that we already have spiritual knowledge within us, and that as we awaken we begin to receive it from within ourselves, and through the life forms around us. There is always an inner teaching for awakened individuals, and an outer teaching, which forms the beliefs of a particular religion. When we awaken to our spiritual reality, and begin to "notice" the inner teaching, which comes through life in each moment when we are spiritually present; the glory of creation — *Being* — is revealed to us, and we feel its presence in all of life. The rules and regulations, dogmas and doctrines of belief systems are not needed, because we live the teaching from within through direct experience of the unity of life. This is the revealed glory, and what is meant by the disciples believing in Jesus; the abundant flow of life from the Spiritual Body, and *I Am or Being* present in you now.

The central message of the Gospel is that each of us has our own connection with the total presence of life, the word (Logos) of God. Whenever we meet life consciously, it brings transformation, through the creative flow of new possibilities, which we then integrate into our life. The full incarnation of the consciously realized *Human Being* begins within us *now*, not in some point in the future. It is happening *now*, despite our lack of conscious involvement, as it always has. It takes place in the everyday lives of people all over the world, whenever and wherever a human chooses to awaken to Being — God within; and it is the essence of all life forms.

The wedding ceremony of the new, awakened human being is followed by an interval of recreation — *re-creation* and lucid reflection, which is to experience space and stillness. *To be* at Capernaum, a name, which means "village of comfort," that is, "to be at peace," and "to purify," indicates the Sabbath. This "period" or "space" of conscious re-creation is essential in any creative process, and is the meaning of the recommendation "to keep the Sabbath Holy." Through conscious participation in this renewal, inner space and outer space can be acknowledged, reflected upon; we allow ourselves *to be*. When we are at peace, we experience a greater sense of unity with life that continually wells up from within. If we do this, through pauses from compulsive thinking throughout each day, we create sacred space, which allows the new and eternal to emerge in our lives.

In Judaism the Shekinah, the Divine presence, is sometimes called the Sabbath Bride or Queen. The Sabbath Bride is the space of the sacred circle of the great wheel of life, and through Her flows the continual renewal of life. Experience of Her takes us from unconscious spiritual darkness, to deeper realizations of the One in the spiritual light of consciousness. The "period" dwelt at Cana therefore marks the realization of I AM that I AM. The focal point of this realized union unites us with the creative universe that underlies the Cosmos. It expands from the heart or center to encompass the circle of Life, to be at one with the Logos, true heart of humanity, one with the source of all life.

Chapter Eleven

Clearing the Inner Temple

Sacred Space Within

There are many ways in which we can realize what the scriptures call "God's presence dwelling in the Temple." It is always present, at your very core, just as it is always present in the Earth and Cosmos that surround you.

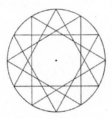

Begin by focusing on your inner center, and breathe from there. This inner center is always present, it is more real than your mind and physical body, and is accessible here and now.

You may feel it as emanating from the Heart center and Solar Plexus, but what is important, is to feel it radiating out from deep within you, and connecting you with all that appears as the objective world. Feel it as the mid-point between your feet, connecting you with the Earth, and the crown of the head, connecting you with the spiritual universe.

You are a point of consciousness within the circle of life, containing space, in which creation takes place. Breathe consciously, and bring your attention to the underlying stillness.

The aim of the exercise is to open up to the space within you, and feel it acutely as living presence. As your awareness increases you may begin to experience that, inner and outer, above and below, and Spirit and matter are only relative truths.

All movement is supported by stillness, in a very real sense, the time that the mind "thinks" is an illusion. Although we can say we are born, grow into an adult, become old and then die, the reality of this movement or change, is always in the eternal present. It is never past or future, it is always rising out of the eternal still center. Only the mind projects time and loses the center, the peace of harmony. The thinking mind cannot hear the silence behind all sound, nor feel the deep presence out of which all movement is continually born.

Sacred Building

When I walk through a Temple as consciously as I can, whether it be a Stone Circle, a Cathedral, Mosque, or Synagogue built using sacred geometry, I become aware of the design, ratio and proportion used by the builders. Some Temples such as the Dome of the Rock in Jerusalem, Ely Cathedral, or the Great Mosque in Cordoba, are sophisticated and refined in their construction. The fine patterning of the tile and plaster work, framed within a beautifully proportioned structure, lifts consciousness to a realization of these patterns and the space which holds them within me, and within the universe. I recognize and feel the life flowing through the natural world and within myself as one. When a Temple is built with awareness of universal patterns, it mirrors, and is mirrored by, the landscape around it, and it mirrors, and is mirrored by any beholder who is receptive to it.

Compared to these places of complex architecture, many stone circles seem quite simple at first sight. There is no wonder at the refined craftsmanship involved, yet the same feeling of awe comes over me, as I feel the conscious intent and knowledge behind the hands that placed the stones in the ground. The stones are precisely and carefully placed to mirror natural features of hill and mountain, and aligned with the position of certain planets and stars in the Cosmos. I experience the same realization of the great Tree of Life within me, as I do when I step into the enclosed temples; the connection and resonance with the structure is the same, an invisible dome above my head, or sphere through which I move. I feel the land around me acutely, the mountains and forest, flora and fauna connected with space — the universe.

I feel the bedrock and core of the Earth beneath my feet, and all the life it supports connected to the planets and the stars. The space through which I am moving pulses in harmony with the space through which the Earth is moving. The flow of life expressed in every living thing, flows through me, and I know as a flock of birds passes overhead, and the clouds move above them to reveal a pale grey afternoon moon, that everything is connected. Nothing is separate. Then I feel the underlying stillness of the One that connects all that moves, from the center of the Earth out though the planets and stars.

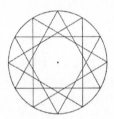

And it was close to the Jewish Passover and Jesus went up to Jerusalem. And in the Temple he found those selling oxen and sheep and doves, and the moneychangers encamped inside. 2:13-14

The festival of the Passover is an important time in the Jewish tradition that celebrates freedom from slavery in Egypt: allegorically, your freedom from the dominance of the egocentric psychological drives. It is a time of purification from sin, and sin simply means, missing your mark, or wandering from your truth. To find your mark or your truth all that is required is that you awaken, become present, and observe your thoughts as they arise in the mind. Acknowledging negative thought patterns as they arise is the beginning of their dissolution, breaking their hold on you; freeing you from your enslavement to the unconscious mind.

This Passover takes place in the holy city of Jerusalem, whose name means "possession of peace," where Jesus is said to go up, literally; *ascend in consciousness*, from the Galilee. When you realize sacred space, time is suspended; form is transparent; all movement an echo of a deeper harmony arising out of Unity. You experience this through inner Peace, which is experienced as inner silence or stillness. When you feel centered, there is a sense of profound quiet, inner calm; the mind is literally stilled, thought suspended; the inner Temple is clear. All movement comes out of this still profound quiet, and returns to it, whether it is a simple movement of the body, or the span of an entire lifetime.

In contrast the physical city of Jerusalem is a stark illustration of the unconscious collective of humanity; a place dominated by egocentric ideas of possession, the antithesis of its inner meaning — possession of peace. Until we realize our inner peace, space, and unity with all of life, there can be no peace in the human world.

This ascension represents a deeper awareness of life, the realization that all egocentric psychological power, all separation from the unity of life is illusion. The values, concerns and expectations of the ego driven world, both our own or those of the human collective, have no meaning; releasing these illusions, we find and enter, the place of peace — Jerusalem and experience conscious presence, the place of beauty, *Tipheret*.

Having reached the place of peace Jesus enters the Temple. Again, remember that Jesus represents your own spiritual consciousness realizing itself, which is to experience unity. The Temple in Jerusalem is a metaphor for the space, which allows life to express itself, containing the dynamic patterns of all life, all of created existence. The Temple is the dwelling place of the

Divine presence of God: The Shekinah, the Divine presence resides within everything that exists in creation.

It may be useful, but it is not enough, to have an intellectual under-standing of the Temple as a symbol for your body, mind, Spirit and Being; to experience it as a living reality, go beyond the symbol. To realize your inner center can be likened to the opening of a flower: it is the liberation of creative space that connects you with the great circle of life. You hold within the breath the realization of intense presence. Take a conscious breath and be aware of the observing presence within you.

The Greek *hieros* used in the Gospel for Temple, literally means hallowed, holy, or Divine; "a sacred space." The realization of Jesus — spiritual awakening — within the Temple transforms your awareness of the life of the cosmos and creation; realizing and embodying that, which sustains all life. Body, mind, heart, Soul and Spirit are a continuous conduit through which *One* consciousness flows freely throughout Heaven and Earth.

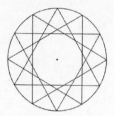

This is a new perception of the great circle of life: *the Kingdom of Heaven is here, now, within you, beyond any form.*

We cannot be consciously present and remain divided. All identification with form is ultimately an illusion; consciousness cannot remain separated by mental concepts; all life is connected. All you think of as inner and outer is One. To consciously enter the Temple, is to realize the creative space of meeting within you, where you feel the presence of Absolute Life acutely.

When we are spiritually conscious we see what needs to be transformed, let go of, made whole. The traders and money-changers that Jesus finds encamped inside the Temple represent the internal, trapped psychological forms that we are locked into. We have invited these *traders* to take up residence within us. The Greek *poleo* translates a Hebrew concept *makar*, the principal meaning of this word is, *to sell someone into slavery,* and principally, *to sell oneself as a slave.*

The Greek *kathemai* means to be encamped — suggesting these slave traders are well established. They represent our misuse of energy, spiritual, psychological and physical, when we are deluded by our identification with the ego. *Any habitual unconscious behavior or thought patterns that have become established in your inner space cannot co-exist with your Being and creative Spirit.* As we saw in Chapter 1:29 your spiritual awakening is "restoring the integrity of the cosmos." If one human becomes spiritually awakened, they affect the whole of life, and, the greater the light of consciousness the more universal the effect. It is only your spiritual consciousness that has the power to drive these traders of your life energy out of the Temple.

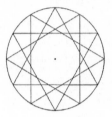

And making a whip out of cords, he drove them all out of the Temple, along with their sheep and oxen, and scattered the coins of all the money changers, and overturned their tables. And he says to those selling the doves, "Take these things from here! Do not make the house of my Father a house of trade." His disciples remembered that it is written, "fervent desire for your house consumes me." 2:15-17

With greater ability to center our consciousness, we observe the games that the ego enjoys playing, and the accumulation of thought forms to which it clings for its identity, and re-energizes as long as we remain unconscious. All of the energy that you invest in ego identification with form must be "set free," and you are the only one who can redeem this energy, even if you are aided by someone more conscious than yourself.

Jesus makes a whip of cords. The verb *poieo* translated as "to make" also means "to perfect," "accomplish," "fulfill," and "to put into execution." We need to be aware of the attention, and focused effort that has gone into finding the cords and binding them together to make a suitable implement for dissolving the shadow of egocentric forms within us. The Greek *Aphragellion*, for whip, translates a Hebrew concept, *showt*, which also means, *to stir up or energize into powerful movement*. This does not mean violent action or self-mortification, but the use of what in Kabbalah is called Gevurah — גבורה: The Hebrew word means power and strength that is connected to the whole of life. It also means precision and efficiency, which maximizes the possibilities of the bourgeoning energy of life. This movement is concentrated and uncompromising, exact, and confident, and it emanates out of the still center of the watcher — Tipheret — תפארת.

Sheep and Oxen have various symbolic meanings, but here they are being sold or traded for sacrifice at the Temple, and we must look at what they mean in this context. The sheep traders that Jesus throws out represent those aspects that enslave us into passive conformity, accepting ideas uncritically from authority figures, and in today's terms, the manipulative propaganda of the media. He also drives out the oxen, unintelligent brute force, castrated to make it docile and compliant.

The moneychangers represent the misuse of trade through the control of prices and manipulation of markets by creating a monopoly. They seek to amass wealth and power through currency and commodity control to exploit whole populations, drawing them in to poverty and debt. Our current economic model is based on this system of Usury, which uses money as system for creating debt and poverty. This poverty is not only an external condition; it comes from an inner state of need and lack, which draws people into external poverty.

At the time when these texts were written the Usury system of illegally extorting interest rates, affected not only the Temple, but the whole of society. The people were being taxed so highly that they were forced to take out loans to pay these taxes against any land or property that they owned. The interest rates on these loans were then increased, sending them into poverty so that they lost their lands.

What we perpetrate in the physical world has its origins in the madness of the collective egocentric nature, at the heart of which is the desire to control and enslave others. In this narrative, Jesus is depicted as overturning the money tables. The Greek verb *Anatrepo,* translated into English as "to overturn," means "to turn upside down," and "to lay waste." In other words, the negative energy of the ego structures, which we rely upon, and institutionalize, is being thoroughly dismantled, broken down, and released. Inwardly we are *overturning the desire for accumulating power and wealth — thus freeing life energy. We are also consciously facing the emotional pain that is trapped within us.*

In the Old Testament Joshua leads an army across the Jordan into the land flowing with milk and honey, and clears out all the old psychological energy patterns that impede the flow into, and out of, the land of the Spiritual Body. He transforms these energies, bringing them under spiritual will, and renews the covenant of the people of Israel with God. In the New Testament Jesus makes a whip out of cords, walks into the temple and clears out — turns around — all the negative energies that have grown up there. He is making a new covenant with God, clearing the way for a new life, which has complete integrity. This is the same motif but in a different allegorical form: clearing out the unconscious shadow that takes away our freedom.

Jesus has a different interaction with the dove sellers, whom he addresses directly. They represent those parts of us, which attempt to sell spiritual enlightenment or salvation, and exploit false ideas and forms of God as an exclusive deity; someone or something that gives us special status and power. This necessitates making God into a separate entity, turning *Absolute life* into "him" or "something" that is only accessible though an ordained lineage, or an extraordinary teacher or leader, or by following a system of prescribed laws.

Many people lay claim to being spiritual leaders, holders of a spiritual lineage, or custodians of enlightenment and salvation. There is nothing new about such claims: the Gospel itself warns us against being taken in by such illusions. This has done nothing to stop their proliferation. It is easy to be beguiled by them, especially when we feel afraid or inadequate. Once hooked in, we may become deluded into spending more money, giving away more of our energy, and told that this is for our salvation.

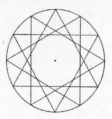

Salvation — spiritual enlightenment, is not a commodity that can be bought or sold — it is always free and abundant, and present within you now.

When we are dominated by the ego, we become trapped and imprisoned by a role or image of ourselves that we cannot escape from, we look for strong and magnetic personalities to lead us, spiritual teachings become dead words, commodities to be bought and sold. It is to this aspect of ourselves, "the dove seller," that the new human consciousness now turns its attention, saying "Take these things from here." These caged birds — these trapped mental energies — have to be removed, as they are not free to move on their own. To let go of old identities takes great courage and can be frightening, but what choice do we have? We cannot hold on to that which divides us, and stops us from realizing the unity of life within ourselves. *Spiritual energy, your connection with Being, is free, without form.* No person, no image or form can stand between you and Conscious presence.

The disciples remember that it is written, *fervent desire for your house consumes me.* The quotation is taken from Psalm 69:9: In Hebrew, Qana (*fervent desire*), means the destroyer of illusion through the generation of the presence Absolute life; Bayith (house, dwelling) — means your dwelling place, containing generative universal life, and the exaltation of life; and Akal (to Consume) means; Absolute life received — molded, into expansive movement.

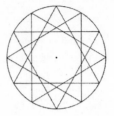

The intense presence of life is here now: To be present to life with all your strength and attention gives you the power that dissolves all illusion, all separation.

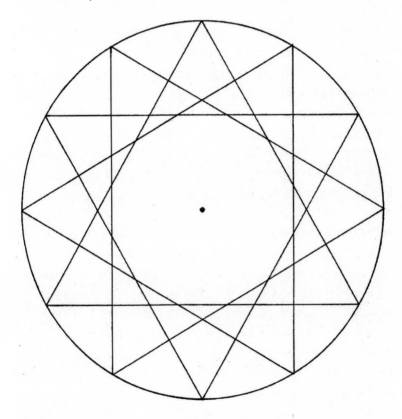

The twelve disciples — the twelve divisions of humanity — stand around the periphery of the great circle of life, experiencing the central

axis as the consuming fire of consciousness, the destroyer of all illusions. What this symbolizes is within you — a point of consciousness that realizes itself within the diversity of the great circle of life. It is universal and free, requiring no external image or authority; nothing can stand between you and Absolute life, between you and God.

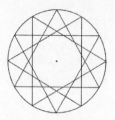

Then the Jews [Judeans] answered, and said to him, "What signs do you show us for doing these things?" And Jesus answered, and said to them, "Destroy this Sanctuary and in three cycles (days) I will raise it up." 2:18-19

The egocentric mind, which is identified with powerful forms, does not want to let go of these images of itself, so it will challenge any awakening consciousness. Either the egocentric "I" turns spiritual experience and the teachings that come from this experience into an authoritative structure, and thus control it, or it seeks to destroy it through conflict and division. These options are not exclusive to each other, since any authoritative structure will create conflict, division and fear, all of which obscure the possibility of realizing inner freedom from form.

There are two important words in verse 19 that we need to look at here to help us understand what the text is conveying. The Greek noun *Naos* is usually translated as "Temple" but in fact means "Sanctuary." The change of word here is significant; until now *Hieron* — sacred space — has been used. The text is now referring to the inner sanctuary of the Temple, the resting place of the eternal presence of God — *Being*. It is your center of conscious presence, your inner most room. The second word is the Greek verb *egeiro*, "to raise up" which also means "to arouse," "to awaken," "to rouse oneself to a better course of conduct," and hence "to rise up in consciousness from a lower place."

We can spiritualize the ego, but the ego can never have spiritual power. The egocentric mind does not want you to become aware of, or to experience anything that means it will lose its exclusive power and special status. But consciousness knows the games of the ego, and replies with the challenge, *"Destroy this sanctuary (conscious presence) and in three cycles (days) I will raise it up (restore conscious presence)."* The old ego dominated thought forms that seek to reassert themselves are denied power by your conscious presence, which exists outside of time as eternal reality.

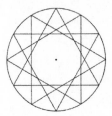

Then the Jews [Judeans] said, "This Sanctuary took forty six years to build, and you will raise it in three days?" But Jesus spoke about the Inner Sanctuary of his body. 2:20-21
Consciousness seeks to express and realize itself through the balance and harmony of the diversity of life. The whole of created existence seeks to do this. When we realize this within us, we have no use for egocentric power.

The Greek oikodomos "to construct, or build" also means, "to advance one's spiritual state." In biblical Greek 46 is the numerical value for Adam, which means universal Humanity. The text is contrasting the old unconscious humanity with the new conscious humanity.

The unenlightened human mind "thinks" that spiritual enlightenment will take time. When we listen to these voices, we do not have the vision or understanding to experience what the new human consciousness is saying. We project outwards, into some indefinite future; we see everything as external and separate. These voices also speak for those parts of ourselves that maintain "things are always done this way, you cannot break with tradition, you cannot undergo a change in three stages — which is outside of psychological time — when it has taken us a whole lifetime to do much less."

Jesus personifies the living Sanctuary within the Temple of Spirit, Soul, mind and body, which is already complete. The opposing voices cannot understand this, which echoes chapter 1 verse 26 where John the Baptist says; *"at your very core stands the One, you have no perception of."* The Greek *eido* means, "to know through attention," and "to be aware of through observation."

Often our spiritual experiences lose their potency because there is insufficient presence in the formless Spirit, which is beyond "our experience." We deny our own beauty, either because we feel inadequate or unworthy, or because we have become inflated through spiritualizing the ego. This is vividly illustrated in Gospel stories where Jesus teaches and heals people. Those who are unable to contain what is revealed to them go out into the world and publicly proclaim that they have found the Messiah. Seldom do we have the maturity to do as the teaching of Jesus advises: *go into your inner room — your inner sanctuary — and commune with God in stillness and in secret.*

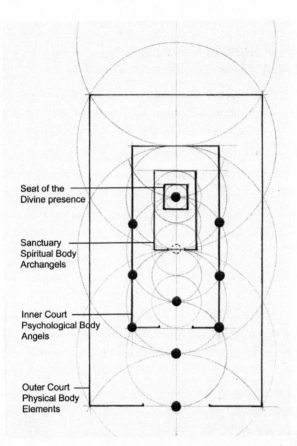

Seat of the
Divine presence

Sanctuary
Spiritual Body
Archangels

Inner Court
Psychological Body
Angels

Outer Court
Physical Body
Elements

The sanctuary in the Temple is your inner most room, the dwelling place within which Being continually creates all that is form and matter. The diagram shows the geometric design, which reflects the idea of moving from the outer world into the inner core of your Being.

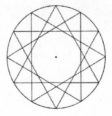

Then, when he was raised from the dead, his disciples remembered that he had said this, and believed the scriptures and the

Word (Logos) that Jesus made known. And as he was in Jerusalem at the feast of the Passover, many put their trust in the name (Logos), beholding the signs that he did. But Jesus did not put his trust in them, because he knew everything fully, and because he had no need that any should bear witness concerning universal humanity, for he knew what was in universal humanity. 2:22-25

The Greek verb translated as dead is *Nekros*, which means "without life," but it also means to be "morally and spiritually dead," and "alienation from God," that is, your own connection with the eternal presence of Absolute Life. Jesus is raised from the spiritually dead; as long as we are unconscious we cannot perceive eternal life within us.

In any transformational journey, there are points when there is a feeling of emptiness, helplessness or barrenness, where we feel we have been abandoned, or that our life is meaningless. These feelings occur as the old ego identities dissolve, as they must, and before we feel our inner vessel filling with new life — new wine pouring into new wineskins, creative space into which new life is continually flowing. The three days of John's transformation into Jesus, and the three days Jesus spends in the tomb, mark the stages where the old dissolves, so that the new can emerge and be realized within you.

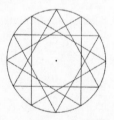

Either sit with the spine straight but not tense, or lie on your back with the legs folded at the knees, so that the soles of the feet connect with the Earth. First, consciously connect with the Earth, allowing it to support you. This requires your presence, in which the mind becomes still.

Be aware, that as the spine is relaxed, it elongates; as you breath in and out from your center, you are allowing space between the vertebrae from the coccyx to the cranium. The shoulders and arms should also be free of tension allowing the chest to open, and for you to feel space opening up from out of your center.

Once you gain a deeper sense of inner stillness, you remember that this presence of life is connecting you to all life. From greater awareness of life expressing itself in diversity on the Earth, become aware of your connection with the planets in the Solar system. Be aware of the central point — the Sun, and through the Sun, your connection with the Cosmos.

As you breathe in bring this awareness back to the center within you, beyond body and mind, beyond form. As you release the breath be aware of the formless that breathes you, be aware that you are being breathed. As your sense of presence increases, the sense of I and mine begin to diminish.

In consciously allowing the old to pass into the new, Jesus is taking part in the festival of the Passover. In Hebrew, this is called *Pasach*, a sacred feast, in which an inner awakening takes place. As we saw in verse 29 of the last chapter, Jesus — the Spiritual Body, conscious of Being — is the Paschal Lamb, the force of life which is your salvation, and which means *safe passage home*. The verse states that many are able to "behold" what he "is," which comes from the Greek *theoreo*, "to gaze upon", and more significantly means "to come to a knowledge of something through experience." When we come closer to who and what we truly are, there is no longer any need to make the small self (ego) big, we no longer have anything to prove to ourselves or the world: we simply find peace in being who we are. In accepting, and knowing who we are, we gain our freedom. Your ego may say "but I don't like who I am," the answer is, you are more than a mere ego; you are life, consciousness expressing itself in form, but much more than any form.

Spiritual consciousness — Absolute presence — knows all

that is in created existence from the beginning, to the end of time in form. More poignantly, spiritual conscious knows all the weaknesses of humanities collective nature; Jesus is depicted in the last verses of this chapter, as having no need of peoples' adoration or attention. Divine presence is realized within our inner center or sanctuary, each in our own way; this is *"the way"* spoken of. *I AM* — Being — (is) *the way*. This is to dwell in the sanctuary, to dwell in solitude, which is held wherever you are. It is not withdrawing from the world, or from other people. Anything you then "do," any words you speak, come from this peace. You hold the potential of your own salvation within you: there is no need of any other to find it for you, once you have released yourself from identity with form.

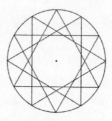

Meditation: The Inner Temple

Sit in a comfortable position for meditation. When preparing to enter your inner Temple begin by breathing consciously from your center. Your life is one great journey that passes through many forms. Become aware of the energy sustaining your body; still the mind allowing no thought to distract you. Whatever outer journeys you may make, everything you see, hear, and touch, is a reflection of the life within you, the life that continually flows through you in the here and now. The One great journey that you make is into the heart of who you are. Your outer journey then synchronizes with your inner awakening — your inner journey. When you are present, which means, when you meet life consciously, you allow the new, the creative patterns of life to bear fruit within you.

All Temples and spaces constructed with awareness of the Creative Universe are built to aid your awakening to the eternal presence of life that exists within, and sustains every living thing. This means awareness of beauty, harmony, and proportion in the connections between all things, and awareness of the space that allows them to be. All the places you feel to be sacred, reflect back to you, the patterns of creation that exist within you now. Many of us pass through life without noticing the sacredness and beauty of things, because we are too preoccupied with our thoughts to experience what is here, now.

Within the sacred space of the sphere of the Earth, flow all of the energies of the planets, which are manifestations of the Sun's life force. Solar light continually sustains all physical matter. The Sun and its planetary system are in balance and harmony, the manifestation of the abundant life that sustains the Cosmos. All of these patterns are alive within you now, and as your presence increases, you begin to feel and hear this as an inner reality. Breathe and sense their presence with all your attention.

As you turn within, become aware of your inner peace, a presence, out of which all movement occurs: This is to enter through the door spoken of in the Gospel. *I Am the door, if anyone enters through that which I possess they shall be made whole (healed), and will go within, and go out, and meet with the abundance of life. John10:9 (my translation.)*

I Am — Being supports all movement that flows through all of the life within and about you in abundance and harmony. As you breathe, you are clearing the way to realizing inner space. This space is transpersonal, it is always present within you, and is only lost through the weight of thought forms that remove the peace of presence. In your innermost room, your sanctuary, cleared of all thoughts and emotional distractions, there is nothing to separate you from the eternal presence of life.

Focus all your attention on your inner space and be aware of your breath emanating from it. As you bring your consciousness to rest in your center, you exist within the continual renewal of life. As you breathe, be conscious of the presence that fills your inner space. This is your true nature beyond any form; it is engraved upon your heart.

Let go of all that is form, all that is "I" or "mine." Feel the space expanding, filling you with the abundance of life. Feel the web of interconnecting life, like a great net cast upon an open sea. As the net is drawn in on the breath, it teams with divergent life. As it is cast out again on the out-breath, the divergent life swims forth into the Cosmos. You are the great sea, and the casting of the net across its surface.

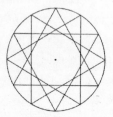

Ehieh Asher Ehieh: I AM that I AM; all life issues forth from the One and returns to the One. This is the eternal breath of life: to be at-One with the great circle of life.

Continue to breathe deeply with a freedom unfettered by the weight of thought or time. If your mind wanders in to thought, use the breath to re-center yourself. Keep alert and listen to the silence behind all the sounds and feel the presence of life within you now.

To finish, be aware of the energy in your feet connecting you with the Earth; Feel the currents of life carried on the breath, flowing along your spinal cord from its base up into your skull, and down again into the soles of your feet. Feel your body upon the chair, your feet on the floor, and the air in your lungs.

Chapter Twelve

Union with God — Death and Resurrection

The symbols of death and resurrection are ancient and universal, and exist in every culture because they are synonymous with our primal understanding of life and its continual transformation. They exist in the Gospel precisely because they convey such fundamental, archetypal principals; all life is *One*; all forms arise out of this formless unity, and all forms dissolve on their return to the One source of all life. The "thinking mind" that is dominated by ego cannot conceive of life beyond form, because it is itself a product of form: Being gives birth to Spirit and Soul, which are merely terms used to denote the formless creative life within you, and the creative expressed in form. From the Soul comes mind; it is through mind that we have come to identify with form.

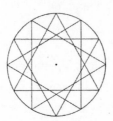

When we are silent and still, Being speaks to us through its many voices; through the diversity of life. Listening is an art, and as we enhance our power of listening, we can begin to experience the fullness of life, through silence and stillness; this is to receive; this is presence. From our spiritual center, our thoughts and actions become clear; we speak and act with our full attention, without fear or distraction. We pierce the veil of form and matter for creation to reveal its inner beauty.

We may hold beliefs of an afterlife with God for all eternity, but as long as we identify ourselves with the ego and its forms, this "I" and "God" are two things, both existing as separate entities, and "eternity" an immense span of time. Ultimately, all are illusions; *Union with God — realizing unity with the source of all life, means there is no other. Union is beyond all our concepts of time; it exists as timeless reality, here and now. Union is the reality behind and beyond all form; it is the reality that the symbolism of death and resurrection points to.*

Death is a part of life, equally as important as birth. Yet, as long as we are identified with form, believe ourselves to be a separate entity from the rest of life, we inevitably suffer the fear and pain of separation; and experience deep-seated feelings of loss, lack, and incompleteness. We cannot suppress these feelings, nor can we hide from our spiritual center and Union indefinitely. The Unity of life is ultimately stronger; its pressure is unyielding as it seeks to know and be known within all that it gives life to; through the birth of form, which contains death, the passing of forms.

Most of us have lost the ability to experience the passing of a loved companion into the spiritual universe in the way we would the birth of that same Spirit into the flesh of a newborn baby. Physical death is birth into new life, and presents the opportunity of awakening to the deeper connection we have with life. When we lose someone, we love our grief is felt acutely and deeply; our foundation is shaken, leaving us vulnerable. In our pain, we are taken to the edge of physical life, to the edge of what the mind understands and thinks of as real. If we are able to become aware of the space within us, feel our grief without making it into a part of our personality, the pain begins to dissolve. *This means accepting life as it is; the continual passing of forms. With our acceptance comes the opportunity for change, a deepening of consciousness in which we know that we are supported by the whole of created existence and its source; life is experienced as beauty, the ego and its manifestations as an ephemeral dream.*

Death is uncompromising, because life is uncompromising; you cannot avoid what it illuminates in you. To feel the pain of separation reminds you that you are not yet aware of your own completeness, your own wholeness. When you recognize your vulnerability — and by vulnerability I mean openness, which has honesty and humility — you are given a choice: To open out to a deeper connection with life, or to close down, containing the pain that makes you fearful, and results in feelings of bitterness, resentment and cynicism.

The dissolving of form we call death, allows those connected with the departing Soul the possibility of experiencing life in a new way, even though this may be hard to accept at the time. The only departure from life you will ever experience is to be unconscious of its unity and abundance. Many of the stories and parables in the Gospel call this unconscious state, *being insensible of Spirit,* and ask you to awaken from it to an eternal life that is always present and accessible. When you are spiritually conscious, you do not experience physical death as the end of life, only a change from ephemeral substance into greater awareness of *Logos* that is always present, even when you are unaware of it.

The principle teaching on death and resurrection is that the essence of life is eternal; and physical death is not our end. This has nothing to do with belief; it comes from our ability to be present, which is the conscious realization of *Divine Being or Logos* as the foundation of life. Life changes form every moment of everyday, the Spirit of life is free flowing, and the light of Being — Logos, cannot be held as a particular form indefinitely, nor can the mind control the passing of any form into new life. This abundance of life — its continuous flow of creative transformation — produces fear in the mind when we are attached to, that is, identified with, any form. Through fear, we contract into loss and separation, apprehension of the unknown, and the illusion that physical death is the end of life. Yet the continual movement of life dissolves all of the masks we make and try to maintain against the fullness of life. This fullness of life can never be owned or contained or controlled by the egocentric mind, because it is One.

The Crucifixion as a Symbol

The story of the suffering savior can be found in the Old Testament and in various forms in Pagan art and writings. We only have to look at human history over the last two to three thousand years, to see why it has such a hold on the human psyche and imagination: the image is laden with so much of our collective and individual pain and suffering. However, in the Gospel it is used not simply as a symbol of suffering but as a symbol of transformation.

The iconography of the crucifixion shows Jesus Christ — our Divine-spiritual essence -fixed to the tree of life. As a Cross, it symbolizes the sacred center of creation, holding beginning and end on the axis of the eternal present. The whip marks on the torso, thirty-nine in number, represent the stages of transformation that the children of Israel underwent on their journey through the psychological wilderness before entering the Holy Land of the human Spirit. The nails fixing the hands and feet, and the crown of thorns upon the head, represent the opening of the chakras associated with these points on the body. The crown of thorns symbolizes the illumination of solar rays that give life, contain all life, in abundant and continual outpouring from stillness. Having been pierced through the heart, the Divine nature descends the trunk of the tree into the roots of the Earth, which symbolize the underworld labyrinth, where all that is crystallized or locked up within is released and redeemed. From here, the fully realized human *being* is resurrected, that is: is known to be *One* with the source of all life; the state of atonement, at-one-ment with the source of all creation.

The archetypal human being suffering on the cross symbolizes the dissolving of all identity with form, the dissolving of the small separate "I" of the ego in the fire of the universal I Am of total consciousness, which brings all suffering to an end.

The crucifixion, death and resurrection of the Anointed Jesus, takes place at Golgotha, *"the place of a skull,"* which symbolizes the point at which physicality and its forms dissolve into formless Spirit. You might remember from the story of John the Baptist that the skull or head was said to contain the human Spirit, that is, the point of connection with the Spirit. This is not meant to be taken literally; your Spiritual Body is not confined to your head or any other part of your body. The Spiritual Body continually breathes form and dissolves those same forms as it draws them back into itself.

Golgotha is an Aramaic word that comes from the same Hebrew root *galal* as that used for Gilgal and Galilee; it means *"to roll," "roll a stone," "to roll up (i.e. dissolve),"* and can also mean *"a round stone,"* or *"to turn in a circle or spiral."* Golgotha denotes the sacred space, or circle of transformation, in which we dissolve our illusions of separation from the unity of life.

The crucifixion takes place during Passover, which signifies deliverance from bondage in Egypt — the dominance of the ego. Here, Jesus is fixed to the cross, (the Greek word translated as cross means "a stake," and comes from a root meaning "to fix,") which is placed into Golgotha. Fixed on the cross or axis of stillness within the circle of time and space, he dies to the illusions of separation, and in this death becomes free from suffering the bondage of psychological time. Time as a mental construction, is an illusion that keeps us from the reality of *Being*, the reality of Logos. Until we are able to raise consciousness to this reality of who we are, the reality that all life is One, we are imprisoned, and bound by the repetitive churning of the mind.

The Tree of Life seen from above stands on Golgotha: Tipheret is repre-
sented by the inner circle within which is Malkut: The central axis is
the stake of the cross, the trunk of the Tree, or the spine, seen through
the top of the skull. Keter — the Crown — is represented by the all
encompassing outer circle, containing the space, which allows Tipheret
to play the game of life, within creation form and matter.

Beyond Suffering

When we fixate on suffering, we lose the possibility of experiencing unity with life and God. The root cause of suffering and
pain comes from our illusions of separation, generated by the
ego-dominated mind. The ego as a separate entity has to create
divisions to achieve a false sense of power and control: Spirit
from matter, mind from body, women from men, friend from

enemy, rich from poor, the powerful from the weak, the natural world from civilization, life from death, etc.

Until we transcend theses illusions, suffering weighs us down with feelings and emotions of guilt, fear, self-hatred, hatred of others — the need for enemies, and ideas of sin and the devil. These illusions disconnect us from the creative energy in the body, cause sexual repression, and are the prime reason for our using the natural world as a commodity that we exploit, pollute and poison. The collective unconscious reinforces our fixation on suffering and pain; it has become like a drug for the mind; we have added to it, spread it as a disease; we have not understood the mystical teaching contained in the crucifixion and resurrection that we can bring all needless suffering to an end.

For thousands of years, these internal shadows that feed and reinforce the ego, have been projected onto others: "enemies," "savages," "infidels," "heretics" and "witches," men and women who were tortured and murdered, often in public spectacles of human sacrifice. These spectacles were deliberately staged by our leaders (focal points for collective egocentric power), appointed through our infatuation with, and worship of authority, allowing it to control our religions and civil life to foster a climate of fear and hysteria within the human collective. This "energy" is then directed into even more violence and hatred. This is deeply connected with the divinization and spiritualization of the ego; emperor worship, the worship of a strong and powerful leader, who speaks as a god, or through whom God speaks. When the ego has virtual control of a group of people or nation, it will commit the most outrageous acts of violence in the name of security, justice, and even peace.

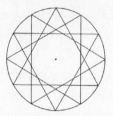

When we portray God as a ruler or king, leading us to war, punishing and killing our perceived enemies, we become slaves to the illusions of the lower human nature, projected by the unconscious mind into a god as a graven image.

Today in the 21st century, we are still held captive by these illusions, which serve to maintain the power of the ego. One of its latest incarnations is called "The War on Terror." A contradiction in terms, it should perhaps be called, "The struggle to maintain terror and fear within the human collective." All such deadly games are perpetrated to maintain the illusion of egocentric power, administered through its institutions.

How do we bring an end to all the *needless* suffering we produce in the world? This, as always, demands that we become spiritually conscious, so that the beauty and abundance of life can live in us. And how do we realize this? By becoming the witness, the observer of the mind as illustrated by John the Baptist; by becoming aware of our connection with *Being;* the permanent presence of Absolute life, the origin of all that is creative in us, and in life.

The pain and suffering depicted in the crucifixion are the darkness that is created and perpetuated by the ego. Its purpose is to obscure the light of consciousness and convince its hosts (humanity) that the light cannot be yours, cannot be experienced by you now. The ego is afraid of your becoming conscious, and will use all its power to control your life. Through awareness of the creative Spirit, all the shadows and misconceptions about who you think you are, and what life is, are intensely illumi-nated, and begin to lose their power over you.

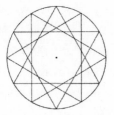

To still the mind is to be present; as you increase your awareness of presence, so, like the Sun, you allow life to unfold within the aura of Being. All that is power, all that gives life, comes from the unity of life, which is free and abundant, and can never be taken as a possession. When we let go of the illusions of egocentric power, we begin to live in balance and harmony with the creative expressions of the unity of life; from this comes the realization of peace and beauty. Breathe consciously now, and feel the presence of life within you as you continue to read.

The Triple Goddess at the Cross

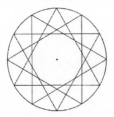

Now next to the Cross/Axis the Mother of Jesus, and his Mother's sister Mary of Cleophas and Mary the Magdalene were stood firm. 19:25

The three aspects of the Goddess; Mother, Grandmother-Crone, and Bride, hold the central axis of conscious life that exists in all things. The Greek *histemi* translated as "were stood" means "as an immovable foundation," and "to be established." They symbolize the awakened watcher, guardianship, and wisdom of the way to the freedom of spiritual consciousness. It is the aspect of Mary Cleophas, Grandmother — Crone, the voice of the abyss: the deep and infinite, eternal and unchanging, who represents death, and through her embodiment of ageless wisdom, knowledge of re-birth. Grandmother — Crone brings the end of time, the *rolling up* of time into the eternal presence of Divine Being. Grandmother — Crone releases us from the cross of time and space, guides us into the stillness of the axis, the central point of the circle of life.

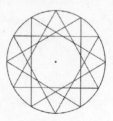

The seed of the Tree of Life begins life suspended in creative space, puts down roots deep into the Earth, and branches out up into the Heavens. When we listen in silence, stilling the mind, the roots tell us where life is going, the branches where life comes from, and to where it returns. The Tree of Life continually creates life out of the universal axis. It takes on form and physical mass. It gives us spiritual air to breathe, absorbs the rays of the Divine Sun, drawing its light into the Earth, into matter.

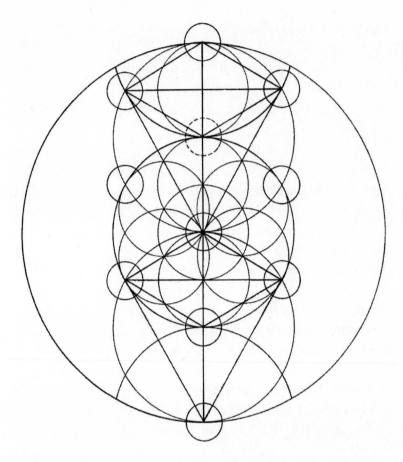

Jesus the fully realized human being, lifted up on the spiritual cross, dies to the illusion of separation in existence. Consciousness realizes Consciousness within the patterns of creative Spirit in form and matter. Heaven and Earth are known to be One, present, here, now.

The Day of Preparation

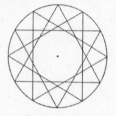

Now in the marked space of the fixed cross, there was a garden; and in the garden a new tomb in which no man had ever been placed. There they laid Jesus because the Jewish preparation day was near. 19:41-42.

The three days in the tomb or cave were understood as purely symbolic in ancient times, marking the winter solstice, a time of rebirth from the darkest point of the year. In astronomical — astrological observations of the winter sky, the Sun appears to stand still for three days in the constellation of the Southern Cross — the symbolic center of the Universe. After which it appears to rise, heralding the re-birth of spring and summer.

The marking of the winter solstice, in turn, is the conscious acknowledgment that creation is continually renewing life, unbounded by the cycles of time. Spiritually it represents the point of passing out of the Cosmos into eternal presence; piercing the veils of form, unveiling new life through the dissolving of all past thought forms which hold us captive, and all future imaginings that keep us from the *eternal presence of Being.*

There is no pain or suffering in this image of the Sun on the cross; it expresses the natural creative cycles of life, and the alignment of human consciousness with the consciousness of the Solar system, and life on Earth. In turn, the Sun is aligned with the patterns and ratio of the Cosmos, with Space in which life continually evolves, and expresses itself. To realize the Sun within the axis of the cross, takes us beyond the bounds of form into the spiritual dimension of creation, where Ideas seed forms that manifest as matter: Unity expressing itself through the play of life in diversity.

The Greek word *Kepos* — "Garden," translates a Hebrew concept meaning, *an enclosed space where life continually regenerates*. This so-called Garden, where the axis of the cross is fixed, is *not* a physical place but a heightened, creative state of awareness, the realization of luxuriant abundant beauty. Here, a new tomb is found, in which the three stages or cycles of renewal take place. Jesus is laid in this Cosmic womb, *because the Jewish preparation day was near*. The time of preparation is an opportunity to consciously acknowledge all that is false within us, all that distracts our attention from our path in life, who we really are, and from union with life; union with God.

In the old myths, the underworld contains a hell-like dimension, where those in it are drawn into collective groups by their own thoughts, emotions and feelings. We enter the underworld to redeem all our unconscious thought forms. The forms we release become new life, the light of consciousness. Physical death and suffering are not necessary for this realization to take place, which is why it is said in an old proverb, "Die before you Die." In other words, die to all illusions that you are separate from the eternal presence of life, die to the illusion of death as the end of life.

The Gospels call this unconscious state, the outer darkness, where we weep and moan, and grind our teeth: that is, the place where we confront the habitual patterns and false personas that we identify with, until we are able to release ourselves from them. Doctrines of eternal damnation are perpetrated in order to frighten and control us, and existed in Pagan as well as Christian teachings. In mystical teachings, hell is simply a state of unconsciousness, and we take it with us wherever we go on our life's journey, whether incarnate or disincarnate. In humanities darkest moments we project it on to the world and people around us, turning our psychological and physical worlds into a desolate hell for others, both human and the creatures of the natural world.

We can choose, now, to raise ourselves up out of these illusions through conscious realization of the sacredness of all life.

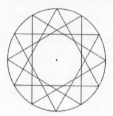

Breathe consciously and realize that you are intimately connected to the abundant creative flow of life that manifests the Cosmos. All that the ego seeks to possess is an illusion, which is a primary cause of all suffering. When we release ourselves from the needs and fears of the ego we become free; free To Be with life, allowing it to support us, becoming One with its creative outpouring. This is the very essence of the teachings in John's Gospel.

Consciousness — the light of the Spiritual Sun — expresses itself through the diversity of life; this is the beauty of creation, it is the eternal spring of life that gives you everything that you need, and that is always present and accessible.

As long as we are in a physical body, we may become ill, the body will grow old and weaken, and we will inevitably experience physical pains; but we no longer perpetuate needless pain and suffering, we are no longer tormented by the mind — nor do we use the mind to torment others. We are no longer destructive but use our energy consciously, that is creatively, which means that we experience ourselves *within consciousness*, as a part of the creative whole, expressing itself through life's diversity.

We experience the day of preparation as an inner centering, a lucidity in which we consciously focus all are attention on a single point.

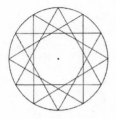

Sit quietly, focusing on the breath for a few moments. Be aware of your spinal cord as the axis that unities the physical and spiritual worlds. Focus all your attention on the energy that manifests and sustains your body. Do not let the mind distract you by attaching judgments or identifying with what you see, hear, or feel. Feel this vital energy as a sphere that is expanding about you from your center. Feel it flowing into every part of your body, and connecting you to all that is perceived as external.

Now, become aware of the space that surrounds the energy — within and about you; be aware of the silence containing all sound, and the ever-present stillness out of which all movement occurs. At your very core, is the center of consciousness connecting you to the whole of life; continually manifesting in the Earth, the Solar system, the galaxy and the Cosmos.

All that is perceived as external is present within you; it is timeless, it is here, now.

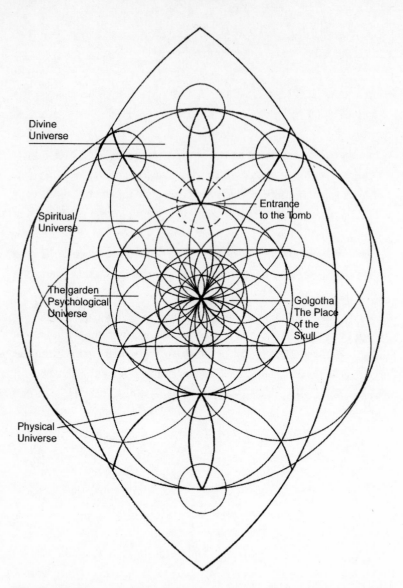

Divine
Universe

Spiritual
Universe

The garden
Psychological
Universe

Physical
Universe

Entrance
to the Tomb

Golgotha
The Place
of the
Skull

The Divine human realizes the central axis of stillness within the whole of existence, out of which life is continually created. This creative pattern is always taking on form and dissolving into new form. Life is continual change yet its source is unchanging containing the Alpha and Omega — beginning and end.

Mary Magdalene and the Resurrection of Life

The resurrection of the spiritually conscious human being has no past or future: It takes place in the present moment, at the core of all life. Every living thing emanates from the intensity of the presence of Being. Into this still center flows the Alpha, and into this still center flows the Omega, the beginning and end are held in eternal presence: I AM, in Hebrew; אהיה Ehieh, one of the Divine attributes of God. One of the ways in which the four Hebrew letters can be heard and experienced is this: *Absolute life* א *plants its seed* י *between the in-breath* ה *and the out-breath* ה. Conscious breath is a doorway into the eternal present.

Mary Magdalene is an extremely important figure in the symbolism on death and resurrection: the continual renewal of life realized as Unity. Yet, all too often, she is marginalized, degraded, or, at best, misunderstood. The Magdalene in Hebrew means "the strong or fortified tower," that is, the fortified conduit of consciousness that connects Divine Being with the physical universe.

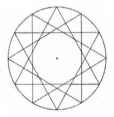

As you breathe consciously from your center, realize your connection with the universal axis of life; feel it through your spinal cord. Through Magdalene, you raise consciousness; realize your inner beauty, and the outer beauty that is expressed in the forms and matter of nature and the Cosmos. All are One; all life in an interconnected creative pattern of the One. Feel its presence in your breath, your blood, and the energy sustaining your body, opening your inner senses to greater awareness.

Mary the Magdalene is the Bride aspect of the triple goddess, which represents the receptive dynamic of every woman and man. You may understand her as the feminine power that lives and breathes the essence of life, in whom inner freedom is met by outer freedom, where you find completion, or peace, in yourself.

At the beginning of her story she prostitutes herself: that is to say, she is unable to realize her creative powers, and so sells herself, gives away her power to the ego; her own, and the unconscious collective, which uses her. If we see prostitution merely as the selling of her sexuality, then we have not understood the teaching. Whenever we are unconscious, we give away our creative powers to the ego and those who would use us; it is this loss of our center, which makes us prostitute the light of life flowing through us; to deny our connection with *Being*.

Realizing the Logos within, Mary directs her own steps on her journey, through the rhythmic powers of creation, flowing through her as abundant life. There is no separation, no loss of strength; she is spiritual awakening, your ability to be at one with the essence of life. She represents stages of transformation within you; from prostituting your life energy, to centered consciousness within the energy field that manifests your physical body. She is the doorway into the formless creative universe and its source; the stillness of the resurrected Christ.

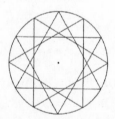

And on the first Sabbath Mary Magdalene came to the tomb early; (Whilst it was spiritually dark), and saw with the power of perception and understanding; the stone had been raised up from the tomb. Then she ran to Simon Peter, and the other disciple whom Jesus loved and said to them, "they have raised up the Lord out of the tomb and we do not know where he is laid." 20:1-2

The Sabbath signifies a pause for conscious reflection. It means little or nothing not to work, yet continue to think unconsciously and compulsively, to fill up silence and space with words and mental images. Sabbath is a period of stilling the mind as part of the continual creative process, allowing space and silence to be observed. That this is the first Sabbath after Passover, gives it extra significance, and marks an opportunity to realize and experience, our connection with the whole of life in a new way.

Arriving at the sealed tomb in which Jesus was laid, Mary the Magdalene, finds that the stone has been *rolled up*, the Greek *airo*, means *to be raised up* in a spiritual sense, so that she is able to see into the open and empty tomb; the pregnant and fertile womb of creative space that surrounds all things. In Hebrew, this is Da'at, a point of transition between dimensions. It exists within every living thing, and in human awareness it represents inner, that is, realized knowledge and perception. At the same time it is the point of unknowing; all our intellectual thinking and under-standing dissolves in the face of spiritual realization.

The Darkness of Unknowing
To look with deep perception into the empty tomb is to be stripped of all form. When your body is taken back into the Earth, who will you be? When the persona you identify with dissolves, who will you be? When all that you thought to possess and build in your earthly life is taken away, what is left; who are you? This is what confronts the perception of the prophet when she looks into the tomb.

The verse tells us that it is still spiritually dark, before the dawn of a new awakening. All that served as the old foundation of life has been rolled up, dissolved by the pressure of conscious presence. Through the opening, she experiences the spiritual foundation of pregnant fertile space that generates life.

Mary runs, (the Greek *trecho*, also means "to strive hard" and "to focus all ones energy,") to find two of the disciples. Simon Peter the keystone, the potential new foundation, and the disciple whom Jesus loved, the one who is closest to his heart or center. Although traditionally seen as John the Evangelist, the two are aspects of the one, acting in unison; lower and higher aspects of one conscious conduit from Spirit into matter.

She tells them that the body of Jesus has been "raised up," and they run to the tomb and find it empty. "John" arrives first and looks inside with all his attention but does not enter. Peter, the foundation stone, symbolic of the center of the world, goes inside and finds the linen in which Jesus was wrapped. Only then does "the other disciple" follow Peter into the tomb. He sees the linen wrappings from his body, and the linen head covering set apart, rolled up, in a unified marked space. The teaching describes their state as follows; **"For not yet could they experience the inner scripture, that he — Logos, must rise up in consciousness from spiritual death."** 20:9. So the two disciples return to their homes leaving Mary weeping outside the tomb.

Only Mary stands firm, she looks, again, into the tomb, and now she sees two angels in white, sitting at the head and foot of the place where the physical body of Jesus had lain. This evokes the image of the Ark of the Covenant in the sanctuary of the Temple in Jerusalem, which was said to be a seat or dais with winged arm pieces, on which the presence of God — the Shekinah — descended. Mary has pierced the veil of the sanctuary; now she sees into the holy of holies. The two angels ask her why she is weeping, and whom she seeks? She replies that she weeps because her Lord has been taken, and she does not know where he has been laid. Her weeping expresses her desire for reunification with Logos; her tears symbolize the glory on the face of the Divine presence, the outpouring Spirit, uniting all things through Logos.

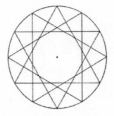

Mary the Magdalene embodies the Shekinah, the stillness sustaining all movement, the pulse of all life, flowing into, and out of, the patterns of diversity as the steps of a dancer. She continually receives the axis around which the ages revolve in their continual movement through the pulse of life. She is the power to bring life into expressions of diversity, sustaining their connections with their eternal source.

Mary now turns, which in Greek means that she is turning within to meet the Christ in herself; raising her level of consciousness. Ascending on a spiral of deepening spiritual awareness, she sees a figure who she supposes to be a gardener. He also asks her why she is weeping, and whom she seeks? In the symbolism of the Bible, a gardener is someone who tends paradise, Eden, the bright Yetziratic universe of forms. Mary answers him saying, *"Sir, if you have carried him away, tell me where you have laid him, and I will take him away,"* (Literally — *"raise him up."*)

Now Jesus calls her by her name, "Mary — Miriam." She hears her name, that is, understands who she is: the great sea of *prima materia* — the formless source of all matter — the initiator of change; *the flow of creative mutable power, containing the seeds of absolute life; creative presence in Space, giving life to the Cosmos.* Again, she turns on the spiral of rising consciousness, and recognizing him in the Spiritual Body, says "Rab-bi'ni!" (Teacher — Lord.) She has realized Logos in the creative union of spiritual Gnosis.

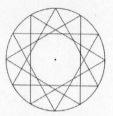

Jesus says to her, "Do not join to me yet, for I have not yet ascended to the Father; but go to my brethren and say to them, I am ascending to my Father and your Father, to my God and your God." 20:17.

The usual translation of Jesus' words "do not hold me yet" do not do justice to the full meaning in the text. The Greek verb *hapto* translated as "hold" in the RSV, means "to cling to" and "fasten to," and is used of sexual union between a man and woman. This is the Divine conjunction that takes place within us when we realize the fulfillment of our humanity in *Being*. Jesus-Mary represent the inner and outer faces of the Christos; and the active and passive creative dynamics spiraling out of the central axis. Together these three principals create and form the great circle of life.

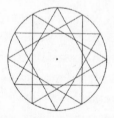

What is important is to see beyond what the figures of Jesus and Mary symbolize; and awaken to them as living realities within you; the dynamics of creation come from the One in a continuous flow; creation is not a past event it is here now: "The Kingdom of Heaven is here now," to know this connects you to the great circle life through its axis.

In the story Jesus asks Mary not to join with him yet, *"because I have not yet ascended to the Father but go to my brethren and say to them, I am ascending to my Father and your Father, to my God and your God."* Through the spiral of creation, Mary carries this Divine radiance from the center out to the circumference represented by the disciples; the twelve divisions of humanity in the great circle of life. For union with the One to become a reality for humanity, each of us has to awaken; those of us already awakening can only communicate this through *Presence;* unconscious words and actions only serve to reinforce the ego; so if you speak in this communion, first be aware of *Presence.*

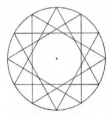

To realize what Mary personifies first become receptive with all your attention; breathe consciously to help you center. Your spinal cord is a caduceus, the staff of the thrice born mystic turning on the spiral. Feel its presence within you; a central axis projecting active and passive dynamic arcs, spirals from the Divine presence, through Spirit and form into the physical universe.

Be aware of the energy it carries from the cranium down to the souls of the feet and back up its spiraling arcs again. The more presence you bring into your life, the clearer your path becomes. Be as present as you can in all that you do, this is the art of remembering: the realization of the Divine essence continually creating the circle of life in every moment.

In the Creation story in Genesis, universal humanity is called Adam — the androgynous Spirit of everyone who takes on male or female form. As the feminine aspect of the androgynous human Spirit, Mary-Eve is Sophia, opening our eyes to the way of wisdom. This wisdom receives the fruit of the tree of knowledge planted in paradise: knowledge that the creative force building up life into form is held in balance through its opposite: death in life. In mythological teaching stories, we await the awakening of the second Adam: the fully realized — universal human being. This is our awakening to unification as Logos — Christ, and Mary-Eve seeks to lead us through the circle of life, asking us to open our eyes to its wisdom. The spiritually awakened Adam (humanity) holds the axis between form and the One, Eve (the circle of life) is the communion throughout its great circle.

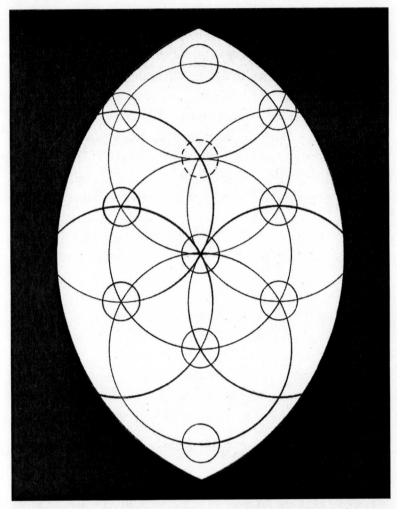

During the period when the Gospels were written down, the most widely known and loved image of the Divine feminine was Isis, the triple goddess; Mother — creation, birth; Bride — wisdom, fertility and diversification of life; And Grandmother/crone — ancestral wisdom and death. The Maternal aspect of the Goddess calls you into consciousness, so that the Bride can unify with Jesus as the Solar Logos — the feminine aspect of the Christ. Mary is the enveloping womb of space: the creative space within you, carrying the life feeding and clothing you. Mary is your ability to recognize and draw into yourself,

the spiritual and Divine essence of life, and distribute it throughout the Cosmos.

It is for this reason that in verse 18 Mary tells the twelve aspects of humanity, that she has perceived with the inner eye, and knows through experience of spiritual consciousness, the resurrected body of Christ. As inner realities, Mary and Jesus take us in a dance through and with the whole of creation. In this dance, Unity is experienced through the diversity of life in all its myriad expressions. Life is fully realized in this consummation of the marriage ceremony, which took place at Cana. Mary-Eve and Jesus-Adam meet as they did at Cana, only now they are in the garden, symbolic of paradise or Eden. Whether you are a woman or a man both these principles exist within you, don't get fixated on the separation of gender; you are Adam, and within you also, is Eve: *Adam means universal humanity, and Eve, the circle of life.*

The underworld that Jesus emerges from on the third day is a doorway through paradise, into the kingdom of heaven, and the kingdom of God. The underworld is where the death process becomes a womb, and from out of this pregnant space a new humanity, with a new perception of Heaven and Earth emerges.

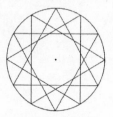

On the evening of that day, the first day of the week, the doors being shut where the disciples were, for fear of the Judeans, Jesus came and stood among them and said to them, "peace be with you." 20:19

The term Judeans symbolizes the egocentric shadow, which seeks to destroy the greater state of consciousness before it can take root in the Cosmos, and awaken humanity from our unconscious state. Only after Mary has gone to the twelve disciples when they are shut up in their houses in fear of the shadow in themselves does Jesus come and stand in their midst. To "stand in their midst" means, at the core of any human who is able to receive Logos or Being. The Greek for door, which has been closed tight, or obstructed through fear, also means "an opening," "an opportunity," and "the door to the Kingdom of Heaven." Jesus and Mary illuminate the twelve divisions of humanity, breathe the Holy Spirit into them, and they are brought into the great unifying dance, with the words *peace be with you; meaning — experience the stillness of eternal presence.*

As he breaths the Holy Spirit, or Shekinah into them, personified by Mary Magdalene, Jesus says, **"If you forgive the sins of any, they are forgiven; if you retain the sins of any, they are retained." 20:23**

If we hold that anyone has sinned against us, then the unconscious thought form clings to us, re-presenting itself to us over and over again as it seeks release. If we release people from sin against us, then we ourselves are free, and the Holy Spirit can flow through us unobstructed, in abundance. When we release ourselves from carrying our burdens through forgiveness, we are set free, and those that we release also have the opportunity to be free, if they so desire.

Chapter Thirteen

The Logos and the Patterns of Creation

The Gospel concludes with an old Hellenistic teaching story that expresses the harmony and Unity of life, through geometric patterns and ratio. Its symbolism has been combined with those of the Jewish mystical tradition, in which the resurrected Jesus as Logos is revealed to the twelve disciples for a third time; that is, creation and form expressed in matter are experienced as *One*.

The story begins when seven of the Disciples are on the shore of the Sea of Galilee at night, and Simon Peter tells the others he is going fishing. They reply, "we will go with you." This is not a landscape of the physical world but depicts the World Soul. The sea is Mara — Mary the great circular Sea, Mother of all things, containing space, in which stars are continually being born and dying, where countless galaxies turn on their axis.

The seven Disciples set out onto this sea at night. The Greek *nyx* (night) is a metaphor meaning the time of death, and an unenlightened state, and they are unable to catch any fish. Just before dawn, Jesus appears on a beach, but they are unable to recognize him. Addressing them as "children," Jesus asks them if they have any food to eat; they answer no. He tells them to change their orientation — their outlook — and they cast their net into the sea of the World Soul, which is constantly moving with abundant life, on the right side of their boat. They now experience the net, which symbolizes the Cosmos, as full of this abundant life. They have awakened to the underlying pattern of life that supports the physical universe, and that exists within them: Logos.

This geometric pattern, which is used to symbolize the stone vessels set out in the wedding at Cana, is also used to illustrate the seven disciples in the fishing boat on the Sea of Galilee.

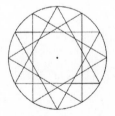

Therefore the disciple whom Jesus loved made it known to Peter, that it is the Lord. When Simon Peter understood that it was the Lord [Logos], he put on his upper garment, for he was laid bare, and threw himself without concern into the shimmering sea. 21:7

Simon Peter standing in the center of the boat realizing the presence of Logos, girds himself in his "upper" spiritual garment, and enters the sea on the opposite side of the boat to the Cosmic net; the side that faces the shore of the spiritual universe, and swims to meet the Logos. The other disciples haul the Cosmic net bursting with fish onto dry land of the creative universe: the universal principles of life.

As they bring the net to the shore, they see a fire of hot coals, with fish and unleavened bread laid upon it. Jesus tells them to bring the fish they have caught to him, 153 great fish in an unbroken net. This is a Pythagorean mathematical and geometric equation for unity in diversity. In an equation of Archimedes, 153:265 was known in the Hellenistic world as the measure of the fish, the Vesica Pisces.

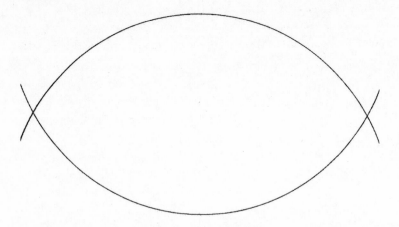

This portrays Jesus as the personification of Logos, recognized in the geometric symbolism of the Fish. As we have seen, the name of Jesus comes from the Hebrew Joshua, who was originally called Hosea son of Nun. The name Nun means fish, the sustaining presence of the One in a sea teeming with the fertile diversity of abundant life.

Now the risen Christ is shining brilliant light upon the waters of the Galilee, the circle of life, at the dawning of a new day, providing sustenance for all who are aware enough to receive it.

On the spiritual shore of creative existence, everything is seen to burn with spiritual light, every living thing is shining with its own light of consciousness.

The circles and geometric patterns that make up the Tree of Life as given in the story of the disciples in their boat (the central circle), casting their net into the sea of World Soul (the bottom circle). The top circle depicts the spiritual universe - dry Land - on which the Logos — Being is established. Logos holds the balance and harmony, ratio and proportion, the laws of life or Torah, that govern all the expressions of diversity out of unity, and unity in diversity.

The disciples are invited to dine with the Logos, and when they have eaten, Jesus addresses Simon Peter as the son of Jonas — the dove — symbol of the Holy Spirit, and says to him, if you love Logos, then distribute and feed those who seek the sustaining presence of Logos. He tells the disciples: **Truly, truly I say to you, when you were governed by your inferior nature, you carried a burden as a slave, and went wherever it took you; but when you become mature you take hold of your creative Spirit, and this creative Spirit will cleave about you, and lead you where your inferior nature would not. 21:18**

The disciple who is close to the heart of Jesus then joins with him in atonement and Simon Peter seeing this, also becomes one with Logos, from beginning to end; Alpha unto Omega. The last verse tells us that, **There were so many things that Logos made known, that if they were inscribed from the greatest to the least, I suppose that the Cosmos itself could not contain all the created things inscribed in their books; it is so. 21:25.**

Every living thing is a book inscribed with the word — Logos — of God; there is not one living thing in created existence, in form or made manifest in the Cosmos, that is not of the Logos. Yet the Cosmos only reflects the forms and outer appearances of created existence. As human beings, we have a choice; to awaken now, as Logos, or continue to live under our inferior nature. We do not need to wait for some future time to awaken; we can realize the fullness and abundance of life now. The end of the Gospel brings us full circle: *In the beginning, the Logos was, and the Logos was with God, and the Logos was Divine.* Being is beyond Alpha and Omega (Beginning and End), and gives birth to created existence — the Alpha and the Omega. Logos is experienced as *fastening* for all time, the diversity of life into Unity, and sustaining the patterns of created existence. It is One, the permanent presence of the Divine universe of Being, the perfect reflection of God the Absolute.

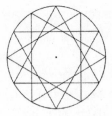

The reason for your existence as a human being is to awaken spiritually, to be at-One with the great circle of life. Everything you then do is at-One with Logos, which sustains you: Be conscious, "Knock," and the doorway of inner perception will be open to you.

Conclusion

All mystical teachings preserved in the Bible point to the same truth. Nothing that exists does so outside of the eternal present moment, which is here, now, within you, and within every living thing. The Gospel of John uses the concept of Logos to represent the formless and timeless eternal source of life that cannot be comprehended by the mind, and in fact cannot be represented at all: it simply *Is*.

As you begin to awaken to the eternal point of consciousness that Logos represents, you become present to life in full consciousness.

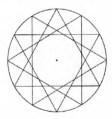

Logos is stillness and every movement of life that is observed. Logos is silence and every sound that is heard within that silence.

Contemplation and meditation are not separate from our daily lives. To awaken to a higher or greater consciousness, is our natural state. Whatever techniques or practices we use to do this become a part of all that we do in our daily lives. When we awaken spiritually, we realize that life supports us, opportunities open up for us to be with life, fully, in appreciation of its beauty and abundance. We will still be met with challenges, but we no longer turn them into negative thought forms that weigh us down, distract us, or make us anxious.

Conscious presence brings to an end all creeds and their systems of belief, worship, and authority; all philosophical and theological interpretations and their dogmas and doctrines, all of which are projections of the mind. The Torah — the teaching — is not written on a scroll, or in the pages of a book; it is living reality within you. Its teaching is expressed in the beauty of harmony and ratio that underpins the fabric of the whole of existence. In the Gospel of John, it is called Logos, the light of created existence, the light of the Cosmos, the glory of the One. *Unification with the One source of all life is a present reality, the axis of Being is here now, the Kingdom of Heaven is here now; all creation awaits your awakening in this eternal moment, to the presence of Being.*

Chapter Fourteen

Historical Background to the Text

This chapter provides a brief historical overview of the development of ideas and symbols that can be found in the Gospel of John.

The writings known to us as the Gospel of John, come from the combining of the Jewish mystical tradition, with the wisdom of the Greek philosopher-mystics, and the teachings and initiations, which were part of the Hellenistic — Greek cultural, and other pagan mystery schools of Ancient Rome. All of which drew on earlier teachings, and the mythologies and symbolism, from Egypt, Mesopotamia, and Persia. In centers of learning such as Alexandria in Egypt, and Ephesus in Asia Minor, mystics and philosophers of the Jewish Diaspora, used the Greek concept of Logos to describe the unity out of which all life has emerged. Logos expresses the One source of life, and the balance, ratio, and beauty of the creative patterns of diversity that emerge out of unity.

John's Gospel clothes these symbols and ideas with the events of a story that unfolds within a definite historical and geographical setting; but it is essential to understand from the outset that the Gospel is not, and was never intended to be, a historical document. Indeed, one of our greatest misconceptions has been to see it as the account of one unique man's teachings, fixed in a remote time and place, and removed by two millennia from our present reality. The Gospel is a perennial teaching story, the written, *outer face*, of a much larger body of oral mystical teaching, which cannot be taught or received through the written word.

The written works of what is sometimes referred to as the

Johannine tradition are not all included in the authorized canon of the New Testament. Those that are, consist of the Gospel, the Revelation, and three short letters also attributed to John. However, the Revelation differs in literary style to the other documents, and for this reason, there has been much debate amongst scholars as to whether they all originate from a common source. Other books from the Johannine tradition exist outside the Church's Canon, such as the Apocryphon of John, found among the Nag Hammadi scrolls, which was considered either as "heretical" or unsuitable by the early Church. There is also *the Gospel of Peace of Jesus Christ*, which is more explicit in its presentation of the teaching as a process of individuation through self-knowledge and healing. All of these writings emerged from a much more extensive oral tradition or *inner face* — ideas and teachings whose origins can be traced to the Hellenistic (Greek cultural) and Jewish mystical teachings of the time, and the ideas, writings, and teachings that pre-date the period.

No one knows with any certainty when and where the Gospel of John was written down. Theologians, scholars, historians, have all speculated on this question over the centuries. Opinions vary, but it is usually dated c.90–110 CE. The places where it was written are plausibly Ephesus in Asia Minor (modern Turkey), or Alexandria in Egypt due both to their association with the concept of the Logos (see below), and to their large and prosperous Hellenized Jewish communities. (Although some scholars have postulated that it originates from Syria.)

When we look at history — and this is true of any history — it is worth remembering that it is usually written by the winners, and that historical events inevitably become embellished over the centuries with myth to become legends in which real historical figures are adorned with the attributes of psychological, spiritual and Divine archetypes.

The word myth is often misused and misunderstood. It comes from the Greek *Mythos*, which in its widest sense originally meant, "anything delivered by word of mouth" and "potent reality." It does not mean "fantasy," as we now so often wrongly use it.

It is important for us to remember how this process of mythologizing works, because as human beings involved in history, we are influenced by, and live out these archetypal energies and patterns, which are a part of the unfolding and development of human consciousness. In the biblical texts, mythological concepts, such as the universal Human being with Divine origins, were consciously and deliberately combined with historical anecdotes to convey the inner meaning of the spiritual teaching. It is of little use to look at biblical stories as accurate and definitive historical sources: the stories contain perennial knowledge and wisdom, which were intended to be reworked in each new era.

The authors of the Gospel were not concerned with documenting history, rather they sought to pass on the spiritual and philosophical teaching they had received orally from their own teachers in story form. Their task was to preserve this teaching in such a way that it could be adapted for use by later generations. The gospels, like most biblical texts, were never intended to be read as history, or fixed in a historical past. This is because the mystical understanding of the Divine Human being and the creation of life exists outside of time in the eternal present, or *now*, and the function of the text is to lead us beyond physical and psychological time and space.

Pagan Philosophy and the Concept of Logos

John's Gospel is unique amongst the Gospels in its description of Divinity as the *Logos*. The first use of this term to describe Divinity, is attributed to the Greek philosopher and mystic Heraclitus, who lived and taught in Ephesus in Asia Minor (modern Turkey) in the late sixth century BCE. Little is known about Heraclitus: only a single written work carries his name, entitled *On Nature*. Like many of the pre-Socratic teachers of his time, Heraclitus called God the "unknowable One", "source of all Being". He used the term Logos to describe "the Being" of God, a reflection of the One, Absolute, and unknowable God, and he left two sayings about the Logos that help define its deeper meaning as the Divine name — *"All things happen according to the Logos,"* and *"it indwells every human being."* The term Logos was taken up by the Platonist schools that followed some three hundred years later, and one of the things they said of it was; *"the Logos pervades all things."* By the third century BCE, the term Logos had been amalgamated with Pythagorean ideas and was understood as the all-pervading Divine presence, the source of all life, all creatures, and the life-giving core of every woman and man. This understanding is highly significant because it accords humanity Divine origins, integrated within, and inseparable from, the web of a harmonious and perfectly proportioned creation. Other Pagan teachings were also a significant influence on the early Christian tradition, and we shall look at those in greater depth later.

Ancient Jewish Mysticism

In the sixth century BCE, around the same period, Heraclitus was forming his ideas on the Logos, over a thousand miles to the east in Babylonia, the book of Ezekiel records the vision of a Divine image in human form, seated upon a throne and riding in a chariot. This vision came as a consequence of the traumatic events surrounding the enforced captivity and exile of around 25,000 Jews from their native land, following two invasions by the Babylonians. During the second invasion, the Temple in Jerusalem was destroyed, effectively separating the Israelites from their place of worship. Ezekiel's experience is induced because the extreme experiences leading up to the vision have put him under intense pressure, pushing him to the edge and then beyond, of what he once thought of as a familiar and seemingly certain life as a priest in the Temple.

Ezekiel's vision must be understood allegorically and not just literally; his name means "God strengthens" and he is called son of Buzi, which means "my contempt". His visionary experience is expressed through *the work of the chariot* (Merkabah), the realization by an individual of the unity of life. His vision takes place as he sits gazing into the waters of the river Chebar in Babylon, where through his own reflection he sees a vision of the universes of paradise, heaven, and the Divine. He sees the Divine glory in human form, seated upon a throne, symbolizing the Spiritual Body. It rides in a chariot, a vehicle, which symbolizes the Soul. The wheels of the chariot represent the physical body and the Cosmos with all its patterns, cycles and processes. In the man Ezekiel, Being realizes itself. At the same time the Glory of God, is perceived by the man Ezekiel, as the eternal presence pervading life in all its creative ideas and forms. As his name is meant to suggest, he is strengthened by experiences, which have temporarily paralyzed his ordinary thought processes. The Cosmos, human body, individual and World Soul, and creative Spirit of life, are known as the real Temple of God, in which the Divine presence can realize itself.

The first chapters of the book of Ezekiel and other sources (such as chapter 6 of the book of Isaiah, and chapter 7 of the book of Daniel) form the biblical writings, of what came to be known as Merkabah Mysticism, *riding in the chariot:* the ascent in consciousness of the Soul from the physical universe, through the seven halls of paradise, and the seven heavens, to be at one with the whole of life. This depiction of "the levels" of paradise or Eden and the heavens is given in the Book of Genesis, and acts as a frame of reference for mystical ascent.

The enforced encounter with Babylonian culture during exile, changed Judaism dramatically, and its cosmology was expanded through close contact with this ancient culture. This period was also the cradle of Pharisaic Judaism, which preserved the oral tradition for a community without a formal functioning priesthood, or external focal point of the Temple, which symbolized the spiritual center of the World. Pharisaic teaching brought ritual and practice into the home and the family. This had important repercussions because even after the Jews returned to Judea and Jerusalem, and the second Temple was built, much of the focus of the spiritual teaching remained in the community, where the Pharisees taught. This teaching in the home, in towns and villages, and in the synagogues, would form the foundation of Rabbinic Judaism some six centuries later in the first century CE, Palestine, bringing the esoteric teachings into the daily life of the Jewish community.

Hellenized Jewish Teachings

The language and style of John's Gospel points to an origin in the Hellenistic (Greek cultural), Jewish communities of the Diaspora. However it is important to recognize that much of its oral source came from Palestine where the drama is set. The spoken language at the time of Jesus was Aramaic, and Biblical Hebrew sources are also used in the text. Whether the text was first written in Greek or Aramaic is open to debate, but the text we have inherited incorporates Aramaic idioms and phrases into the Greek translation. The Greek text, which is the source of most translations, could well have been put together in Alexandria, where the term Logos came into popular use through a Jewish teacher and middle Platonist philosopher, called Philo Judaeus (c 20 BCE– 50 CE).

Alexandria was a center of learning for all the esoteric and exoteric teachings of the period, and the culture of its schools, libraries and places of worship embraced a rich diversity of symbols and images. Here Philo would have come into contact with Pagans from all over the Roman Empire, as well as teachers from the East, such as Hindus and Buddhists. This exchange of ideas was particularly prevalent among the Greeks, and

Hellenized Romans, and with the native North Africans who carried the legacy of the ancient Egyptian culture.

Schooled in Platonic and Pythagorean ideas, Philo and others like him brought together the Greek philosophical and Jewish traditions, making Judaism acceptable to the Greek mind, and Greek philosophy accessible and understandable to the Hellenized Jewish Diaspora. Like the pre-Socratic philosopher mystics, and Jewish sages before him, Philo saw God as transcendent, beyond human understanding, or description. Philo used the term *Divine Logos* to signify the image or name of God. That is, the Divine garment, the immanence of the unseen and Absolute God who is transcendent, beyond existence, and who cannot be contained by existence. The blending of Jewish and Greek mystical teachings by Philo is illustrated very clearly in his description of the Logos: *"Having made the whole of the universe to depend and cling to himself, he is the charioteer of all that vast creation."* Here the Logos is described in the terms of the Merkabah mystics as the "charioteer," or rider in the chariot, the only begotten Divine image of the Absolute, unseen God.

The Holy Land During the Second Temple Period

At the time of Jesus, in Palestine, the Jewish teachings came through three main schools; the Essenes, the Sadducees and the Pharisees. The Essenes are usually viewed as a strict community, who saw themselves as fighting for the light against the forces of darkness. Their beliefs are described in detail in the surviving manuscripts of the community rulebook, known as *"the manual of discipline."* The first archaeologists of Qumran, where the Dead Sea scrolls were found were monks. Not surprisingly, they saw the Essenes as some kind of strict monastic sect. However, the Essenes were spread throughout the Holy Land, and had centers in Jerusalem. But their main community, for which they are famous, was next to the Dead Sea, almost certainly at En-Gedi, which was a relatively green oasis on the western shore of the

Dead Sea. Here they distanced themselves from Jerusalem and the Temple, which they viewed as totally corrupt. For the Essene community it was not enough to have been born a Jew to gain salvation: joining their sect required making a second or new covenant with God.

The school of the Sadducees controlled the Temple and trained the priesthood. They had a ritual technique called the Moses Seat for ascending in consciousness through the halls of paradise and the heavens, in which one of their number would undertake a mystical ascent, and then describe his experiences to his companions, sitting in a circle about him in a meditative state. The Sadducees left no writings of their own, and we only know about them through their opponents who wrote about them in derogatory terms. They were largely distrusted and despised by the other groups and schools for their collaboration with Herod and the Romans. Many of the Priests were appointed by Herod from communities in the Hellenistic Diaspora, and were seen by many Jews as not only corrupt, but also as outsiders, with little cultural connection to their own.

By far the largest and most diverse group of teachers were the Pharisees. Although they had a presence at the Temple, they mostly wandered from town to village using parables as a method of teaching. They related ideas in the mystical teaching to things found in everyday life — for example, comparing a grain of mustard seed to the Kingdom of Heaven, and were called, Rabbi, meaning "Lord," "Revered," and "Teacher," by the population.

Just as during the Babylonian exile, some of the Rabbis were involved in transferring the focus of the teaching from the Temple in Jerusalem to the interior life of the men and women in the communities where they taught. This emphasis on the inner life is the essence of the experiential knowledge gained through the practice of Merkabah mysticism. It is also to be found in the books of the Torah (the five books of Moses) and forms much of the esoteric teaching behind the books of Genesis and Exodus. Some Rabbis also took the spiritual teaching to the Gentiles (non-Jewish nations or peoples), often combing Hebraic concepts with those from Hellenistic philosophy and mysticism.

In stories on the life and teachings of John the Evangelist, he is depicted as one of the Rabbis who spread the Messianic tradition — teachings focusing on the Messiah (in Greek Christos) — that would become Christianity, to both Jews and Gentiles. According to a tradition of the Church Fathers, John was exiled to the Greek island of Patmos by the Roman authorities some time after the death of Jesus. There, John is said to have received the book of Revelation directly from the risen Christ. Later he was given a reprieve by Rome, and went to live in Ephesus in Asia Minor. He arrived at a philosophical school there, and began to transmit the teaching he had received from the Christ. It was then passed on orally to a Greek called John the Elder, and it is said that the teaching has been passed down the generations to this day by word of mouth.

Although this story cannot be substantiated historically, and can even be seen as propaganda since the Greek schools vied with each other to be seen as direct lines of descent from the apostles, its real value is in the link it implies between the Gnosis of the philosopher mystic Heraclitus and the teaching found in the Gospel of John in the school at Ephesus some six centuries later. At some point during the late first century – early second century, the teaching was written down, most likely from an Aramaic and Greek oral source, and subsequently reworked with a Hellenic overlay containing teachings from Philosophy, Gematria, and Sacred Geometry.

Further Developments in Jewish Mysticism after the Second Temple

During the first and second centuries CE Judaism was in turmoil due to the uprising of Zealots against the Roman occupation of the Holy Land. This culminated in the destruction of the second Temple and the devastation of Jerusalem by Roman legions in 70 CE. For the Judaic tradition to survive it had to consolidate in a new form, and to a certain extent it turned in on itself. Yohannan ben Zakkai, said to have been a pupil of Rabbi Hillel, the greatest sage of the second Temple period, became an important figurehead in the reformation of the tradition. Ben Zakkai, took Judaism back to its roots by consolidating its Hebraic form, and through the Merkabah Mysticism, preserved the chain of esoteric tradition for following generations. He said that *the work of the chariot* could only be taught to one who already knows; meaning, that it is only possible to impart knowledge of mystical teachings to someone who is mature, that is, already experiencing spiritual awakening. His academy, in the town of Javne near the Mediterranean coast (outside modern Tel Aviv), ushered in what is called the Tannaitic period 70 – 200 CE. This simply means the repeating or recounting of the tradition. It is at the end of this period, the late second – early third centuries, that the term Kabal — the root of the word Kabbalah — began to be used for the receiving and passing on of the oral tradition.

Because of the disruption of the old way of life and the loss of their spiritual center in Jerusalem, the Rabbis decided upon a fixed canon of books for the Bible, 39 in all — representing the stages on the journey from Egypt to the Holy Land. In addition to this, a whole library of other manuscripts began to be written, that come from the pool of ideas, symbolism and teachings that also found their way into the Gospel of John and the New Testament. Although, there are different emphasizes on how these teaching were interpreted by the emerging messianic sect (Christianity), from its parent tradition (Judaism), their source is the same.

A particular development of Merkabah Mysticism that emerged from the visionary experiences of mystical ascent produced some important esoteric texts called the Hekhalot

(Halls or Palaces). These descriptive passages of paradise, the heavenly realm and the Divine presence were written from the second century onwards. Although these texts are later than the Gospel of John, they contain the formulation of an oral esoteric tradition, parts of which are found in earlier writings connected with Talmudic and Midrashic teachings of the first and second centuries CE (Rabbinic commentaries on biblical texts.)

Of more significance, are the writings of what are now called pseudepigraphic texts (lit: falsely inscribed), written between circa 200 – 300 BCE and 200 – 500 CE, depending on varying scholarly opinion. Using the names of ancient biblical figures and prophets, such as Enoch and Abraham in their titles, these texts are apocalyptic — revelations on the Divine image of God. They follow a similar style to Ezekiel, with the climactic vision of the mystical ascents of the chariot riders in the appearance of the Divine image of God, sitting upon a throne, riding in a chariot. This Divine image is often referred to as the "Glory of the Lord," in the pseudepigraphia; "*And the Great Glory sat thereon* [the throne/Merkabah] *And his garment shone more brightly than the Sun...*".*(1 Enoch 14:20)*. In these texts, the frequently used terms "Glory of God" and "Power of God" are synonymous with the name of God, Ha Shem [YHVH], which is sometimes also called the "Garment of God," and is seen as the creative agency or "hand" through which God operates in existence.

Midrashic sources (Rabbinic commentaries on biblical texts) also speak of the Garment of Glory as a pre-existent Unity or Presence, out of which creation occurred. Mystical circles within Judaism also affirm humanity's Divine origins that pre-exist creation. There were conflicts among some of the Rabbis about the idea of a created human becoming identified with the Glory of God, much of the division of opinion surrounded the figure of Metatron, who is important in Jewish esoteric literature. In the pseudepigraphic 3 Enoch 16 he is called *"Prince of the Divine presence, the Glory of the highest Heaven."* Whilst in 3 Enoch 7–15

Metatron is made synonymous with the Glory of God. He is the transfigured patriarch Enoch, called the lesser JHVH (Yahweh), who embodies the name of God, and acts as God's messenger in creation, guiding the ascending mystic.

Similar attributes are given to Jesus in the Gospels; in whom Divinity and humanity are united as One. In John's Gospel the language and symbolism has the same quality as that found in the Jewish mystical writings of the pseudipigraphia. John refers to the Divine image or Logos as the "Glory of God," "the only begotten" of the Absolute — (1:14), and again in (1:18) the Logos is called the "garment of God." The same language, ideas and concepts are also to be found in other Christian and Pagan Gnostic sources, which tells us that these ideas and concepts were circulating widely during the time the teaching was being transmitted and written down.

The Birth of Christianity: From the Founding of Christianity to the Founding of the Church

The early Christian movement began as a Jewish messianic sect within the Synagogue in the middle of the first century CE, and the first disciples extended the teaching to both Jews and gentiles. It became very popular in some of the synagogues, where feelings about the coming of the messiah were high amongst a population who were hoping for liberation from the rule of Herod and the Romans.

By the end of the century, Gentiles pre-dominated, in what was now a fledgling messianic movement, growing more and more distant from the reformed Judaism of Johannan b.Zakkai at Javne. This separation of Jewish esoteric ideas from their source, and their amalgamation with those of the Pagan world molded the teaching into the Christian form. This is especially true of the Eastern half of the Empire where the teachings began to be written down in both Aramaic and Greek.

The impact of the Pagan mysteries — especially the cult of Isis and the Mithraic cult — on later redactions of the Gospels and the theology of the early Church was immense. Both cults were very popular in the Roman Empire during the first centuries of the Common Era. The cult of Isis — the triple Goddess; Mother, Crone and Bride of the Son of God, is represented in the Gospels by the three Maries; the Madonna, Mary of Cleopas/Bethany (or Mary Salome), and Mary Magdalene. Representing the Goddess in her three aspects, Isis-Mari (Mary) is crucial to our understanding of mystical teachings hidden in the Gospel. They symbolize the connection of Divinity and the human Spirit with the physical body and the Cosmos, and the awakening to the Divine presence in the everyday world. In the Gospels, Mary personifies what remains of the teachings on the Divine feminine without which we only have half of the mystical teachings on Divinity in humanity. Mary in her triple aspect also personifies the passage of spiritual and Divine knowledge through the conduit of human consciousness, which allows the manifestation of the Divine Presence to take place through the body and psyche in the outer world of appearances.

Divine Mother and Bride

The figure of Mary contains the amalgamation of many goddesses such as Isis, Aphrodite, Demeter and Hera. For example, Hera is the Queen of heaven who renews her virginity by bathing in the river of life, after joining with her consort Zeus. She is both Virgin and Mother, who gives birth to a half Divine and half-human child. Her child has to grow into a Divine and spiritual adult, and go through the process of death and rebirth to obtain union with the One. Mary is the Great Mother, enveloping all humanity in her cloak or aura of Divine sustenance. As such, she is the Earth Mother giving life to all creatures and all living things. She is the birth-giving Goddess and the Queen of heaven, the second Eve and the embodiment of wisdom — Sophia. As Sophia, Mary is Mother, Daughter, and

Bride, and as the personification of wisdom, she is the guiding archetype of human evolution, which belongs to, and exists within every human being. In short, She is the Feminine face and image of the Logos and Christos. It is important that we understand clearly that Logos and the Christ are neither male nor female but contain the essence of both in harmony, balance and unity; in the ancient world the Divine and the perfected human representing Divinity on Earth were depicted in both male and female form. However, the feminine aspect of the One has long been suppressed and marginalized in Western culture, and its institutionalized religions, and this now needs to be rebalanced if we are to understand the mystical teachings and ourselves fully.

In some Gnostic texts the original teachings on Sophia, while rejected by the Church, survived. Here she is the great Mother, consort of the Father, and their only begotten child is called both Sophia and Christ. This is represented by an equal-armed cross, used in early Christianity, with two masculine and two feminine faces, male above and to the right and female below and to the left. The One, containing both male and female in balance and harmony was understood when reading the terms used in the Gospel, of Father, Son, Logos and Christ. In one respect the use of the term Father and its predominance in spiritual literature is simply of its time, yet extensive teaching on the Divine Mother, also existed at the time. While they are not present in the writings we have now in the authorized New Testament, this does not mean that they were not present in the original Christian teachings.

Together the Divine Mother and Father present with a unity, a quarternity of Male and Female, the active dynamic and passive dynamic in balance. It is a perfect reflection of the One. Without the passive dynamic of the feminine, we cannot be whole, and we cannot perceive the whole. We cannot know ourselves, or the created universe in which we live, nor grow to be at One.

The Figure of Jesus and the Pagan Sun Gods

During the period from the second century to the fall of the Roman Empire, the figure of Rabbi Joshua of Nazareth was given many of the attributes of popular Pagan Sun Gods and Savior figures. An examination of the attributes of the Roman god Mithras throws light on some of the key symbols in the Gospel, the themes of death and resurrection and the concept of a Divine savior. The figure of Mithras appeared in the collective imagery of the time as an archetype through which teachings on the nature of Divinity and its relationship to the created universe were expressed. The Mithraic Sun god was adopted as the patron and protector of the Roman legions, and his sanctuaries were established all over the empire, from as far north as Scotland to Egypt and North Africa. He was worshipped in underground Temples designed as models of the universe, some of which had vaulted ceilings depicting the starry constellations of the heavens. His popularity only receded in the fourth century when he was superseded by the figure of Jesus Christ.

Early scholarship pointed to Mithras being an adopted Persian God, but more extensive research has shown that he was transformed through his amalgamation with other hero Sun gods of the Roman Empire, Perseus, Apollo, Aeon, and Horus from Egypt. As Aeon, he is the personification of Divine Being. The name Aeon means, "all time," that is, the eternal unmoving center of creation, the cause of causes, the still point around which the great ages of cosmic time revolve and unfold. Mithras represents the Spiritual Sun behind the visible Sun (Helios), the cause of all life, and the door though which the initiate passes on their spiritual ascent. He is the axis of the age, the beginning and end of time. Mithras was the personification of the redeemer, said to have been born in a cave, or from a rock, on the 25th of December — celebrated in ancient Middle-Eastern and Mediterranean cultures as the shortest day of the year.

In the stories that connect him with Aeon, Mithras was said to have been born on the 6th of January, the day of epiphany, which means the manifestation of the Lord; the birthday of Aeon symbolizing timeless Being entering into time. Mithras as Aeon is the first and the last, the beginning and ending of time, the One who is, was, and shall be. The birth of Mithras signified the return of Sol Invictus the unconquered Sun, and was witnessed by shepherds. After a life of wandering as a spiritual teacher with his twelve companions — the twelve divisions of the Cosmos and humanity — he died and was buried in a tomb, but rose from the dead after three days. His resurrection was celebrated every year at the spring equinox (Easter), and he was called savior and mediator of the unseen God. This deeply ingrained cross-cultural motif already existed in the pre-Christian Roman Empire.

As Perseus, Mithras embodies the forces, which govern the procession of the equinoxes — the slow movement of what appear to be fixed stars over thousands of years, leading to a shift in the astrological ages that govern the twelve divisions of life and humanity. The central icon of his cult shows Mithras seated astride a bull (Taurus) thrusting his sword into its torso. For something new to be born or come into existence, something must die or pass away. This is a universal principal: death is necessary for the eternal renewal of life. This act symbolized the atoning sacrifice through the life-blood of Divinity in created existence. As slayer of the bull, Mithras ushers in the age of Aries, changing the time and space governed universes forever, and bestowing eternal life on his followers, who were reborn into the light. An inscription to him reads, "Us too you have saved by shedding blood which grants eternity." Just as Mithras slays Taurus and brings in the age of Aries, so too Jesus, the sacrificial lamb of God, brings an end to the age of Aries and ushers in the age of Pisces with its symbol of the fish; a symbol used so frequently by the early Christians. This motif is used in the last chapter of John's Gospel, where Jesus is depicted cooking fish on a beach. (John 21:1–12)

Mithras and Jesus are both manifest forms of the One God in the different cosmic ages of the zodiac. The creators of the Gospels understood that the consciousness they personify exists in the heart of every woman and man; simultaneously the eternal center of existence around which creation, and time and space revolve.

As a consequence of the movement of the ages, the image and form of the One will inevitably change again in the age of Aquarius. This transition into the next Cosmic age is given in the Gospel of Mark 14:13, where he tells two of his disciples; "you will meet a man bearing a pitcher of water: follow him." These Comic symbols revolve around the Divine center, as humanity evolves in connection with this spiral through the ages, our image of the eternal and our relationship to it changes. On an individual level, as we move towards this center within us, we go through deeper — more cosmic levels of time, until we reach the timeless or all-time of the eternal now.

During the late first century BCE to the early second century CE, the messianic movement in Judaism was increasing in popularity, and anthropomorphic teachings on the Divine image of God became more prevalent, particularly in the Hellenistic Diaspora. At the same time, Gentiles were beginning to predominate in the Messianic movement that was to become Christianity. As Christians began to assert the Divinity of Jesus, they came into conflict with the Orthodox Rabbis, many of whom saw the equating of a human being with God as blasphemous. In the Jewish mystical teachings of the time: God is unknowable; it is through direct experience of the Divine Glory of God — through knowing ourselves, through experiencing paradise and creation in mystical ascent, that we come to unification with the whole of existence. The mystic experiences the unity of Life: Divine Being, creation and formation through the physical body and the outer world of appearances. To both Paul and the evangelist John, Jesus personifies the Glory of God, which is not the unseen Absolute. In the Pagan world the Absolute is called the One, the Divine Glory equates with Logos.

As Christian concepts of the Messiah began to incorporate a blend of teachings on the Divine human from the Merkabah traditions, with Pagan teachings on the Solar Savior, this caused greater rifts with Judaism, which was consolidating and reformulating itself around its Hebraic roots. As the rapidly forming institution of the Church began to sever its connection with its Jewish origins during the second and third centuries, Gentile Christianity became increasingly hostile towards Judaism. This separation also affected the ability of Christian theologians and biblical translators, to understand the Hebrew texts they were interpreting. This has resulted in mistranslations and problems of interpretation of Hebrew concepts and symbolism that have continued to this day. One example is the misinterpretations of the Genesis creation story: Christian interpreters have rarely if ever been able to understand the nuances in the Hebrew texts. Early commentators often took their readings from Greek translations. Justin the translator of the Latin Bible from Hebrew had a very superficial understanding of the Hebrew language. The days of creation were taken literally to mean 24 hour periods, rather than continuous cycles; Adam was seen as a man, rather than universal humanity containing both male and female; the Divine names of God were taken as "someone" or something" rather than the Eternal Presence of Being, and so on. Gnostic teachers fared little better: Although Valentinus was correct that the Creator in Genesis is the Divine agent, or name of God, and not the unknowable One, he equated the Hebrew name Elohim with the figure of a King or Judge, rather than the creative power of Being which is beyond form, and cannot be associated with human qualities.

The Christian movement was itself, developing in an increasingly hostile environment where it came into conflict with the Roman Pagan state. It began to be viewed as a dangerously subversive sect due to its resistance to the divinization and worship of the Emperor, and many Christians were killed in public spectacles in the arenas all over the Empire. Christians became convenient scapegoats for anything that went wrong, and it is well documented by writers of the time that, if the Tiber flooded or the crops failed Christians were blamed. During the reign of the Emperor Nero (54–68 CE), the persecution of Christians escalated, and when a great fire destroyed a third of the City of Rome, the Roman authorities blamed Christians as the cause.

This only served to make Christianity more popular, particularly amongst the poor, and slaves, and by 312 CE, the situation had changed to the point where the Emperor Constantine was to take a tolerant view towards the practice of the new religion. This culminated in Christianity becoming the leading religion of the Empire in 324 when Constantine became Sole Emperor of both the Eastern and Western provinces. In 325 CE, he convened a council in Nicea where the Bishops were told establish a universal doctrine for the whole of the Church. Although a later emperor tried to reverse the position of Christianity and reinstate the Pagan cults, by 391 CE, Nicene Christianity had become the official religion of the Empire. The Church gradually took the place of Paganism in the daily and yearly ritual cycles of the official Roman calendar, and the Church slipped further and further into a centralized authoritative institution, preaching an increasingly dogmatic Christology and doctrine, which among other things, made Jesus uniquely synonymous with the Divine Glory/Garment of God.

Gnosis and Gnosticism

During the period in which the Church was trying to establish itself as an accepted religion within the Roman Empire, many Christians once persecuted as insurgents, now became regarded as heretics by the Church. As Christianity became the leading religion of Rome its positions of authority such as Priests and Bishops, became filled with displaced Pagan administrators who were appointed by the Roman authorities. At the same time, the Church was becoming increasingly centralized. This caused a rift between many of the separate churches or communities, and further marginalized many of those who were trying to keep to the essence of the mystical and still largely oral teachings. As the written word became associated with authority, and polemical writings against heresies increased, the Church inevitably became more doctrinally based, and its teachings more dogmatic.

The Gospel of John was seen by many Gnostics as one of the most important Christian texts. The word Gnosis occurs many times in the Gospel of John, as it does in the New Testament. However, it was interpreted very differently by the Ecclesiastical Christians of Rome, who began calling themselves orthodox Christians, and saw Gnosis as referring to the Knowledge that came from apostolic succession. Those who called themselves Gnostics, did not recognize an ecclesiastical hierarchy, and saw Gnosis as inner knowledge gained from spiritual awakening.

The idea of *"Gnosis"* is knowledge of your spiritual Self or Center: knowledge of Being — the Divine Glory of God, gained through personal experience. The word itself can be traced back to the pre-Socratic schools of the philosopher mystics, and many philosophical schools became associated with Gnosis as a concept of inner awakening. Different schools were influenced by different ideas and traditions, encountered through the expansion of the Greek and Roman Empires, across the Middle East, and into Persia, and Egypt. There is no single Gnostic doctrine because Gnosis can have no central authority; the disciple followed a teacher and teaching that made sense to them, and they adapted the teaching through their personal experience.

By the time the Gospel of John was written, Gnostic sects could be found all over the Roman Empire, including Rome itself. As well as the Pagan schools of Gnosis, there were Jewish, and later, Christian forms, separated by cultural differences, and different interpretations of what Gnosis is. "Gnosticism" as a group belief is marked by a diversity of conviction ranging from dualism and extreme asceticism to an understanding and knowledge of existence as the reflection of God. As a group movement, it is a derivative of Gnosis, which has lost the inner connection and meaning becoming largely a theoretical aberration. The Gospel of John contains ideas from "Gnosis" rather than "Gnosticism," which comes through direct experience of Logos; the Divine image of God.

The problems and differences in the early Christian movement can be roughly categorized as follows: Generally speaking the Roman Church believed in the authority of its Priests and Bishops: For the Gnostics; knowledge of the Divine essence of life and Self knowledge need no intermediary, no external authority, and so bypasses the need for a, Bishop or Priest. In many Gnostic sects women were seen as equals, and conducted rituals, gave the sacraments, taught, and were seen as prophets or wisdom keepers. Orthodox Christians did not see Women as suitable for any of their offices and introduced a rule that they should be silent, and segregated from the men.

Gnostics were accused of dualism, and some of their writings confirm this belief, which saw a division between a God of light and spirit on the one hand, and matter and the devil on the other, and which, also appeared to be elitist. Despite this, dualism and elitism became ingrained in the theology and doctrines of the Orthodox Church, culminating in institutionalized ascetic practices and the segregation of the sexes, the demonization of others. Humanity also came to be seen as hopelessly fallen, the desires of the body, the physical universe and the natural world as creations of the devil. Women have suffered particularly as a result of this institutionalized dualism, which is also largely responsible for our destructive behavior towards the natural world.

The mystical teachings in the Gospel of John differ radically from these doctrinal teachings — whether the Orthodox Church or Gnosticism. John's Gospel affirms that the physical world is both good and holy, coming from God, and that, although mostly unconscious and separated from our Divine source, human beings are also essentially good. We are not merely passive receptacles of Spiritual and Divine agencies; we can communicate with and have an effect on the physical universe, the solar system, and the heavens of the collective spiritual world, as well as comprehend the Divine world of Being. This is the meaning of Gnosis, to know through spiritual awakening, our true Self or center of consciousness, God and creation. This is beyond mind, beyond intellect and thinking, it is our ability *To Be-Being*.

Chapter Fifteen

Kabbalah

The principal meaning of the word Kabbalah is to receive: To receive and accept life; and through knowledge of the unity of life, realize the presence of God. We can only receive if we are awake: spiritually conscious: present in this moment now, with all our attention. With this comes the ability to be, and in *Being*, accept instruction. This means *to meet*, in ourselves, the teaching or Torah, and the eternal presence of God.

Kabbalah is a way of living life as consciously as possible, and can only be revealed, that is, passed on by word of mouth from one person to another and from one generation to the next, or directly from God. This is only possible when we awaken sufficiently to meet in conscious presence. To be taught directly by God, does not necessitate visions of fiery chariots and angels. We receive the teaching through our daily lives, and the circumstances, people and creatures of the natural world around us; life is our teacher. This mystical Gnosis, called Merkabah up until the early centuries of the Common Era, is the journey of the awakened Soul through life. It is this lucid personal experience that gives us the three Kabbalistic principals of knowledge, wisdom and understanding.

Kabbalah is not a complex system of numerology or philosophical opinions, nor an elaborate enigma of Hebrew ciphers. Although these aspects may be studied and meditated upon, its theory is of little use if we are not prepared to awaken, and go beyond our mind-made attachments, held by the ego. What the theory does give us is a map to help train the mind about the different levels of consciousness within each of us, and within what is sometimes referred to as the mirror of existence.

The Kabbalistic principles laid out below all appear in various books in the Bible, primarily Genesis, Exodus, and also in the prophets such as Isaiah and Daniel, and the Psalms and Wisdom tradition. John's Gospel is no exception to this, in that the authors of all these writings either personified the energies represented through the sephirot or laid them out in the landscape as geographical place names in the areas where they lived and journeyed. These interactions in story form, present to us the principals laid out on the mandala of the Tree of Life. The form of this mandala, as it appears in this book, was first made public from the eleventh century onwards.

The aim of the use of kabbalistic terminology in this book is to help to clarify some complex ideas in the text of the Gospel of John, which belongs to the same mystical tradition. It is not the purpose of this book to go into kabbalistic symbolism in any depth, as there are plenty of books that have already done this. I have laid out some of the Hebrew terms as simply as possible and suggest that you meditate and contemplate upon their meanings, allowing them to speak to the heart and inform the mind of something of their essence.

Kabbalah is concerned with consciously realizing our relationship with God and life. God is not limited by existence and cannot be said to exist in the terms that the human mind understands by existence. God is beyond and cannot be contained by existence. Kabbalistic mystics therefore gave three attributes to God who is simply referred to as the Absolute.

Attributes of the Absolute

אין – **Ayin:** which is translated as No-thing. The no-thingness of the Absolute: No Mind, nothing that we can say is anything.

אין סוף – **Ayin Soph:** which means without end, the Infinite, Absolute all. Absolute all: Total Presence.

The Absolute is both No-thing that we can say is anything and All that "Is" — Total Presence. No mind or thought, and total presence are one. Unity.

אור סוף אין – **Ayin Soph Aur:** is translated as "the endless light". אור – Aur in Hebrew is translated as light because it symbolizes the sustaining presence of life; the essence of life or existence. Existence simply "Is." Inner and outer light: The power of Being. The three letter-numbers of Aur, Aleph, Vav, Resh, connote the limitless and unknowable One, connected to the universal container of existence.

Ayin

Ayin Soph

Ayin Soph Aur

The Birth of Existence
The birth of existence is sometimes described through a Hebrew concept called **Tzim-Tzum,** which means a "contraction", a dimension-less point or space called negative existence, into which the power of Being — Ayin Soph Aur — can emanate. This "space" allows existence to be. It is the power of Being (light —

Aur) that links the Absolute to existence and which causes existence to be.

The philosophical concept of Tzim-Tzum is a way of explaining to the mind that there is no separation between the Absolute and existence, but that existence cannot contain the Absolute. It is also a way of informing the mind that any conceptual image or form of "God" is an illusion. It is useless to speculate about what God "is" or "is not." All we can know comes through *Being: our experience of presence* — in and through the Divine image of the Absolute that contains existence, the unity of life, here and Now.

The Absolute gives birth to existence as Being — total presence, which in mystical language is called the perfect One, that is, a Unity, without separation, uncreated.

The Mirror of Existence

The ancient Jewish mystical tradition understands existence as divided into what are referred to as four worlds or universes, only one of which is a physical place. These universes are not separate, but interpenetrate each other from the center outwards, to make up one seamless garment, the mirror of existence, in which God beholds God.

אצילות – Atzilut.

The first of these universes is called Atzilut in Hebrew, which contains many meanings: *Root, origin, to join, conjunction, proximity — to be near, by the side,* and is translated as, *to stand next to.* It symbolizes *Being, total presence, the Divine essence of existence.*

It is the eternal, and can be understood, and known as the timeless now. It is Unity, the emanation, or Glory of God — the garment or the names of God. In Greek, this is the first principal of the name Logos.

From a human perspective it is the light body of Adam Kadmon, which means primordial humanity, containing the essence of the human race in One being, beyond what we understand as male and female. It is symbolized by the element of Fire. In the book of Genesis it is referred to as *the Tree of Life*, which is *the universal and eternal essence of all life.*

בריאה – Beriah

The second universe is called Beriah. The Hebrew root means; *to create, shape, to cut — carve out,* and for this reason it can be translated as *creation*. It is the spiritual universe of the creative powers of existence, called *Genesis in Greek* and *Bereshith* in its original Hebrew. Its teachings originate from mystics who experienced life at its deepest level through higher states of conscious awareness.

Beriah is the universe of the Archangels, which can be understood as containers of pure ideas, without form or physical substance. It is where the Idea of every living creature emerges during the six cycles or pulses of creation. These pulses are not a past event but are happening now. It is where the created Adam, which means universal humanity, is conceived in the sixth cycle of creation: the androgynous Spiritual Body of human beings.

Beriah is referred to in the Bible as the heavens, and is symbolized by the element of Air. As such it is dynamic movement, potent force, the unfolding of sequential pattern in space. We may understand this unfolding as the beginning of time-in-space; but it is not time as we think it to be in our daily lives. Through dynamic movement in space, creative pattern brings the first separation from pure Being or Unity; movement out of stillness. It is for this reason that Genesis calls creation, *the Tree of Knowledge of good and evil.* The Hebrew terms translated as *good and evil* mean: the force to build up and concentrate life, and the force to break down and dissipate life. In other words, through polarity, creative life contains its own resistance, which allows the play of diversity in life to begin.

יצירה – Yetzirah

The third universe is called Yetzirah from a Hebrew root, meaning; *to form, to fashion, imagination, and purpose.* It is therefore translated as formation — the universe of forms, which develop out of the ideas of Beriah. It is the universe of the angelic hosts, which mould the Archangelic ideas. It is symbolized by the element of water, because its nature is fluid and ever changing, a concentrated, dynamic, mutable, realm.

In this mutable universe, the androgynous human Spirit enters into form as a Soul; male and female appear as objective to each other; through this greater sense of separation, we seek out relationships in order to learn more about the unity of life. Women and men reflect the opposite polarity to each other in diverse patterns of our psychological body.

The movement started in Beriah as a series of dynamic ideas, is slowed, expanded, diversified, and experienced as psychological sensation through what the mind understands as, image, color, sound, and smell. Genesis calls it the *Garden of Eden*, paradise, a place of great beauty and vibrant flowing change.

אשיה – Asiyyah

The fourth universe is called Asiyyah, which comes from the Hebrew root meaning, *shaping, making, and physical action.* It is symbolized by the element of Earth. This is the manifest Cosmos we see through our telescopes and microscopes, and where we experience the natural world around us in its myriad expressions, all of which are a reflection in symbol, of the universes of form, idea and Being.

For humanity, the emphasis is to be fully conscious in the physical body. The physical universe is where time is slowed down and stretched out further, where existence is under the most laws, and where life is more fully objectified. What we experience through the five senses, all the creatures that we share life with, appear to us as outer and other. It is where we learn to awaken and connect with the diversity of life, and start the evolutionary journey as receivers of the Unity of life. God beholds God in the mirror of existence; for us to join with existence in this great creative outpouring means that we awaken to the greater consciousness that exists as the core of our Being.

Each of the four universes is a tree in itself. That is, each level contains the dynamics of the universe above but in more complex patterns and movement. These divisions or levels of existence are only for the mind and must not be taken as literal truth. All the levels exist in the same "place" or "space" simultaneously, and cease to exist as separate worlds as we become more conscious. The three created universes of Beriah — creation, Yetzirah — formation, and Asiyyah — physicality, are all interactive expressions of the One universe of *Being* — Atzilut, which is the pure unchanging reflection of the One. Thus, Divinity is in matter and all of creation is an expression of the One, and is sustained by the One. For this reason, existence is called a seamless garment, and *Merkabah* is to journey in the Soul through the worlds of making, form, creative idea, to experience the Being of Atzilut. This is Kabbalah.

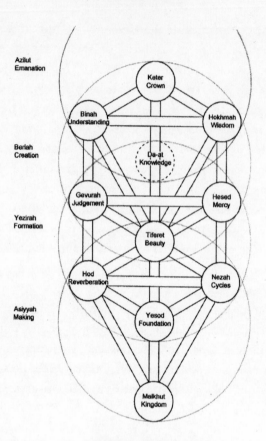

Sefirotic Tree of Life

The Sephirot

The Tree of Life — symbol system or mandala of kabbalah — represents the living reality of existence. It cannot be understood through written words but must be experienced through our awakening higher consciousness, which connects us more deeply to the life around us, wherever we may be. The Tree of Life is multi-dimensional, ever moving, changing, and alive. The mandala as shown in this book provides a mere snapshot through geometric representation of the unity of life; the mirror of existence. The sephirot illustrate principles, which govern life, and interact as a unity. These principles appear in the Gospel of

John portrayed through human characters moving through a landscape, their names and the names of the places that they come from, or visit, symbolize the dynamic movement between the sephirot within the Tree of Life.

These principles called "sephirot" (sephirah — singular) in the Hebrew, come from a root meaning *vessels, numbers, dimensions and dynamics*. Tradition tells us that there are ten not nine, ten not eleven sephirot. Ten symbolizes a complete unity, yet there are eleven names. In addition to the ten principles or dynamics is the "non-sephirah" Da'at, which is a doorway or a membrane from each universe or dimension to the other: the opening or gateway between the four universes, and between existence and God. Each Sephirah expresses the life of a dynamic within the One, in the physical world of making, psychological world of forms, Spiritual world of Ideas and the Divine world of Being.

The sephirot follow what is called the "lightning flash" from the crown at Keter to the kingdom at Malkut. (See diagram.) This is a process that flows from equilibrium at the top of the tree — Keter, to active dynamic and passive dynamic until it resolves itself in equilibrium at the foot of the tree — Malkut — the kingdom, and flashes back to the source. The attributes given to the sephirot below are approximations of the Hebrew roots. What they and the schema of the tree of life represent in diagrammatic form can only be truly understood through direct experience, when you become aware that they are alive within you — and in all of life.

Jewish mysticism uses the 22 letters of the Hebrew alphabet to give insights into existence. The letters make up the Divine attributes of God and principals or universal laws that create and give form to life. The Hebrew letters are ciphers or symbols that make up the Aleph-Bet, and can only be understood through meditation. In an old myth we are told that once there was only א – Aleph; Aleph was alone, nowhere we can say is anywhere. א

– Aleph reflected upon itself until ב – Bet emerged out of nothing that we can say is anything: ב – Bet contained all of life, all power and knowledge, and ב – Bet moved where before there was only silence and stillness. ב – Bet provided a dwelling place for א – Aleph; ב – Bet became polarity – two, and has the power of multiplication expressing itself in all the letters of the Aleph – Bet. א – Aleph is only known through Silence, Space, and the stilling of the mind; it is the principal of creation yet it is uncreated; it exists yet it is nothing that we can say is anything, without past or future it is the eternal present moment out of which all life emerges.

The Names or Values of the Sephirot

Although the standard English translations of the sephirot are given below, we are also going to look at their meanings through the Hebrew letters. Each letter is a symbol with a depth of meaning that can only be understood through meditating upon them, and their relation with each other.

כתר – **Keter:** This Hebrew word is usually translated as *Crown*, it means, *a diadem of a King or Queen, a circle of gold, and also to surround, to encompass, a loop containing all within its bounds.* On the tree of life diagram it is at the top of the central column of equilibrium, it symbolizes a point where the will of the Absolute manifests existence.

To experience the crown is to be centered in stillness within the circle of life; to experience existence through heightened awareness. In the human form, it is the crown chakra, felt at the top of the head and above. In stillness and silence, we receive the fullness of Absolute life. The three letter symbols are: כ – kap, to receive, to mould and reflect. ת – taw, universal resistance to life. ר – resh, universal container of life.

חכמה – **Hokhmah:** Means *revelation, a flash of Gnosis, and also wisdom.* The word is made up of two particles, חכמ – Hokm, which connotes; ח – Het, raw undifferentiated power, כ – kap, received

254

and molded, into מ – mem, mutable dynamic energy. The letter, ה – hay, at the end symbolizes, *universal breath of life, ground and holding,* a receptacle causing the charge to flow into a flash of brilliance and illumination. Hokmah symbolizes concentrated life force, containing all, released in a split second. On the tree of life diagram, it is placed at the head of the active dynamic column. From out of stillness and silence, we receive the revelation of life.

בינה – **Binah:** Is translated as *understanding* and means *to distinguish, intelligence, discernment, and prudence.* It is a passive dynamic holding principle; the first three Hebrew letters of ב – Bet, dwelling; י – Yod the universal seed of life; and נ – Nun, generation and offspring, give the connotation of the containment and generation of new life. The letter ה – hay at the end symbolizes the breath of life as space holding the presence of life. All life held in a single moment. On the tree of life diagram, it is placed at the head of the passive dynamic column.

Hokhmah and **Binah** work together as active and passive dynamics respectively; each, like the yin and yang symbols, has an element of the other within. In the human form, they govern the chakras associated with the hemispheres of the brain, the face and third eye.

דאאת – **Da'at:** Called the "non-sephirah," *the eleventh dimension,* is the space within the frame of a doorway, or a membrane through which energy may pass between universes, a point of transition from one state to another. The Hebrew root means to *Know* — *through experience, to perceive, the perception of the eye, both physical and non-physical.* It also means *to discern, and to know intimately and sexually.* Its place on the column of equilibrium below Keter is shown as a dotted line or black sphere signifying that it is, yet is not. It is a paradox — a place of unknowing and a place of knowledge. To know that we do not know allows the possibility of experiencing real knowledge. On the human body, it is equated with the chakra placed at the throat.

חסד – Hesed: Sometimes called Gedulah — *greatness*, it is usually translated as *Mercy*. It has an expansive quality — the will to expand, and also means, *benignity, goodness and kindness, it can be translated as love of, and amongst humanity.* Understood through its three letters it is; ח – Het, raw power, ס – Samek, circulatory movement, ד – Dalet, nourishing and expanding created existence. It is placed on the middle of the active dynamic column.

נבורה – Gevurah: Means strength, power and might. The word is used of military virtue, the valor of a great warrior, and in this sense also means precision through controlled fine movements, and judgment or severity. ג – Gimel, Organic movement contained in ב – Bet, which is linked through ו – Vav, connecting and transformative power to ר – resh, cosmic containment in the universal life breath ה – hay.

As the counter balance to Hesed, Gevurah is placed on the middle of the passive dynamic column. Together they symbolize the expansive and contracting principles, which govern life. Along with Tipheret below on the central column of consciousness, they make up the triad of the Soul and govern the chakra of the heart center, and the chakras associated with the lungs, arms and hands.

תפארת – Tipheret: Can mean *beauty* and also *adornment*. It comes from a root meaning *to dig down, to explain, and to declare oneself.* It therefore means *the beauty of the Heart or Soul, a glorious raiment, and the core of a person or given thing.* On the diagram of the tree of life, it is the central focal point holding equilibrium between active and passive dynamic and between Keter and Malkut. It is associated psychologically with the higher self of awakened consciousness. To hold Tipheret is to experience the dynamic flow of life into and out of the core of one's *Being*, like a radiant star or sun.

**תפארת – The Hebrew letters place א – Aleph, the essence of existence, at the center: Framed by two ת – Tav's, cosmic resistance to life. This enables א – Aleph to create through פ – Phey, the emanation of the patterns of life, and ר – raysh, universal containment of all existence, the flow of life into form and matter.

On the system of chakras, Tipheret can be felt through the solar plexus, as it is concerned with balance and harmony and the flow of life force. When taken with Gevurah and Hesed it can symbolize true love, that is, Judgment and Benevolence held in balance.

נצח – **Nezah:** Is translated as *to eternally repeat, and perpetuity* — the cycles of life, both great and small, from whole galaxies and universes to the cycles of the natural world and sub-atomic particles. Netzach can also mean *endurance, to conquer* and hence is sometimes called *victory.* On the tree diagram, it sits at the foot of the active dynamic column, and represents the instinctive drives of nature and the passions in a human being. נ – Nun, the generation of life צ – tsadde, exalted feminine, gestating life, and ח – Het, the raw power that is taken and gestated into new generations.

הוד – **Hod:** Means *reverberation, resonance, and the rhythmic patterning of life.* It is therefore translated as *glory, splendor,* or *brightness.* Governing the rhythms of the natural world, it is associated with communication and the gathering of information. ה – hay, the universal breath of life, is linked through ו – Vav, the transforming power of life into ד – Dalet, the quarternity, nourishing and expanding life.

Hod sits at the foot of the passive dynamic column, and along with Netzach forms the patterning of life throughout the three created universes. In the human form both Hod and Netzach are associated with the Chakra of the sacrum, and the hips.

יסוד – **Yesod:** Is translated as *foundation,* and further means *to establish, ordain, or decree* something. It can also mean *to consult together in a unity,* therefore giving the idea of a foundation. י –

Yod the universal seed of life, in circulatory movement ס –
Samek, linked through ו – Vav, the transforming power of life to
ד – Dalet, nourishing and expanding abundance of existence.

It sits on the central column below Tipheret and the active and
passive dynamics of Hod and Netzach. Yesod with Hod and
Netzach makes up the dynamic energy that governs the ebb and
flow of life. In the human psyche, it relates to the ego, which in
its pure and unadulterated form is the interface between the
inner life of the Soul and the outer senses in the body. It is
associated with the chakra that governs the genitals and coccyx.

מלכות – **Malkhut:** *The Kingdom,* also means *dominion, to rule and
reign.* In essence, it is the ground of Being in life, where seeds
sprout and bear fruit, returning the expression of their energy
though diversity to the source of life. In each of the four
universes, it is the place of resolution and expression. It is
perhaps best understood in relation to the Earth, the physical
universe and the physical body as the receptacles of all the other
dynamics in the tree. מ – mem, mutable dynamic energy is given
direction through, ל – Lamed, life in extension and elevation,
received and molded through כ – kap, and linked through ו –
Vav, the transforming power of life with ת – Tav, cosmic resistance to life which brings all form and matter to its end. In the
body, it relates to the chakras, which govern the knees and feet.

All the Sephirot work together as a single organism, *on the tree
of life,* and are connected by twenty-two paths or conduits. Keter
represents the source of all life: Being. It becomes an active-
dynamic potency at Hokmah, whose charge is contained and
checked by Binah, where it is gestated and understood before
being released or birthed through Da'at, the membrane which
transforms the energy, and gives it what we understand as
gravity and knowledge. At Hesed this weighted charge is
expanded, and this force itself, gives rise to the counter force at
Gevurah, which both holds its expansive power and gives it
precise direction and flow. Equilibrium is reached at Tipheret

where the charge becomes a radiant out-pouring and in-drawing pulsating heart or core. It is the holding center point of all the sephirot, where the spiritual, psychological and physical universes meet.

From here the life energy is channeled through cycles and rhythms — Nezah and Hod — which diversify it into more and varied forms, and draw it onward into the sphere of Yesod, where each form achieves an identity, and is filtered and energized for its physical expression at Malkhut. Here in the world of appearances, all the other principles of the tree are made manifest through the diverse patterns and rhythms that make up life, the final expression of the ideas brought forth from the One. Here they reflect back to the source from whence they came. All that exists is a manifestation of Being, a reflection of the One source of life, to which we are intimately connected; the more so when we awaken to its abundant eternal presence.

Appendix

Full translation from the Greek of Chapters One and Two

Verses 1-5. The Relationship of God to Existence
1:1

In the beginning the Logos was, and the Logos was next to God, and the Logos was Divine.

1:2

This One had its Being in the beginning next to God.

1:3

All things came into created existence on account of the Logos, and without the Logos not even one created thing came into created existence.

1:4

In the Logos life had Being, and the life was the radiance of Humanity.

1:5

And the light was made visible in the spiritual darkness, and the spiritual darkness could not take possession of it.

Verses 6-8. Awakening the Soul
1:6

A human being named John came into created existence as an envoy of the Logos.

1:7

This John came as a witness, in order that there might be a witness about the light, so that all might believe through that light.

1:8

This John is not the light, but is a testimony concerning the light.

Verses 9-13. The Revelation of Divinity in Matter
1:9

The Divine light is the true radiance, which illuminates every human being coming into the Cosmos.

1:10

The Divine light was in the Cosmos and the Cosmos came into created existence through the Divine light, but the Cosmos did not perceive this Divine light.

1:11

The Divine light came to its rightful dwelling place and its own kin did not admit it.

1:12

But as many as received (gave hospitality) to the Divine light, those it empowered to become descendents of God, for they put their trust in the Divine Name.

1:13

Who came into created existence not by blood, nor of the will of the flesh, nor of the will of man, but of God.

Verses 14-18. Stilling the mind: The Realization of Sacred Space
1:14

And the Logos became flesh and dwelt in us (as in a tabernacle), and we beheld its glorious manifestation, like unto the splendor of that unique issue of the Father, perfected grace and truth.

1:15

John witnesses concerning the glory of Logos, and cries out
saying, "This One is of whom I said, 'The One who comes
after me has come into created existence before me because
The One precedes me.'"

1:16

Because out of the perfection of the Divine we all receive grace on
top of grace.

1:17

Because the Torah is given through Moses, grace and truth come
through the Anointed Jesus.

1:18

No one has ever gazed upon the Absolute at any time: the unique
issue, who lies in the heart of the Father, is revealed through
the Christ.

Verses 19-28. Witnessing the Ego and Psyche
1:19

And this is the witness of John when the Jews of Jerusalem sent
envoys, Priests and Levites that they might ask, "who are
you?"

1:20

And he acknowledged, he did not deny but acknowledged that "I
am not the Christ."

1:21

So they asked him, "what then are you Elijah?" And he said "I am
not."

"Are you a prophet?" And he answered "No."

1:22

Then addressing John they said, "Who are you that we may give an answer to those who have sent us, what do you to say about yourself?"

1:23

"I [am] a voice crying in the wilderness, `make straight the way of the Lord,' as the prophet Isaiah said."

1:24

Note that these people were envoys from a school of Pharisees.

1:25

And they questioned him closely, and said to John, "Then why do you baptize if you are not the Christ, nor Elijah, nor a prophet?"

1:26

John answered them saying, "I baptize in water, but at your very heart there is a permanent presence of which you have no experience."

1:27

"This One who is coming after me, the latchet of whose sandal I am not worthy to untie."

1:28

These things occurred at Bethabara beyond the Jordan where John was baptizing.

Verses 29-34. The First Day of Transformation
1:29

The next day John perceives Jesus coming towards him; and says "Behold! the lamb of God removing the sins of the Cosmos."

1:30

This is the One about whom I said, "After me comes a man who has come into created existence before me, because he has preceded me."

1:31

"And I did not know him. But in order that he be revealed to Israel, I came baptizing in water."

1:32

And John witnessed saying that, "I have discerned the spirit coming down as a dove out of the Heavens and it indwells him."

1:33

"But the One sending me to baptize in water, that One says to me, 'On whomever you see the Spirit descend and indwell, this is the one baptising in the Holy Spirit.'"

1:34

"And I have beheld and I have witnessed that this one is the Son of God."

Verses 35–42. The Second Day of Transformation
1:35

On the next day again, John was confirmed with two of his disciples.

1:36

And observing keenly how Jesus was conducting himself, says, "Behold! the lamb of God".

1:37

And the two disciples understood exactly what was said, and accompanied Jesus.

1:38

And Jesus turned to examine closely the nature of their conduct as they followed him, and said to them, "What do you seek"? And they said to him, "Rabbi", which means teacher, "Where do you dwell?"

1:39

He says to them, "come and see for yourselves." They went and, themselves transforming, saw where he dwelt in close settled union. And they abode with him that day. It was about the tenth hour.

1:40

One of the two who understood John and accompanied him was Andrew, the brother of Simon Peter.

1:41

This Andrew first seeks out his own brother, Simon, and tells him, "we have found the Messiah," which, when translated means Christ.

1:42

He led him on to Jesus, and observing him clearly Jesus says, "You are Simon the son of John, you shall be called Cephas," which when translated, means Peter.

Verses 43-51. Day Three of Transformation

1:43

The next day Jesus purposed to go out into Galilee. And he seeks out Philip, and Jesus says to him, "walk with me step by step."

1:44

Now Philip was from Bethsaida, the city of Andrew and Peter.

1:45

Philip seeks out Nathanael, and says to him, "We have discovered the one whom Moses wrote about in the Torah, and of whom the prophets have written; Jesus, the son of Joseph, from Nazareth."

1:46

And Nathanael says to him, "Can anything good come out of Nazareth?" Philip says to him, "come and see."

1:47

Jesus beheld Nathanael coming towards him, and said of him, "Behold! truly an Israelite in whom there is no deception."

1:48

Nathanael Says to him, "how do you know about me?" Jesus answered and said to him, "before Philip called you, I perceived you under your fig tree."

1:49

Nathanael answered, "Rabbi, you are the son of God, you are the king of Israel."

1:50

Jesus says to him, "because I told you that I saw you under the influence of the fig tree, you believe this! You will be admitted to witness far greater things than these."

1:51

And he says to him, "Truly, truly, I say to you, you will be admitted to witness the heavens opened and the angels ascending and descending on the Son of Humanity."

Ch 2 verses 1-12. The Conscious Realization of Divinity in Earth.

2:1

And on the third day, there was a wedding in Cana of Galilee, and the mother of Jesus was there.

2:2

Jesus and his disciples were also called to be present at the wedding.

2:3

And there being no wine, the mother of Jesus says to him, "They have no wine."

2:4

Jesus says to her, "what has that to do with you and me madam? My hour is not yet come."

2:5

So his mother says to the servants, "do whatever he says to you."

2:6

And there were six stone waterpots set out for the Jewish purification ceremonies, each containing two or three measures.

2:7

Jesus says to them, "fill the waterpots with water," and they filled them up to the top.

2:8

And he says to them, "draw out now and bring forth to the master of the feast," and they brought forth.

2:9

But as the master of the feast experienced the water that had been created wine without knowing its origin — but the servants who had drawn the water knew — the master of the feast calls the bridegroom.

2:10

And he says to him, "Every human being sets out the good wine, and when they have become intoxicated, sets out the inferior: You have kept the good until the present."

2:11

This marked the beginning of the signs of Jesus in Cana of Galilee, and it revealed his glory, and his disciples believed in him.

2:12

After this, he went down to Capernaum and his mother and his kindred spirits, and his disciples went with him, and they dwelt there for a while.

Verses 13-25. The Clearing the Inner Temple.
2:13

And it was close to the Jewish Passover and Jesus went up to Jerusalem.

2:14

And in the Temple he found those selling Oxen and Sheep and

doves, and the money changers encamped inside.

2:15

And making a whip out of cords, he drove them all out of the Temple, along with their sheep and oxen, and scattered the coins of all the money changers and overturned their tables.

2:16

And he says to those selling the doves, "Take these things from here! Do not make the house of my Father a house of trade."

2:17

His disciples remembered that it is written, "fervent desire for your house consumes me."

2:18

Then the Jews [Judeans] answered, and said to him, "what signs do you show us for doing these things?"

2:19

And Jesus answered, and said to them, "Destroy this Sanctuary and in three days I will raise it up."

2:20

Then the Jews [Judeans] said, "This Sanctuary took forty six years to build, and you will raise it in three days?"

2:21

But Jesus spoke about the Inner Sanctuary of his body.

2:22

Then, when he was raised from the dead, his disciples remembered that he had said this, and believed the scriptures and the word [Logos] that Jesus made known.

2:23

And as he was in Jerusalem at the feast of the Passover, many put their trust in the name [Logos], beholding the signs that he did.

2:24

But Jesus did not put his trust in them, because he knew everything fully,

2:25

and because he had no need that any should bear witness concerning universal humanity for he knew what was in universal humanity.

Bibliography

I have listed my sources under the most relevant chapter headings, and in order to save repetition they are not repeated under each chapter. It will be understood for example that the Greek lexicons and Bibles are used throughout the whole of the book.

Preface and Chapter One
In chapter one, I would refer the reader to James M Robinson (general editor) *The Nag Hammadi Library*, revised edition, Harper San Francisco, 1988. This is valuable to get a feel of the diversity of manuscripts that were being circulated at the time of the birth of Christianity. It also contains works attributed to John the son of Zebedee.

Chapters Two to Fifteen
My main source for the Greek text is the United Bible Societies, *Greek New Testament*, third edition (corrected), published by German Bible, Society Stuttgart, 1983. Editors, Kurt Aland, Matthew Black, Carlo M. Martini, Bruce M. Metzger and Allen Wikgren.

I also reference Jay P. Green, Sr. (Gen Editor and Translator). *The Interlinear Bible, Hebrew-Greek-English*, second edition, Hendrickson publishers, Peabody, Massachusetts, 1986. In the book, I use the, *Revised Standard Version of the Holy Bible*, Collins, New York, 1973.

For my translation of the Greek text, I use several standard Greek lexicons, the main one being Harold K. Moulton, *The Analytical Greek Lexicon Revised*, The Zondervan Corporation, Grand Rapids, Michigan, seventh printing 1981, of the 1978 edition. I also found very helpful and illuminating, Walter Bauer, *A Greek-English Lexicon of the New Testament and Other Early*

Christian Literature, second edition, University of Chicago Press, 1979. And for further detailed referencing I also consulted Liddell and Scott, *A Greek — English Lexicon,* fifth edition, Oxford University Press, 1861.

At certain points during the translation, I cross-reference the Hebrew text which has been quoted or referred to by the gospel writer. For this, the main Hebrew lexicon that I used was *The New Brown-Driver-Briggs-Gesenius Hebrew-English Lexicon,* Hendrickson publishers, Peabody, Massachusetts, 1979.

I have consulted many and various commentaries and books on the Gospel of John and the Gospels and New Testament writings in general over my years of study, I list the most important ones here. A very important work is that by M. Black, *An Aramaic Approach to the Gospels and Acts,* Oxford, 1967. An appreciation of the Aramaic gives a deeper flavor of the Jewish and Middle Eastern nuances that exist in the Gospel. Also Neil Douglas-Klotz, *The Hidden Gospel — Decoding the Spiritual Message of the Aramaic Jesus,* Quest books, Illinois, 1999. Finally, I would like to cite the work of C.F. Burley, *The Aramaic Origin of the Fourth Gospel,* Oxford University Press, 1922.

Maurice Nicoll, *The Mark,* Watkins publications, London, 1981.

Maurice Nicoll, *New Man, an Interpretation of Some Parables and Miracles of Christ,* Robinson and Watkins, London, 1968.

Beryl Pogson, *Commentary on the Fourth Gospel,* Quacks Books, York, 1993.

Rudolf Steiner, *The Gospel of St. John,* Anthroposophic Press, New York, 1962.

James M. Pryse, *The Magical Message According to Johannes,* The Theosophical Publishing Company, New York, 1909.

John Ashton (editor), *The Interpretation of John,* SPCK/Fortress Press, London, 1986.

John Ashton, *Studying John — Approaches to the Fourth Gospel,* Clarendon, Oxford, 1994.

Ravi Ravindra, *The Yoga of Christ — In the Gospel According to St. John*, Element, Shaftsbury, 1990.

Elaine Pagels, *The Gnostic Gospels*, Penguin Books, London, 1990.

Gershom Scholem, *The Messianic Idea in Judaism — and other essays on Jewish Spirituality*, Schocken Books, New York, 1971.

Bede Griffiths, *The Universal Christ*, Darton, Longman and Todd, London, 1990.

Bede Griffiths, *New Creation in Christ*, Templegate, Illinois, 1990.

Clark M. Wiliamson and Ronald J. Allen, *Interpreting Difficult Texts*, SCM Press, London, 1989.

Gareth Lloyd-Jones, *Hard Sayings — Difficult New Testament Texts for Jewish-Christian Dialogue*, The council of Christians and Jews, 1993.

Edward F. Edinger, *The Christian Archetype — A Jungian Commentary on the Life of Christ*, Inner City Books, Toronto, 1987.

Edward F. Edinger, *The Bible and the Psyche, Individuation Symbolism in the Old Testament*, Inner City Books, Toronto, 1986.

Edward F. Edinger, *The Mystery of the Coniunctio — Alchemical Image of Individuation*, Inner City Books, Toronto, 1994.

Specific to Chapter Five

James H. Charlesworth (editor), *The Old Testament Pseudepigrapha — Apocalytic Literature and Testaments Volumes 1 and two*, Doubleday, New York, 1983. Of particular interest are the books of Enoch in Vol 1 and the fragments of Judeo — Hellenistic works in Vol 2.

Carlo Suares, *The Qabala Trilogy*, Shambala, Boston, 1985. From this work, the section on the Cipher of Genesis.

Z'ev ben Shimon Halevi, *A Kabbalistic Universe*, Rider and company, London, 1977.

Z'ev ben Shimon Halevi, *Kabbalah and Exodus*, Rider and company, London, 1980.

Specific to Chapter Six

Harvey Falk, *Jesus the Pharisee — A new look at the Jewishness of Jesus*, Paulist Press, New York, 1985.

Abraham Cohen, *Everyman's Talmud — The Major Teachings of the Rabbinic Sages*, Schocken Books, New York, 1995.

Adin Steinsaltz, *The Essential Talmud, Basic Books*, New York, 1984.

Specific to Chapter Eight

Abraham Cohen, *Everyman's Talmud — The Major Teachings of the Rabbinic Sages*, Schocken Books, New York, 1995. For the sayings of Rabbi Hillel.

Specific to Chapter Nine

Alois Podhajsky, *The Complete Training of Horse and Rider*, The Sportsman's Press, London, 1991.

Specific to Chapter Ten

Teilhard de Chardin, *Hymn of the Universe*, Collins, London, 1965.

Teilhard de Chardin, *Phenomenon of Man, Collins*, London, 1959.

Jacob Neusner, *A Life of Yohanan ben Zakkai — circa 1 — 80 C.E.*, second edition, revised, J.E.Brill, London, 1970.

Jacob Neusner, *Development of a Legend: Traditions Concerning Yohanan ben Zakkai*, J.E.Brill, London, 1970.

Specific to Chapter Eleven

Ancient Egyptian Myths and Legends, by Lewis Spence, Dover Publications, New York, 2001

Specific to Chapter Thirteen

David Fideler, *Jesus Christ Sun of God — Ancient Cosmology and Early Christian Symbolism*, Quest Books, Illinois, 1993.

Robert Vincent, Geometry of the Golden Section; second edition, Chalagam Publishing, 2007.

Chapter Fourteen

Edward Carpenter, *The Origins of Pagan and Christian Beliefs,* Senate, London, 1996.

John Romer, *Testament — The Bible and History,* Channel 4 Books, 1988.

C D. Yonge, *The Works of Philo — Complete and Unabridged;* New updated edition, Hendrickson publishers, Peabody, Massachusetts, 1993.

Susanne Schaup, *Sophia — Aspects of the Divine Feminine past and present,*

Nicolas-Hayes, Maine, 1997.

Anne Baring and Jules Cashford, *The Myth of the Goddess — Evolution of an Image,* Arkana, London. 1993.

Thomas Schipfliger, *Sophia-Maria — A Holistic Vision of Creation,* Samuel Wiser, Maine, 1998.

Joseph Campbell, *Creative Mythology — The Masks of God,* Penguin Books, New York, 1968.

Joseph Campbell, *Occidental Mythology — The Masks of God,* Penguin Books, New York, 1964.

Carl Jung, *Man and his Symbols,* Pan Books, London, 1978.

Carl Jung, *Answer to Job,* Ark Books, London, 1992.

Carl Jung, *Aion: Researches into the Phenomenology of the Self,* Bollingen, Princeton N.J. , 1951. Chapter 5 of this series of theses is on Christ as a symbol of the Self.

Williston Walker, *A History of the Christian Church, fourth Edition,* T & T Clark, Edinburgh, 1986.

Boniface Ramsey, *Beginning to Read the Church Fathers,* Darton, Longman and Todd, London, 1986.

J Stevenson, *A New Eusebius — Documents Illustrating the History of the Church to AD 337,* SPCK, London, revised edition 1986.

Henry Chadwick, *The Early Church, Pelican,* Harmondsworth, 1967.

C Jones, G Wainwright & E Yarnold, Sj, (Editors), *The Study of Spirituality,* SPCK, London, 1986.

J.N.D. Kelly, *Early Christian Doctrines*, fifth edition, A&C Black, London, 1985.

Terence Irwin, Classical thought, Oxford University Press, Oxford, 1989.

John Sallis, *Being and Logos — Reading the Platonic Dialogues*, third edition, Indiana University Press, Indianapolis, 1996.

Richard Tarnas, *The Passion of the Western Mind*, Pimlico, London, 1991.

Bertrand Russell, *History of Western Philosophy*, Routledge, London, second edition 1961.

Edmund Wilson, *The Dead Sea Scrolls*, W H Allen, London. 1955.

G. Vermes, *The Dead Sea Scrolls in English*, Pelican, Harmondsworth, 1962.

Chapter Fifteen

Aryeh Kaplan, *Meditation and the Bible*, Samuel Wiser, Maine, 1978.

Aryeh Kaplan, *Meditation and Kabbalah*, Samuel Wiser, Maine, 1982.

Dion Fortune, *Mystical Kabbalah*, Williams & Norgate Ltd, London, 1935.

W.G. Gray, *The Ladder of Lights*, Helios Books, Toddington, 1975.

Gareth Knight, *A Practical Guide to Qabbalistic Symbolism Vol 1*, Helios Books, Toddington, 1976.

Zev ben Shimon Halevi, *Adam and the Kabbalistic Tree*, Rider & co, London, 1974.

Plotinus, *The Enneads — new unabridged version*, translated by Stephen MacKenna, Larson Publications, New York, 1992

AXIS MUNDI
BOOKS

Axis Mundi Books, provide the most revealing and coherent explorations and investigations of the world of hidden or forbidden knowledge. Take a fascinating journey into the realm of Esoteric Mysteries, Magic, Mysticism, Angels, Cosmology, Alchemy, Gnosticism, Theosophy, Kabbalah, Secret Societies and Religions, Symbolism, Quantum Theory, Apocalyptic Mythology, Holy Grail and Alternative Views of Mainstream Religion.